PREHISTC
DORS

PREHISTORIC
DORSET

JOHN GALE

TEMPUS

For Julie

First published 2003

PUBLISHED IN THE UNITED KINGDOM BY:
Tempus Publishing Ltd
The Mill, Brimscombe Port
Stroud, Gloucestershire GL5 2QG

PUBLISHED IN THE UNITED STATES OF AMERICA BY:
Tempus Publishing Inc.
2 Cumberland Street
Charleston, SC 29401

British Library Cataloguing in Publication Data.
A catalogue record for this book is available from the British Library.

ISBN 0 7524 2906 X

Typesetting and origination by Tempus Publishing.
Printed in Great Britain by Midway Colour Print, Wiltshire

CONTENTS

PREFACE

This book is largely about places; places which, for the most part, survive as earth-works that represent some of the earliest locations occupied by our ancestors, within the geographical framework that conforms to the modern county boundary of Dorset. These places are sometimes those that people lived in, in which the business of survival was maintained largely in the pursuit of farming. Frequently it is also about those places in which some of our ancestors were laid to rest. Death, and the circumstances surrounding the disposal of the dead have always provided great insights into the 'lives' of our ancestors, and frequently the survival of monuments associated with the dead have survived the passage of time in a more complete state. There is a third group of monuments, however, for which there is a great deal of ambiguity, in which the identification of activity and purpose is obscured by a lack of information and understanding. The archaeological literature is littered with the euphemisms of 'ritual activity' and 'ceremonial activity', which is often the most that can be claimed for material evidence that we cannot explain effectively through analogy with our own contemporary culture. The problems of interpretation are, of course, as much to do with cultural diversity as with the limited availability and accessibility of suitable data from which to comprehend the past. We are all, individually and collectively, products of our own time and culture, interacting with our environment intuitively because we understand its complex language and rules. The language and rules of a community are a cultural package that evolves over time and is an essential part of its identity. Our ancestors were, of course, living in a cultural environment which was technologically, economically, politically, socially and spiritually structured in ways that we would almost certainly find alien to those of our own. The solutions to living in the world would accordingly, at times, result in the production of cultural material (artefacts – monuments – are of course artefacts, just very large ones!) that directly relates to the community of the time and which may appear inexplicable to those of a different time or place.

As this book is about places and monuments it is also constrained to the later prehistoric period, beginning with the introduction of agriculture around 4000 BC. Accompanying the introduction of agriculture (but not necessarily as a result of), communities erected permanent dwellings through which nearby land was farmed. Such permanency of settlement allows for the construction of fixed structures of a more substantial nature than would be associated with more mobile hunter-gatherer communities that prevailed in the preceding Palaeolithic and

Mesolithic periods. Also associated with agriculturalists is their huge effect on the wider landscape with the enclosure of land. The ownership and demarcation of land has to be undertaken for the effective management of crops and the successful rearing of livestock. The ordering of the landscape in such a way marks a fundamental change in human interaction with the physical world that has left a surprisingly large number of remains that have survived into the present day. Fragmentary remains of fields, settlements and territorial boundaries are to be found across the county whose origin is clearly prehistoric, and represent the sole remnants of ancient landscapes that span 4,000 years.

Chapters 2–4 are divided in the traditional manner ranging from the Neolithic to the Iron Age and are done so for the sake of easy reference. The use of such terms is, of course, nothing more than a useful chronological device for charting activity in relation to a common framework, which only becomes problematic at the junction with the next or previous period when such artificial divisions become somewhat fuzzy. Within each chapter and period, I have made liberal use of the terms 'early', 'middle' and 'late' where required. The use of 'middle' in any of the periods has a degree of formality that has gone in and out of fashion over recent years. My use of the term does not predicate the acceptance of a Middle Neolithic or for that matter of a Middle Bronze or Middle Iron Age, it has been used rather simply, and generally when early and late seem inappropriate. I have as a matter of choice restricted my use of absolute dates (normally radiocarbon dating) to a minimum. Where they have been included, I have used calibrated dates to ensure compatibility with calendar years and they are expressed as a range calculated to two standard deviations.

I have attempted to utilise as many of the major monuments observable in the county within the main narrative of this work, but at times this has been impossible due to shortage of evidence, or when doing so would have resulted in much repetition or redundancy. Included, as a final chapter, is an extensive gazetteer of Dorset sites, which includes all those places and spaces that are worth visiting. Within the pages of the gazetteer I have endeavoured to include a précis of available archaeological information for each of the entries. The intention of this was to provide important information for those who wish to venture out and experience as far as is possible ancient places without doing too much homework.

The origins of this volume lie very much in a decision made in the winter of 1990, when I accepted the offer of employment at the then Bournemouth Polytechnic. I had until that point, spent the majority of my working life in the English Midlands, where comparatively speaking, upstanding prehistoric monuments are a little thin on the ground. For the opportunity to work in a county whose landscape contains such wonderful prehistoric archaeology, I must thank Alan Hunt who steered me through my first steps at teaching Field Archaeology. Since then it has been my pleasure (mostly) as part of my professional duties to introduce students from the HND Practical Archaeology and BSc Archaeology courses at Bournemouth University to many of the monuments discussed in the following pages. During this time, I have frequently benefited from the views and comments of many students that I have taught, who have on occasion provided me with alternative views and opinions, as well as pointing out features in the landscape that I had previously missed.

Earlier draft versions of the script benefited hugely from the many helpful comments and suggestions provided by my colleagues Bruce Eagles, Mark Maltby and Miles Russell. They are, of course, free of all blame for any remaining errors, omissions and contentious issues. Whilst the great majority of the line drawings have been redrawn by myself, I would like to thank Mike Butter for his persistence with CAD in the production of the distribution maps which accompany most of the following chapters. My wife Julie has had to endure more than my normal quotient of mood swings during the last few months of the preparation of this volume, which probably exceed those that she signed up to. In addition to providing a number of photographs and drawings, she has also visited many of the monuments with me and has been a constant source of encouragement and support. I am very grateful to Dorset County Council for their support provided for this book. In particular, I would like to thank Claire Pinder for allowing me to spend five days looking at the complete SMR (Sites and Monuments Record) for the county; the staff of the reference library in Dorchester and Steve Spring for allowing permission to use some of the excellent 1997 aerial photographs from the CD ROM 'Dorset, a photographic atlas'. I would also like to thank Peter Woodward and Val Diker of Dorset County Museum, particularly for their kind assistance in searching the museum's photographic archives. Text illustrations **1**, **2** and **35** are reproduced with the kind permission of The Dorset Natural History and Archaeology Society at the Dorset County Museum. Similar thanks are also due to the staff at the Aerial Photographic section of the NMR (National Monuments Record) in Swindon. To my employers Bournemouth University, thanks are due in providing some financial support for the funding of copyright fees and reproduction costs. Special thanks must also go to Francesca Radcliffe for providing a number of aerial photographic images, who did so with friendliness and professionalism.

John Gale
Winterbourne Abbas
April 2003

1

INTRODUCTION

MONUMENTAL LANDSCAPES

The landscape of Dorset is today the home of approximately 700,000 people, most of whom reside in the urban centres surrounding the Poole basin with smaller concentrations in the rural centres to the east and west. Dorset has for centuries been very much a rural county, traditionally relying on agriculture and fishing to support its relatively diminutive population, which in more recent years has benefited from tourism as a major source of revenue.

Many visitors come to the county from all parts of Britain and the rest of the world, attracted by a landscape that is not only of great scenic beauty, but which also contains a wealth of ancient monuments that evidence the county's rich cultural heritage. Many of these monuments are of such antiquity that they date to a time before history, and consequently are in themselves the only surviving record of past events which require the methods and techniques of archaeology to analyse and interpret. Many of these monuments are massive in extent, none more so than the Iron Age hillforts which are to be found in all parts of the county, whilst others form discrete, often fragile, earthworks of even greater antiquity. Many of the smaller earthworks are in constant danger of destruction, and indeed, many are destroyed each year through the actions of both nature and human activity.

My colleague Miles Russell in the introduction to his recent study of *Prehistoric Sussex* (Russell 2002, 13) highlighted his disconcertion with the level of misunderstanding that surrounds the public perception and understanding of the prehistoric period in general, and prehistoric monuments in particular. My own experiences in this regard mirror his own, and I suggest that the difficulty lies principally with the failure of our educational system to provide a core curriculum which includes basic information about our Island's pre-Roman roots. Fortunately ,however, for those with the motivation and access to the landscape of Dorset, this lack of knowledge and understanding can be remedied through a study of its ancient monuments, aided I humbly suggest, by this volume. The breadth of prehistoric monuments still extant in the Dorset landscape and consequently accessible to the visitor are almost unequalled in any part of the British Isles, and many of them have been investigated by some of the most distinguished archaeologists of the last century or so.

Dorset 'diggers'

The prehistoric monuments of Dorset have long attracted the attention of antiquarians and archaeologists, but few have been as prolific as those who dug into prehistoric barrows during the eighteenth and nineteenth centuries. As in other parts of the country, the nineteenth century was a time in which the curiosity of the educated classes was in part directed towards unearthing our cultural past quite literally through the opening up of burial mounds (tumuli), chiefly of Neolithic or Bronze Age date. The attractions for the investigators must have been very tempting. Not only was there the possibility of unearthing the physical remains of their distant ancestors, but also the chance of finding accompanying cultural material in the way of grave goods. Unfortunately the great majority of this work, however well motivated and intentioned, was undertaken prior to the development of adequate archaeological techniques and with hindsight it is possible to see that much valuable information was lost. However, the work of such people as Charles Warne, Sir Richard Colt Hoare, William Shapp, the Reverend John Henry Austen and Edward Cunnington amongst many others, paved the way not only for a better understanding of the county's ancient past, but also for the development of modern archaeology.

Of all the early diggers there is one name which does tend to stand out above all others, that of General Pitt Rivers (formerly Augustus Henry Lane Fox). The General inherited the Rushmore estate on Cranborne Chase in 1880, where over a period of a few years he conducted a range of excavations that he subsequently privately published. Among the sites he investigated were the Bronze Age enclosures at South Lodge and Martins Down (neither technically in Dorset, but close enough to make the fact irrelevant), which even today are vital components in our investigation into the origins of Dorset's prehistoric landscape. The quality of his excavations and their subsequent recording and publication has led to his broad acknowledgement as the 'father' of British archaeology.

Following Pitt Rivers, the twentieth century saw a progression of important excavations in the county, many of which were directed by some of the most influential archaeologists of their time. It is impossible to extensively summarise the extent of the contributions made by numerous archaeologists during the last 100 years in this volume, but the following précis does allow for a brief review of some of the most significant contributions.

Harold St George Gray, who had previously worked with Pitt Rivers, confirmed the Neolithic origins of Maumbury Rings in Dorchester through his excavations at the site at the end of the first decade of the twentieth century. The photograph (1) taken during 1909 of a section through the enclosure bank, clearly

1 *Maumbury Rings during excavations of 1909 directed by Harold St George Gray.* Courtesy of Dorset County Museum

shows aspects of a careful and planned excavation that would not be out of place on an excavation today (although the garden trowel in the hands of the elegantly dressed woman standing at the edge of the trench might well be frowned upon).

The years leading up to the Second World War saw a great deal of excavation activity in the county. Stuart Piggott's excavation of two Neolithic barrows, one close to the southern terminal of the Dorset Cursus on Thickthorn Down (**2**), and the other, a rare example of a long barrow located off the chalk in Dorset at Holdenhurst between Bournemouth and Christchurch, provided some insights into the variety of forms and deposits found in such monuments. These two monuments are still the most complete examples of the genus to be excavated and published in the county to date, although further information about Neolithic long barrows can be garnered from examples excavated elsewhere in Wessex.

The investigation into the county's Iron Age hillforts also advanced signifi-cantly in the 1930s with excavations at Maiden Castle, Chalbury and Poundbury. Those at Maiden Castle are certainly the best known, and were directed by Mortimer Wheeler, the results of which were published in 1943. His excavations are a classic example of the advancement of archaeological techniques from those of earlier in the century, utilising the then favoured method of box-grid excava-tion to recover in detail the stratigraphic sequence of archaeological deposits, crucial in the phasing of events in such a complex site.

2 Thickthorn Down barrow during excavation in 1933. Courtesy of Dorset County Museum

Following the Second World War, and an understandable decline in the number of large excavations, the field investigation of hillforts was still very much an active pursuit. Mortimer Wheeler continued his interest in the prehistory of the county and hillforts in particular with the sampling of the huge enclosure on Bindon Hill on the coast close to Lulworth Cove. This was followed by Sir Ian Richmond's excavations at Hod Hill, carried out between 1951 and 1958. This campaign of excavations was particularly informative with regard to the organisation of hillfort interiors during the Iron Age, and provided a rare glimpse into a hillfort that had clearly been attacked by Roman soldiers following the Imperial invasion of AD 43.

During the 1960s and 70s, the pace of excavation once again picked up with a number of research and rescue excavations that still greatly underpin current interpretations of the county's prehistory as well as southern Britain as a whole. The work of three archaeologists during this period has been particularly enlightening, amongst a great many other valuable contributions made by numerous archaeologists at this time. The excavations at Shearplace Hill and Hog Cliff Hill directed by Philip Rahtz have in many ways characterised settlement on the chalk downs during the Later Bronze Age and Early Iron Age. Similarly Barry Cunliffe's excavations at Eldon's Seat and Hengistbury Head have provided much evidence for the nature of settlement activity, particularly the results from Hengistbury Head that established comprehensive evidence for Continental trade in the years preceding the Roman Invasion.

One of the most prolific of excavators in Dorset during the 1960s and 70s was Geoffrey Wainwright, who recently retired as the Chief Archaeologist for English Heritage. Wainwright's excavation of the stone circle at Hampton, north of the village of Portesham, highlighted the danger of taking for granted the modern positioning of stone settings on some megalithic sites, which in this case proved to be a false representation of the original layout (see chapter 3). His excavation of the Neolithic henge at Mount Pleasant, to the south-east of Dorchester, was undertaken as the last in a series of investigations into similar monuments in the Wessex region, without which our knowledge of these colossal later Neolithic monuments would be much diminished. Arguably his most productive sites have been the Iron Age settlements at Gussage All Saints and Tollard Royal, both located on Cranborne Chase. Both sites have been used extensively to characterise Iron Age enclosed farmstead settlement on the chalk downs, straddling the whole of the Iron Age period.

During the last two decades of the twentieth century, continued progress has been made across the county in both the excavation and survey of archaeological sites. A great deal of excavation has been undertaken by way of relatively small scale evaluations, usually in response to planning constraints as part of development control processes. Such planning controls have enabled new discoveries to be properly excavated prior to subsequent destruction, an excellent example of which being the extensive findings of prehistoric monuments along the line of the Dorchester by-pass (A35) in the 1980s. In addition, there have been a number of projects of a larger scale such as those conducted by Lillian Ladle at Bestwall Quarry near Wareham, where extensive later prehistoric deposits are being discovered and analysed prior to destruction during quarrying. Amongst the most well-documented and prolonged of archaeological investigations are those ongoing at Down Farm on Cranborne Chase. Martin Green, a local farmer and archaeologist, has been systematically investigating the landscape on and around his farm for nearly forty years. Often working with the collaboration of others (chiefly Richard Bradley, John Barratt and Michael Allen), he has managed to shed new light onto one of the most intensely studied parts of southern Britain (Green, M., 2000; Barrett, J., et al. 1991).

Literary milestones in the archaeology of Dorset

Whilst Dorset is blessed with a rich and extensive archaeological heritage, the synthesis of such remains in literary form is largely disparate. The publication of archaeological survey and excavation is abundant, finding expression in monographs as well as national journals and the county-based proceedings of the Dorset Natural History and Archaeology Society. If it were not for such a rich collection of reports this volume certainly would not have been possible, and for the most part, the availability of archaeological information on Dorset sites mirrors that from counties elsewhere in the British Isles. Bringing all this data together to form a coherent narrative is by its nature a difficult task, which largely explains the shortage of syntheses not only in Dorset but for many other regions also. However, Dorset has benefited from a number of excellent publications in the past, which the reader might find useful in getting to grips with the ancient cultural landscape.

Foremost in all of the publications of the past half century is the excellent set of volumes (in five parts) compiled by the Royal Commission for the Historical Monuments of England (now integrated within English Heritage). The volumes relate to a Royal Warrant commissioned in 1946 by King George VI, instructing the appointed commissioners to make an inventory of the ancient and historical monuments in the counties of England dating from the earliest times to 1714 (plus significant monuments of more recent date). Unfortunately the publication of such a vast task proved to be prohibitively expensive for the whole of England but Dorset was published before a final decision was made in this regard. The complete set of volumes published progressively between 1952 (West Dorset) and 1975 (East Dorset), is an excellent resource describing the then known monuments in great detail. Of course, such works contain information that can become quickly outdated in a relatively short space of time because they are describing features within landscapes which are continually evolving. New inter-pretations and new discoveries are constantly adding to our understanding of the past and the destruction and disturbance of many known sites necessarily requires a recording and inventory system which has greater flexibility than the published paper volume. However, even today the earliest of the volumes provides a great deal of accurate and relevant information which can be updated from English Heritage archives at the National Monuments Record centre in Swindon if required.

John Hutchins' *History of the Antiquities of Dorset* dominates earlier accounts of the ancient monuments of Dorset. First published in 1774 and eventually reaching a third edition in the second half of the nineteenth century, the work was published in four volumes. This exceptional early history of the county frequently describes and illustrates monuments as they appeared in the landscape as much as two hundred and thirty years ago (**3**). Records of ancient monuments made many years ago can often be used in their subsequent analysis, frequently shedding light upon episodic activity that has nothing to do with the original articulation of the moment. In volume 2 of the 1861 edition, a description of Kingston Russell Stone circle (see chapter 3) made by the Reverend James-Knight Moor (in 1815), indicates that the stone circle contained a single upright stone with a further twelve recumbent and even included a plan of the monument. By 1939 when Stuart Piggott reported on the known stone circles within the county, all of the stones at Kingston Russell were recumbent, which is how they are to be found today. The question as to whether or not any of the stones were ever upright is obviously made partially redundant by the nineteenth-century observation.

By the later half of the nineteenth century, the zeal within which the Victorians were enquiring into the ancient monuments of the Dorset landscape can be seen in the writings of Charles Warne. As we have already seen, Warne was an inveterate digger of barrows in the Dorset landscape between 1839-62 (Marsden, 1983, 56). Whilst his techniques of excavation were as limited as many others of his generation, he did manage to publish two texts which, to some

3 *The Hell Stone.
A print of the partially
collapsed monument before
its rebuild in the nineteenth
century. Compare with*
colour plates 2 *&* **3**

extent, contain his archaeological observations coupled with reflections on the
findings of those of his contemporaries. The publication of his *Celtic Tumuli of
Dorset* in 1866, was followed by the more expansive *Ancient Dorset* in 1870.

The thematic approach begun by Warne on the prehistoric barrows of Dorset
was certainly adopted by the archaeologist Lesley Grinsell, who published his
account of Dorset barrows nearly a century later, in 1955. Grinsell's analytical
work on barrows in Dorset was only a small part of his lifelong interest in the
subject of barrows, which included the publication of inventories for several other
English counties. His inventory and discussion must form the starting point for
any subsequent analysis of barrows in Dorset, which he revised with the publication of a supplement in 1982.

At the same time that Grinsell was working on barrows in the 1950s, the
academic examination of early landscapes was under fundamental review, particularly through the growing number of discoveries being made by the rapidly
evolving discipline of archaeology. Historians, many of whom naturally relied on
documents as their main resource, had largely dominated the academic debate on
the origins and evolution of the English landscape. Consequently, recognition of
the great antiquity of elements of our landscape was frequently underestimated.
The publication of *The Making of the English Landscape* by the landscape historian
W.G. Hoskins in 1954 actively encouraged the integration of contemporary field
observation with that of historical documentation, which has in part led to the
better understanding of relict landscapes and their origins. In 1970 Christopher
Taylor published an account of the development of the Dorset landscape, which
was very much influenced by the methodology of Hoskins, and made great use of
the findings of the increasing number of archaeological excavations and observa-

tions that were being made at the time. Taylor's account remains the most recent synthesis of the evolution of the cultural landscape of Dorset, which even after thirty years retains a great deal of relevance to the modern scholar.

Dorset – the bare bones and settlement distribution

Whilst we are primarily engaged with the investigation of 'cultural' activity in prehistoric Dorset, it is impossible to do this without reflecting upon the natural framework that in part has influenced human habitation and settlement from the earliest times to the present day.

The county of Dorset is located on the south coast of Britain and is bound by the counties of Hampshire to the east, Wiltshire to the north and Somerset and Devon to the west. The county boundaries enclose an area of 1024 square miles (265,216ha), approximately half of which is designated as an Area of Outstanding Natural Beauty. The boundaries of modern Dorset are, like those found elsewhere, a product of centuries of administrative development, which have little likely relevance to prehistoric land division, or indeed to the occupants of the region during those times. They do, however, form such a fundamental part of our current society that it is difficult to avoid them. I have accordingly not slavishly omitted sites of significance from the narrative if they lie outside of the county's boundaries if they are of consequence to the overall theme. This was particularly necessary in relating parts of the settlement evidence for the Bronze and Iron Ages, for which the sites excavated by General Pitt Rivers are of some importance, although they are located in each case no more than 5km to the wrong side of the county boundary.

Topographically Dorset can be divided into three regions that broadly relate to the general trends of the underlying geology (4). The underlying geology has always been a factor of influence in the human settlement pattern, as it in part influences soil formation processes on which agriculturalists are so dependent. Cutting a huge diagonal swathe through the central region of the county are the beds of Cretaceous chalk on whose light soils the greater proportion of prehistoric monuments are to be found. To the west and south of these deposits lie the older Jurassic deposits consisting of limestones, sandstones and clays, which form the vales of Blackmoor and Marshwood. These vales have yet to reveal extensive evidence for earlier prehistoric habitation although by the Iron Age the heavier clay soils of the area were able to support settlement, evidenced by the presence of hillforts, hilltop enclosures and remnants of extensive field systems which probably date to the period. To the east of the chalk lie the most recent geological deposits in the area, those of the Tertiary period. These deposits include sandstones, clays, and gravels that for the most part are topped by extensive heath-lands, which envelope Poole Basin, and extend eastwards into Hampshire forming the New Forest and the Hampshire Basin.

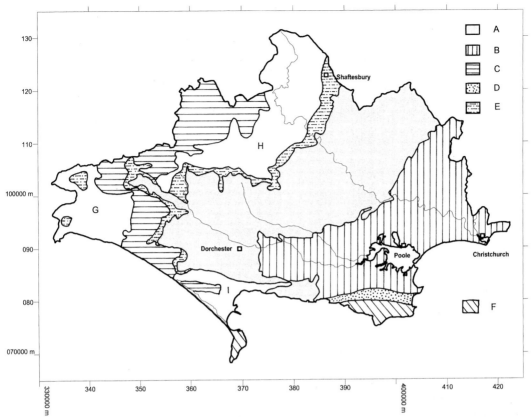

4 *The geological zones of Dorset. A simplified map of the county's geology including the major river basins.*
A − Chalk, B − Tertiary beds, C − Oolitic Limestones and Cornbrash, D − Wealden beds, E − Greensands,
F − Portland and Purbeck beds, G − Lias, H − Clays, I − Oxford Clay

The rivers of Dorset are relatively modest channels that have nonetheless played an important role in the formation of habitable landscapes both ancient and modern. The three major river systems consist of the Avon to the east, the Stour in central Dorset and the Frome to the south and west. All of these rivers have a network of tributaries which form the major drainage basins which predominantly outfall into Poole Bay. All of the rivers could have performed as communication and trade routes throughout the prehistoric period and would have been navigable for some distance by the small craft at such times. By the Iron Age, the trade of materials to and from the distribution centres on the south coast would have been made possible through use of these rivers, and settlement can be found near them on the interior. A significant number of hillforts are to be found strategically placed overlooking these rivers, probably positioned to protect and possibly administer effective trade and communication and perhaps in some cases linking in to a wider network of distribution.

The current distribution of archaeological sites found in the county (see distribution maps at the beginning of chapters 2-4), is in part a reflection on where sites have been observed and recorded, which in itself is not necessarily a true reflection of the total population or distribution in antiquity. There are many factors that can influence the recovery and survival of ancient sites and monuments, which can and do skew the evidence, resulting in possible unrepresentative distributions. The survival of a number of monuments on the chalk downs of central Dorset have been aided by the lack of intensive cultivation of soils in some areas after the monuments went out of use. Many areas of the chalk downs probably remained little cultivated for centuries. The relatively recent availability of chemical fertilisers combined with the general light and free draining soils has led to a marked intensification of cultivation of much (but not all) of the Dorset chalk downscapes which has intensified the destruction of a great deal of archaeological sites. That some round barrows survive as upstanding earthworks on the chalk downs today, whilst others have been flattened, is largely attributable to the land that they are located on having been largely given over to grazing in the ensuing centuries. Those areas that retained periods of intensive arable farming are consequently much more likely to have been denuded over time. A good example of this variable survival can be seen on Cranborne Chase where a large proportion of the round barrows in the barrow cemetery at Oakley Down are remarkably well-preserved. At Knowlton Rings, just a few miles to the south-west, very few barrows have survived (beyond that determined recently through aerial photographic remote sensing) because of intensive periods of cultivation. Consequently, the northern barrow cemetery at Knowlton has no observable barrows surviving above ground.

Increasingly the distribution of archaeological sites is also being affected by their identification through so-called 'rescue archaeology'. Thanks to planning policy guidelines introduced in the 1980s and with the co-operation of a large number of developers, many archaeological sites have been recorded prior to destruction, thereby rescued by record at least. However, the pattern of distribution will be skewed to reflect where development is taking place as well as that of past presence of activity.

Monuments as messengers

As I have indicated in the Preface, this book is very much about monuments and places rather than about 'things' or objects. As a prehistorian much of the information that I need to investigate the past is locked up in the places which were inhabited by our ancestors. Much necessary archaeological endeavour has been spent during the last century investigating places via the artefacts contained within them. Such artefacts frequently provide much information about human activity related to technology, economy and social intercourse. However, the monuments themselves are nothing if not artefacts, which although frequently damaged are still *in situ* and available for investigation through a variety of techniques. Although excavation is one of the fundamental tools available to the archaeologist, much important investigation can be undertaken without recourse to what is in effect controlled destruction. Increasingly, field archaeologists are using a vast array of techniques (geophysical and geochemical prospection are amongst the most productive) to extract information from monuments in the field that are non-destructive, all of which help in the task of piecing together the history and purpose that such monuments represent.

As will become apparent, many places in the landscape are used time and time again, sometimes after considerable interludes of apparent inactivity. One of the best visual examples of this is the Church Henge at Knowlton in East Dorset. Here, a henge monument was constructed towards the end of the Neolithic period (c.2500-2000 BC) which was certainly a focus for activity of some significance (5). During the Early Bronze Age, the importance of the immediate environs of the henge (and that of its companion monuments – see chapter 2) is reinforced by its adoption as a funerary complex with the construction of at least 170 round barrows. At this stage the henge itself may have been reused, as is likely with the larger southern henge nearby, perhaps with a change of use linked to the ceremonial utility of the wider landscape. During the later prehistoric period,

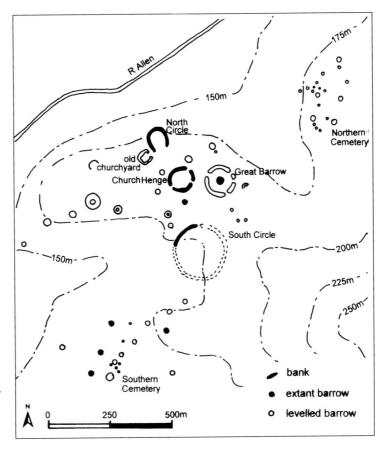

5 *The Knowlton complex. A complex of henge monuments, barrows, ring ditches and other features, yet to be defined*

there appears to be little evidence that the henge was formally used, although it would have been a major earthwork that would have been difficult to ignore. At some time during the Early Medieval period, the place was adopted by the Christian Church as a focus for the worship of God which culminated in the building of a chapel on the site during the twelfth century. The use of such pre-Christian sites as centres for Christian worship is not particularly unusual, but it does hint at the power of places to act as focal centres for gathering long after their original purpose and function has been forgotten. This is not to imply the presence of some mystical indefinable quality to the site, but rather that such sites retain a measure of elevated status beyond bare utility, passed on from generation to generation. No doubt such status can easily be corrupted into misplaced veneration when original explanations of purpose are lost over time, but this does not detract from the importance and continued value of such places. Indeed, it could be argued that new places are given credibility through the adoption of older respected sites that supply a firm foundation for new beginnings.

There are two fundamental questions that an archaeologist will address when examining a landscape that contains relics of the past, neither of which are particularly easy to answer. The questions are fundamental to our collective approach to understanding, and provide a framework from which a more detailed investigation can proceed. The questions are quite simple ones. Firstly, what is it? Any answer to this requires definition as well as classification because we are addressing activity that is probably significantly alien to our own cultural perception. Secondly, what date is it? Which question is asked first is largely irrelevant as in many cases they are dependent on each other. These questions are, of course, also the same questions which archaeologists themselves are asked when approached by others outside of the discipline. Anyone who has been on, or indeed has given a tour of an archaeological site, will be familiar with such questions.

The following pages are, therefore, an attempt at creating a framework for the further study of the prehistoric monuments of Dorset. It is a framework that is constructed upon the foundations laid down by a considerable number of archaeologists over the last century, and it begins around the time of the first agriculturalists.

2

THE NEOLITHIC

A LANDSCAPE OF
HARMONIOUS ADAPTATION?

It is with the period universally classified as the Neolithic that we begin our description of the occupation of Dorset. It is true that we can find substantial evidence for human habitation in the county at considerably more distant times, but it is with the arrival of the first farmers during this period that we see clear evidence for monumental construction and shaping of the landscape. It is this monumental construction, manifest in a variety of forms, which heralds the introduction of so many social, economic and political changes, that has consequently attracted scholars to its description and investigation over many years. Such investigations have understandably tried to comprehend why such changes came about, as well as describing their location and present nature and extent.

However, we must begin by sketching out what the Neolithic means and the fundamental issues that are associated with it. The 'three age' division of time which consists of: Stone (of which the Neolithic is the final stage); Bronze and Iron, which was developed towards the end of the nineteenth century, is a necessarily crude structure into which the progressive development of technology (and the people associated with it) is defined and analysed. It is a structure which has served the discipline of archaeology well, and will no doubt do so for the foreseeable future. Its origins are to be found in the classification of artefacts, which are the products of the cultures that created them and which consequently convey attributes of style and utility associated with those cultures. They are also, however, objects which are essentially controlled by the level of technological competence of the culture that created them, a process which, chronologically, is chiefly (but not exclusively!) linear. The artefacts of these cultures can therefore be compared, contrasted and ordered into a typological sequence which equates to a linear progression. When we examine the artefacts associated with this period compared with those that preceded it, we notice fundamental changes which herald a different way of life from what had gone on before. New stone tools are being manufactured and used, suggesting that different 'tool kits' are now required for daily life. Interestingly, this adaptation

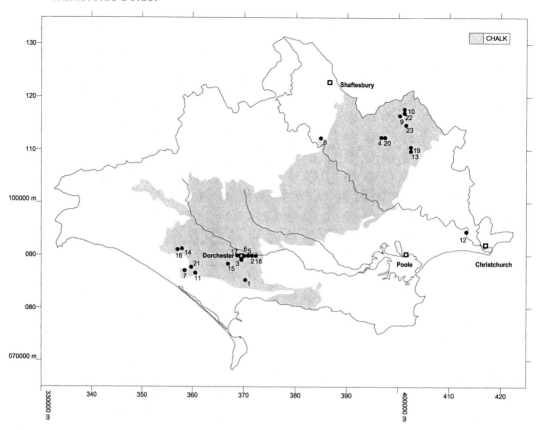

6 *Map of Neolithic sites mentioned in chapter 2. 1 – Broadmayne bank barrow, 2 – Conquer Barrow, 3 – Conygar Hill (pit-rings), 4 – Dorset Cursus, 5 – Flagstones, 6 – Fordington, 7 – Grey Mare and Her Colts, 8 – Hambledon Hill, 9 – Handley Down mortuary enclosure, 10 – Handley Down Neolithic round barrow, 11 – Hell Stone, 12 – Holdenhurst long barrow, 13 – Knowlton, 14 – Long Bredy cursus, 15 – Maiden Castle, 16 – Martin's Down bank barrow, 17 – Maumbury Rings, 18 – Mount Pleasant, 9 – The Great barrow, 20 – Thickthorn Down barrow, 21 – Valley of Stones, 22 – Wor barrow, 23 – Wyke Down*

of stone tools coincides with the introduction of pottery storage vessels, an innovation which would not have been of great use for the preceding Mesolithic communities, who required vessels to be more robust, in order to be able to withstand the demands of mobile communities. However, as discussed in the previous chapter, this book focuses upon places and people and only by association on objects. These changes in the artefactual record, as we shall see, also coincide with major changes taking place in the landscape, evidenced by the construction of great earth and stone monuments and more subtle traces of environmental change in the flora and fauna records of the time.

It is tempting to view such changes as immediate and profound but the evidence points us in another direction. The changes are progressive adaptations, which are largely the product of the gradual introduction of new developments whose impact is likely to have been minimal at an individual and personal level. It is relatively rare for evolutionary change to be so immediate that it impacts greatly upon individual lives, even in our own apparent highly-charged and adaptive western culture; change keeps pace with the generations and more particularly with the pace of communication. In the past, particularly the prehistoric past, the methods and geographical extent of communication were technologically limited and consequently the pace of the transposition of new ideas to new individuals and communities was shackled. Similarly, those great instigators of change, conquest and colonisation, do have a place in our considerations but must be seen in the context of the likely social and political constructs of the time. Whilst no doubt complex, such constructs are unlikely to have been able to mount or maintain widespread control and change over large tracts of landscape without supportive and effective forms of communication. Therefore, changes observable in the archaeological record evidenced by the introduction of new items of material culture or indeed the physical alteration of parts of the landscape, must be seen as evolutionary rather than revolutionary.

What then it might be asked are these changes, what do they consist of, and why did they come about? The description, at least of these changes, is relatively straightforward, and perhaps we should, therefore, begin by looking at the chronological development of the Neolithic landscape of Dorset through the monuments that they have left behind.

The early Neolithic – the beginnings of monumental expression

The first flickers of change in the monumental record of this time are not difficult to see, if for no other reason than the preceding occupation was not essentially predisposed to the construction of monuments to any particular purpose. The inhabitants of Mesolithic Dorset were essentially hunter-gatherers whose way of life was largely mobile. Mobile communities, by definition, need to move around the landscape, harvesting the fruits of that landscape universally governed by the climatic seasons. As soon as the resources available to them in an area are insufficient to meet their needs they consequently are forced to move on to a new one, and so on. The need to construct substantial dwellings or associated structures for such communities is, therefore, largely absent. The habitation site excavated by Susanne Palmer at Culverwell on the Isle of Portland (Palmer, 1999) is probably one of the best known in the county and it is certainly the most recently investigated. An extensive programme of fieldwork and excavation on the site has revealed a large midden deposit containing considerable quantities of occupational material including lithic tools and the debitage from their manufacture. The midden was also associated with a deliberately constructed limestone pavement or floor as well as hearths and working areas.

Such midden deposits and their association with Mesolithic coastal dwellers are a fairly common characteristic of human activity in this period in various parts of

Britain, and for that matter in the world at large. The habitation at the site was dated by the use of both radiocarbon and thermoluminescence techniques resulting in a date of around 5500 BC. Evidence for the construction of a dwelling is limited to a small number of post-holes, which may have supported a roofed shelter. The inhabitants of the site demonstrably made ample use of the resources available to them, chiefly through access to abundant supplies of sea food in the form of molluscs which may have enabled them to be less dependent on mobility than their counterparts inland. The midden contained large quantities of molluscs, but surprisingly little evidence for the exploitation of fish or small mammals. It has been postulated by the excavator that the large quantities of flint 'picks' found on the site suggest that vegetable matter may have formed a considerable part of the diet of the inhabitants, perhaps as a supplement to molluscs or perhaps during those times when molluscs were scarcer.

The site at Culverwell demonstrates quite effectively the features which archaeologists use to compartmentalise behavioural characteristics into technological epochs – in this case the Mesolithic. The lack of evidence for the management of the landscape in the site's material remains hints at a community that required little need for a substantial dwelling beyond that which could easily be erected as a temporary shelter. Similarly, the archaeologically-recovered evidence suggests that the subsistence base was dependent upon making use of what was naturally available to them, with little substantive evidence for the domestication of animals or vegetation.

This type of activity is mirrored throughout the southern coast of England during this period and as fieldwork progresses, more and more sites are coming to light. These sites are providing archaeologists with a firmer foundation of knowledge concerning their basic interpretations of Mesolithic communities. Increasingly, it is possible to enhance our knowledge, not only of the level and extent of activity but also the finer details of the social and political structures which maintained such communities.

Change, however, did emerge and that change is often seen to be dramatic, bringing with it domestication and taming of the environment, more sedentary forms of habitation, and monumental construction, including new forms of funerary monuments. All of these things can be inter-linked with considerable social economic and political change, in what can only be described as a major evolution in the nature of the human habitat. So, when did it occur and what evidence is there for it within the confines of the modern county of Dorset?

As we have seen in chapter 1, elements of prehistoric activity frequently survive in our own landscape, albeit in relict form. Understandably, the further one progresses back in time, the more fragmentary such remains become, and the monuments of the Neolithic can be amongst the most fragmentary of all. However, they do constitute a major cultural resource with which we are able to piece together the past at this important stage in our cultural evolution.

What then are these monuments which appear in the Dorset landscape and herald such fundamental changes in the way our ancestors lived around 6,000 years

ago? They comprise of a relatively small number of 'types', which have been identified throughout southern England, and most of them are to be found within
Dorset. The monuments comprise:

- Causewayed enclosures (also referred to as causewayed camps or interrupted
  ditch systems/enclosures)
- Long barrows and bank barrows
- Long mortuary enclosures
- Cursus

The following descriptions and discussions of these monuments are conducted in no
particular sequence and certainly do not imply a chronological order to their origin
in the landscape. Whilst causewayed enclosures and long barrows are generally
considered to be the earliest of monuments constructed in the British Isles, very few
absolute dates are available for those from Dorset. Similarly, the dating of the bank
barrows, which are a unique phenomenon to the region is poorly defined (particularly if the example from Maiden Castle is discounted – see discussion below). Their
chronological sequence within the scheme of monument building in the region is
therefore based upon a crude, but probably reliable affinity to the long barrows, with
which they share common characteristics and probably ancestry.

Causewayed enclosures

A recent survey (Oswald, Dyer & Barber 2001) has established that 66 examples
of this form of monument are currently known to have existed in the British Isles.
The majority of these are to be found south of a line drawn between the Wash
and the Severn Estuary. Three such enclosures are located within Dorset and all
of them have been the subject of archaeological excavation in recent years.

The term 'causewayed enclosure' defines a group of monuments, which share
some basic constructional elements but do not necessarily all share the same
commonality of purpose. They consist primarily of one or more circuits of bank
and ditch, where the ditches (and sometimes the banks) are discontinuous. There
has been much academic debate concerning these monuments over the last fifty
years but even today we have to recognise that our understanding of them is still
at a very basic level. What they clearly represent, however, is a major investment
by the societies that created them, at least in terms of time and labour. It is perhaps
easy for us to look at the relatively diminutive surviving remains of these
monuments today and be initially under-impressed by their impact on the
landscape (8). However, we must be aware that to the contemporary society that
was responsible for their construction, they would have been engaging in the
creation of an expression of their cultural identity within a landscape that was
quite literally devoid of any other significant similar cultural feature (with the
possible exception of a long barrow or two). All of these monuments are notable
feats of engineering, created with nothing but the simplest of tools and each

would have taken thousands of man-hours to complete. Such an investment speaks volumes for the importance that these monuments must have held to their respective communities, a fact bolstered by widespread evidence of the rebuilding and remodelling that seems to be evidenced in many of those sites that have been archaeologically investigated. Whilst the Dorset examples are perhaps better understood than many, they do highlight quite effectively the differences in archaeological data which result in different interpretations as to their function.

The example at Maiden Castle, on the outskirts of modern day Dorchester, was initially discovered buried beneath the later defences of the Iron Age hillfort by Sir Mortimer Wheeler in 1937. However, the Neolithic origins of the site had been suspected many years previously with the discovery of numerous 'artefacts' of Neolithic date being found in the vicinity (Croft 1907). A further programme of excavations undertaken by Sharples in 1985-6 has increased our understanding of the enclosure and the activity that took place within it. The enclosure consists of two circuits of ditch, possibly constructed at the same time, with no traces of any surviving bank. The results of radiocarbon analysis of material from the primary fills of these ditches suggest that they were excavated around 3800 BC. The presence of the causewayed enclosure ditch was determined in six separate trenches during Wheeler's campaign, but later activity has made it extremely difficult to determine with any certainty the plan of the original enclosure. However, there is every likelihood that the builders of the first hillfort during the Iron Age used the then partially-surviving Neolithic enclosure earthworks as their template for their own enclosure. This would certainly fit with the known location of the ditches below the western and eastern Iron Age ramparts. If this is the case, the original ditch system enclosed an area of approximately 4ha. The two ditches were spaced approximately 14-15m apart, with the inner ditch being the larger of the two in terms of general volume. The inner ditch appears to have been originally constructed in sections, which were subsequently joined together, creating a continuous ditch. The depth of the ditch varied from between 1.2-1.6m and its profile was round-bottomed, with relatively straight sides and varied in width at the top between 3-4m. The outer ditch, where sampled, was noticeably smaller in width than its counterpart (1.7-2.4m) although it was slightly deeper, 1.35-1.8m. This outer ditch was flat-bottomed, which is certainly more common amongst other contemporary monuments. The outer ditch also showed evidence for the presence of archetypal causeways. The apparent differences between the inner and outer ditches have prompted speculation as to their homogeneity, at least in the earliest construction phase. However, the range of radiocarbon dates from the primary fills of each of the ditches was essentially very similar, and consequently, if there is any constructional phasing between the two ditch elements, the interval between them is likely to be in the order of a small number of years, and certainly beyond the precision of radiocarbon determination.

When we examine the excavations of both Wheeler and Sharples to look for evidence of activity which might shed some light as to the purpose of the enclosure, we find only fragmentary clues. Certainly neither campaign of excavations sampled any significant area of the Neolithic interior and what was sampled was compromised by later earthworks and associated activity, particularly during the Iron Age occupation of the hill-top. A series of pits and post-holes sealed by the construction of a linear mound (see below) are potentially contemporary with the enclosure. The difficulty arises not only in determining a date for these features, but also in that there is no pattern discernible to them. The best evidence for the use of the monument comes from material contained within the enclosure ditches, particularly that found in the outer ditch. Although the outer ditch was truncated by later activity, the basal fill contained a deposit of animal and human bones which were accompanied by a scatter of flint flakes and a stone axe. Nearby, a human skull was found, thought to be from an adult male. It is thought that these buried remains represent carefully structured depositions and are not the product of casual dumping from adjacent areas. As to the purpose of such action, it would appear that it may be associated with reaffirmation of the monument's importance to the people that used it, beyond which we can only guess.

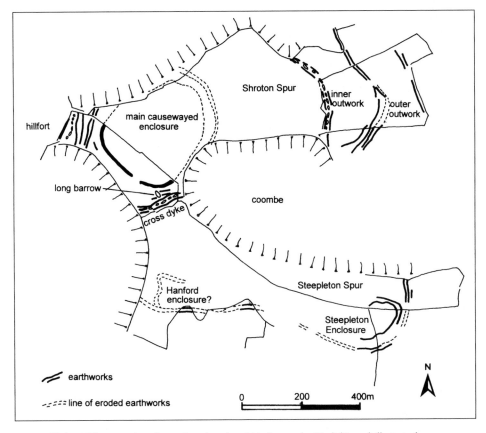

7 *Hambledon Hill: a complex of several earthworks which date to the Neolithic and illustrate the power, longevity and organisation of contemporary society at the time.* Redrawn with amendments from Mercer 1980

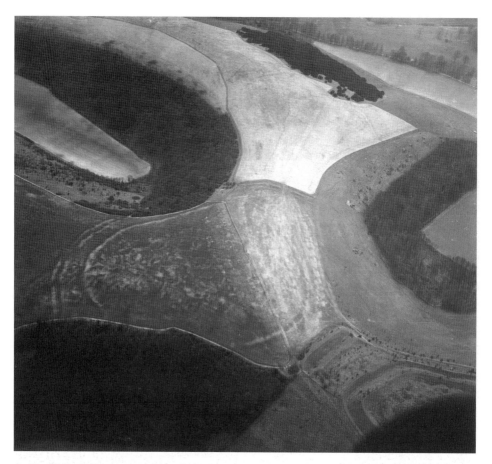

8 *Hambledon Hill: main Neolithic enclosure from the air, 1968. Note the erosion of the earthworks compared to figure* **9**. © Crown copyright, NMR

At Hambledon Hill in the north of the county we have one of the largest Neolithic monument complexes in the British Isles (**7**). As with the site at Maiden Castle, the monument's location was considered to be special as it was also later chosen as the site of an Iron Age hillfort (chapter 4). However, unlike Maiden Castle, the later defensive earthwork did not occupy precisely the same spot in the landscape, and the Neolithic activity consisted of not one but two enclosures, with additional outworks. Although the main enclosure, which is located on the crown of the hill from which it takes its name, is barely discernible today, it was until fairly recent times in a much better state of preservation. Two aerial photographs of the main enclosure at Hambledon demonstrate well the adverse effects of less than 50 years of unchecked agricultural activity on relatively low earthworks. The earlier aerial photograph taken in 1924, **9** clearly shows the earthworks of both the bank and ditch of an irregularly-shaped enclosure, evidenced as shadowed relief (above the more pronounced Iron Age ramparts). The later photograph, taken in 1968 (**8**) shows exactly the same area and it is clearly apparent that the same earthworks

9 *Hambledon Hill: main Neolithic enclosure from the air 1924. The low relief of the enclosure can be seen above the more extensive earthworks of the Iron Age hillfort.* NMR (Keiller Collection)

largely survive only as a soil mark, with the banks of the enclosure having been the main casualty. During the time between these photographs the site was subjected to a number of archaeological interventions which determined the extent of the earth-works and some limited exploratory trenching established their nature and date.

In addition to the main enclosure, surveying undertaken in the 1960s also observed the presence of further earthworks on connecting spurs to the east and south-east. All of these features were the subject of a major excavation programme undertaken by Roger Mercer between 1974-86.

The first stage of this excavation programme concentrated on the main enclosure with parts of the interior and the enclosure ditch and banks being inves-tigated. The interior of the enclosure contained 97 pits, all of which had, however, been seriously truncated by recent agricultural activity. The purpose of these pits remains ambiguous, with many of them apparently containing structured deposits of artefacts within episodes of deliberate backfilling. Amongst quite diverse deposits, which include selected flint tools, greenstone axes and sandstone rubbers there were 14 instances of the deposition of red deer antlers in the bottom of the pits (Mercer 1980, 21-3). Many of these pits had been open for a period of time prior to backfilling, which was identifiable by a thin layer of washed silt in the pit bottoms. Very little additional evidence of a structural nature survives from the interior but this is compromised by the level of truncation of the interior surface that has occurred, particularly in recent times. The excavator estimated that a depth of at least 30-40cm of the interior has been lost since the Neolithic period – significant enough to lose all trace of any lightly built structures. In fact, no post-holes were recorded from the surface of the interior of the enclosure, which is perhaps surprising given the intensity of the pit distribution and the high density of artefacts recovered.

The major findings of Mercer's campaign of excavation were, however, to be found in the ditches of the main enclosure. Ditch fills associated with many of the monumental earthworks from the prehistoric (and historic) periods generally survive intact, and within their fills much of the evidence which enables archae-ologists to partially reconstruct the past is frequently found. Typically material either migrates into ditches naturally from the surrounding area or it is deliberately placed in them by human or animal activity. Of course the material concerned can vary enormously from discarded artefacts to environmental indicators such as molluscs or pollen. Much of this material will degrade over time but many materials survive, if only in fragmentary form, which often allows for effective reconstruction not only of human activity, but also of contemporary environ-mental and climatic conditions. The ditches at the Hambledon Hill Neolithic complex are an excellent example of how this process can work. Careful excava-tion has revealed a complex progression of deposits within the ditch which has provided a tantalising glimpse into aspects of human behaviour practised by our ancestors during the early part of the fourth millennium BC. The ditches of the main causewayed enclosure initially appear to have been intended as a quarry to

enable the construction of a bank on its inner side. The segmented ditches themselves comprised a number of contiguous pits, which seem to be associated with
the method of excavation rather than any particular design feature. Mercer's interpretation of this process suggests that the organisation of labour entailed two or
three individuals working together, excavating material on a predetermined
circuit, stopping only when sufficient material had been excavated to satisfy the
requirements for the construction of the inner bank. The inferred behaviour
seems to be suggesting that at this early stage of the monument's construction
there was a need to create a defined place within the landscape. This place required
definition by the erection of banks of earth and chalk in three concentric circuits.
Although the banks have not survived, their presence could be determined
through their remains slipping over time into the ditches from which they originally came. The banks themselves are unlikely to have been of any great height,
probably no more than 2m and were almost certainly linked to a series of posts
which formed a timber breastwork or palisade, which could have protruded above
the crest of the earthwork as much as 2–3m. This arrangement, however, could be
interpreted in many other ways. As yet, there is no clear indication as to likely
entrances into the enclosure, and certainly the causeways between the ditch
segments are rarely matched by gaps in the inner bank, which further indicates the
suppressed significance of the ditches.

Very soon after the monument was constructed, the bottom of the ditch was
scoured clean, removing initial deposits of primary filling which would have
consisted of primary silts or colluvium washing into the ditch. This activity is
interesting in that it implies a degree of maintenance and explicit control over the
monument presentation to the people or communities that used it. Precisely why
this was done is unknown, but it does herald a course of events which combine
to suggest that the function of the ditches of the enclosure held much more significance as the years progressed.

Following this cleansing of the ditch, deposits of organic material along with flint
waste, pottery and quantities of disarticulated human bone, possibly originally
bound together within organic containers, were laid out in the bottom of parts of
the circuit. Other parts of the ditch circuit have a deposit of human skulls, often
seemingly deliberately placed at the base of the ditch. The circumstances of these
deposits would indicate that these were deposited as skulls and not as fleshed human
heads. In the northern part of the enclosure ditch there are more occurrences of
human remains being interred deliberately, but in these cases in a much more recognisable way. Two intact infant burials were discovered, both within separately cut
graves in the ditch floors. The body position of each case was of a tightly crouched
form, which had been subsequently covered by separate flint cairns.

A further deposit of human remains discovered in the south-eastern sector of
the monument was felt by the excavator to be the key to unravelling the whole of
the monument's purpose. The trunk of a fifteen-year-old male was discovered
lying underneath a pile of flint nodules. The trunk had entered the ditch

articulated, which indicates that at that stage it was still fleshed. The only damage to the surviving skeletal remains appeared to be related to tooth marks caused by animal gnawing on the femurs. The interpretation for this event suggests that the partly decomposed remains of the individual were dragged or thrown into the ditch, during which time they were partially devoured by animals and then buried under a cairn of flints. Following this activity the ditches appear to fill quite naturally, with the internal banks slipping into them, all of which indicates a period of decline for the monument. The monument later displays periods of new activity, with a series of pits being dug into the ditch fills, which are deliberately filled with ash – they also contained fragmentary remains of human bone. It is unclear as to whether or not this material is simply residual within the fills of the pits, having been part of the excavated soil from the pits later mixed with the ash.

Investigation of the second enclosure at Hambledon Hill located on the Stepleton spur commenced in 1977, although confirmation of its status as a cause-wayed enclosure was not confirmed until more extensive excavation in the following year. Its date appears to be broadly contemporary with the main enclosure but it is significantly smaller, consisting of a single circuit of bank and ditch enclosing approximately 1ha. The Stepleton enclosure appears to display little of the complex pattern of recutting and ritual deposits that we have seen within the main enclosure. The ditch also appears to consist of fewer causeways, and its internal bank was primarily continuous and possibly more massive than its near neighbour. An entrance gateway was identified on its eastern arc, which coincided with a wide causeway spanning two ditch segments. Here, as elsewhere with this monument, considerable evidence for a conflagration was discovered, with extensive remains of what appears to have been a torched timber breastwork that would have lain above the bank. The remains of an intact male human skeleton were located in the ditch terminal adjacent to this gateway, which appears to have been deposited during this conflagration and presumably relates to the circumstances surrounding the event. The finding of a leaf-shaped arrowhead in the vicinity of his thoracic cavity certainly provides us with information as to how he met his death, and suggests that the event marks what could be described as a raid. If this is the case, it represents the earliest instance of what one might consider as localised warfare in the county. Elsewhere in the ditches of the Stepleton enclosure, deposits of disarticulated human bone are to be found but their occur-rences are fewer in number and interestingly, the circumstances of their deposition differs significantly to those of the main enclosure. The human crania in two out of four cases appear to have been fleshed indicating that they at least entered the ditch soon after death and presumably, therefore, under different circumstances from those previously noted.

The interior of the Stepleton enclosure has, like its counterpart, suffered badly from post-1950 agricultural erosion. The survival of significant numbers of truncated pits and post-holes, however, some of which seem to be concentrated directly behind the position where the bank once would have stood, have given rise to speculation as to the domestic character of the evidence. However, the data is partial and other interpretations, of equal validity, could be tendered.

We know from evidence taken from excavation elsewhere in the British Isles that the picture regarding the purpose of causewayed enclosures is compromised by our limited taxonomic criteria of classification. The understanding that cause-wayed enclosures simply represent a constructional technique for creating places by bounding space largely confines the classification to the academic dustbin; however, as we have yet to establish a more radical or developed alternative, it remains for the moment a useful vehicle for further study. The evidence from the three Dorset sites in the meantime provides a relatively straightforward interpreta-tion. All the enclosures appear to date to the first half of the fourth millennium BC and all display the same general constructional form of circuits of segmented ditches with internal banks, which are largely continuous. There is fragmentary evidence that all of the enclosures probably had some form of timber breastwork or light palisade associated with the banks, although the example at the Stepleton enclosure was possibly more substantial than the others. Many of the ditches contained structured deposits but in the case of the main enclosure at Hambledon Hill, these appear to be primarily funerary in nature and related to the exposure of cadavers for natural de-fleshing or excarnation prior to interment in more permanent structures (see long barrows below). The other structured deposits found in the ditches at Maiden Castle and the Stepleton enclosure could be associated with more ambiguous votive offerings which affirm the monument's significance not only during their construction but also perhaps periodically during their use. The tentative suggestion that the Stepleton enclosure may be the setting for domestic activity, possibly even settlement, cannot be discounted, but equally it remains unproven.

Long barrows, bank barrows, mortuary enclosures and chambered tombs
Of all the monuments associated with the first Neolithic communities, it is with long barrows that we most readily identify. This is probably because they have, generally speaking, survived as upstanding earthworks better than other contem-porary structures, and their meaning and purpose is on the face of it fairly well understood. The phrase 'houses for the dead' has been used by numerous authors over the decades to describe such barrows but their outward appearance belies a complexity of form and ritual which transcends overly simplistic explanation and interpretation as receptacles for the remains of the dead.

Traditionally long barrows broadly comprise an elongated mound, either parallel sided or trapezoidal in plan, which is usually accompanied by flanking ditches that sometimes conjoin but more typically do not. The mounds follow two basic traditions in southern England, those that are constructed of stone and earth, and those which contain stone chambers which can be further sub-divided into various types. The differences between these two general traditions, manifest in surviving monuments today, are not always apparent and whilst many may outwardly appear to be of the earthen form, they can indeed contain stone-built chambers. Both basic forms exist in Dorset, although the confirmed number of long barrows which contain chambers is very much the minority, a fact which is perhaps partially explained by the distinct lack of stone suitable for the construction of chambers anywhere but in the west of the county. At the time of Lesley Grinsell's study of Dorset barrows in 1959, there were 47 surviving barrows which he considered to be broadly of long barrow form (including those with chambers and chambered tombs). Since Grinsell's initial survey, which also identified a number of possible sites that are referred to in antiquarian records but cannot now be located, a number of additional barrows have also been identified. The total of potential long barrow sites that have some substantive evidence has now risen to approximately 60 examples, but it is unlikely that this figure will grow much higher. The distribution of these barrows is almost exclusively limited to the chalk downlands of the county, with only two recorded examples being located on a different geology (Gillingham on limestone and Holdenhurst on alluvial gravels). The distribution further highlights the two major concentrations of barrows, one located to the east on Cranborne Chase, with the second clustering close to the south western extremities of the chalk downs between Bridport and Dorchester. Those barrows which are known to be associated with chambers or could be considered as chambered tombs, have a distinct distribution pattern located within a very few miles west of Dorchester. This clustering is almost certainly influenced by the availability of suitable sarsen boulders, which outcrop near the village of Portesham in an area known as the Valley of Stones.

The significance attributed to the orientation of long barrows has been the subject of discussion since the early observations by William Stukely in the middle of the eighteenth century. Generally speaking, the orientation of long barrows in the whole of southern England conforms to an east-west articulation, which is usually interpreted as having celestial origins with the rising and setting of the sun. Whilst the examples from Dorset (10) broadly follow the trends observed elsewhere there is a significant group which bucks this trend. The barrows located on Cranborne Chase in the east of the county are more usually orientated south-east/north-west or even south-south-east/north-north-west. Paul Ashbee noticed this apparent anomaly in his study of *The Earthen Long Barrow in Britain* in 1970, and his rationale related the errant barrows to the topography. Many of the barrows concerned are located upon north-north-west/south-south-east ridges with which the barrows noticeably orientate. Why such a universal design should be abandoned will probably never be known, but the example does serve to illustrate that universal schemes or conventions of behaviour were extant within communities during the period, and that a degree of latitude was possible under certain circumstances.

The siting of the mounds, like orientation, can be generalised, with the great majority being located on, or slightly to one side of, ridges. It seems clear that such uniformity of siting implies, once again, universal conventions subject to regional variation. What does appear to be central to the siting of these barrows is their

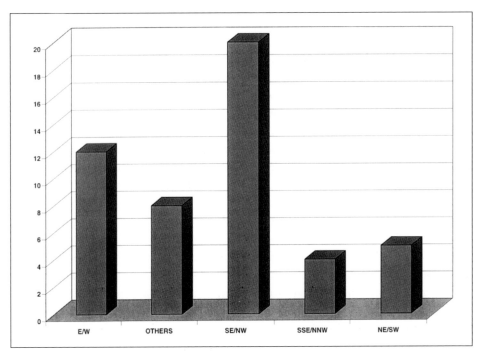

10 *Histogram of the alignments of Neolithic long barrows in Dorset. Data is drawn from Grinsell 1959 and 1982 and includes bank barrows*

dominance within a landscape; they were meant to be seen and therefore could be said to be statements or symbols of a cultural language of the contemporary populations. Some commentators have inferred that the barrows are the territorial markers of groups, perhaps located at the periphery of territorial ranges, whilst others have viewed them as a spiritual focus for communities which perhaps grew out of a reverence for their ancestors culminating in a type of cult-based worship.

At least 17 of these monuments in Dorset are recorded as having been partly or wholly excavated, but only five of them during the last 70 years. Antiquarian interest in long barrows has a long tradition dating back to the early eighteenth century. Unfortunately many of these early diggings were inexpertly undertaken and in many cases the findings were never reported. Probably the earliest examination of a Dorset long barrow occurred at Thickthorn Bar in the parish of Chettle which was opened around 1700. The following account, taken from John Hutchin's *History and Antiquities of the County of Dorset,* gives a flavour of the level of information recoverable in the 1860s:

> Beneath the level of the surface of the field, a great quantity of human bones were found, and with them heads of spears, and other warlike instruments, which were presented to the Earl of Pembroke, and are among his curiosities at Wilton House. (1863, 567)

35

Other barrows fared slightly better in terms of recorded information over the next two hundred years, but it is only with the work of General Pitt-Rivers in 1893 that we see a standard of excavation and recording which approaches modern methods and standards. Pitt-Rivers's approach was notable in many ways, but what stands out is the quality of recorded observations and the academic rigour with which he pursued his investigations. The level of detail found in his privately published reports not only charts his systematic approach to excavation, but also enables a retrospective analysis of the results. In 1893 Pitt-Rivers excavated the long barrow known as Wor Barrow, located on Cranborne Chase, whose remains form part of the later Oakley Down Barrow Group (see chapter 3). The excavation demonstrated, for the first time, a sequence of construction and use for a long barrow. Such was the quality of the collection and recording during the excavation that it was possible to submit a sample of antlers discovered by him from the barrow's quarry ditch for radiocarbon dating over half a century later (3790-3100 BC). The barrow itself has been the subject of reinterpretation since 1893 but it seems clear that the construction of the main mound was preceded by an earlier mound which was itself associated with earlier funerary structures (see mortuary enclosures below).

Of those earthen long barrows excavated within the county in recent times, the excavations at Thickthorn Down on Cranborne Chase (Drew & Piggott 1936, 77-96; Bradley & Entwistle 1985, 174-6) and Holdenhurst near Christchurch in the 1930s (Piggott 1937, 1-14) are amongst the most complete. In addition, more recent excavations at Fordington in Dorchester (Davies *et al.* 1985, 102-110) and on Hambledon Hill (Mercer 1980) have added valuable breadth to our understanding of these often complex monuments.

The Holdenhurst Barrow (**11**) near Christchurch, as we have seen, is unusual in that it is the only recorded long barrow located on the heathlands of Dorset. It was excavated in the winter of 1936 by a young archaeologist, Stuart Piggott. The barrow lay in an area of development and because the barrow had no legal protection it was to be destroyed. Although time and resources would not allow the total excavation of the barrow, a significant sample was undertaken by means of 33 separate excavation trenches. The excavations revealed that the heaping-up of a turf-revetted earthen mound was the final act of closure in the creation of a monument whose earliest phase was much more modest in scale. Predating the construction of the larger mound and located at its southern end, there was a turf mound, measuring approximately 5.5m in length and 3m in width, which had been raised above the old ground surface, covering a patch of charcoal. Piggott's report (1937, 1-14) suggests that this turf mound probably covered human remains, but that these had been subsequently dissolved after burial in the acidic soils of the burial site. Following the burial of these remains with a turf stack, the site was aggrandised by the construction of a larger mound with turf-revetted sides, whose quarry ditches unusually not only flanked the lateral edges but also extended around the southern end. The majority of long barrows

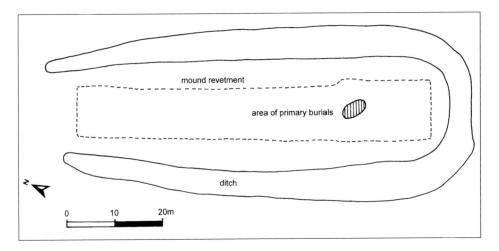

mound revetment

area of primary burials

ditch

N

0   10   20m

11 *Holdenhurst long barrow: this barrow was excavated in 1936 prior to its location's subsequent development. An early example of 'Rescue archaeology' in the county.* Redrawn with amendments from Piggott 1937

have one structurally dominant end, that is to say the focus of activity both functional and ritual, is usually confined to one of the ends, which is visualised in a broader and/or higher structure to the mound itself. In trapezoidal or pear-shaped mounds this is usually self-evident, but barrows that have parallel sides frequently do not display such a characteristic. The Holdenhurst example was of the pear-shaped variety whose dominant end was to the south. The site's investigation was conducted some years before the advent of absolute dating techniques and consequently was dated primarily through the examination of artefacts from stratified deposits within the structure. Pottery recovered from the earliest fills of the ditches is of plain baggy bowl types, similar to the earliest ceramic wares of southern England, comparable with Hembury and Windmill Hill forms.

Piggott's excavation of the Holdenhurst barrow followed his earlier investigation of another long barrow on Cranborne Chase in 1933. Along with C.D. Drew, Piggott's excavation of one of the Neolithic barrows on Thickthorn Down remains amongst the most closely studied and published of this site type in Dorset (Drew & Piggott 1936, 77-96; Bradley & Entwistle 1985). This barrow is one of a pair of long barrows whose alignment seems to be associated with the southern terminal end of the largest of all the Neolithic monuments in the British Isles – the Dorset Cursus (**17**).

Unlike the Holdenhurst excavation, the barrow at Thickthorn was totally excavated, and therefore the monument that you see today is the result of restoration immediately following the excavation. The results of the excavation revealed that the barrow was entirely of earthen construction, and comprised a rather short mound enclosed by a ditch on its lateral sides, with the ditch extending round its

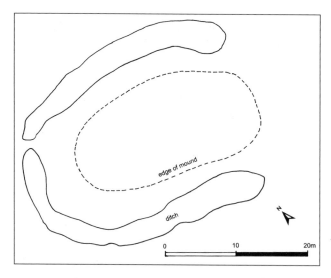

12 *Thickthorn Down barrow: excavated in 1933 by Drew and Piggott this site is conventionally interpreted as a long barrow. It does however, have an oval mound and an unusual ditch layout not unlike others on Cranborne Chase which have given rise to a possible variant form.* Redrawn with amendments from Drew and Piggott 1936

north-western end. The mound itself could be said to be more oval in form (**12**), certainly with no clear topographical evidence of a dominant end. Along with a number of other barrows in Dorset, the example at Thickthorn comprises a regional variation of form seen nowhere else, and is defined largely by the U-shaped form of the enclosing quarry ditch. This type was initially defined by Ashbee (1980, 15) but has also been discussed by Barrett, Bradley and Green (1990, 36).

The Thickthorn barrow contained a number of inhumations within the mound itself, but all were the product of secondary interments of the Early Bronze Age (**35**). Although not unique, Thickthorn is a relatively rare example of a long barrow which appears to contain no primary interments. As with the Holdenhurst example, the excavators identified the existence of what they assumed to be another example of a turf mound which had preceded the erection of the final chalk and earth barrow. This feature appeared to have been very ill-defined and it has been suggested by Bradley and Entwistle (1985, 174-6) that the trace obser-vations made by the excavators might be more readily explained as part of a bayed construction technique for the whole of the later mound. This involved bays or partitions formed along the axis of the monument which were probably constructed of turf and subsequently filled in. This method of constructing mounds is very well paralleled in an example from Beckhampton near Avebury in Wiltshire (Smith & Evans, 1968, 138-42) which also shares the distinction of having contained no primary burials.

The dating of the Thickthorn Barrow, like the Holdenhurst example, was achieved typologically through the ceramic and flint materials recovered from the excavations. The earliest pottery, plain Windmill Hill types, was found in small quantities in the primary fills of the barrow ditches, with greater quantities of later impressed wares in the upper fills. An attempt to date the barrow more accurately was made by Bradley (Bradley & Entwistle 1985, 176), using a piece of red deer antler recovered from the old ground surface under the barrow mound. However, the antler had been contaminated by PVA and the returned date is almost certainly too early (4040–3810 BC).

Two other long barrows have been excavated in Dorset since the 1930s. The most complete example is that excavated by Roger Mercer as part of his investigations into the Neolithic complex at Hambledon Hill (1980, 41–44). The barrow was located immediately to the south of the main causewayed enclosure, between the enclosure ditches and the cross ditches, which cut across the Hanford spur. The barrow had been badly damaged by bulldozing in the 1960s to such an extent that its mound had been destroyed, surviving only as re-deposited material in the general vicinity of the remaining area defined by the barrow ditches. The ditch fills provided the bulk of the material for the interpretation of this monument which suggests that although the barrow was probably constructed before the causewayed enclosure, it was later remodelled in a similar manner, evidenced in the main enclosure ditches themselves. The ditch was re-cut, filled with deposits of ceramic, flint and bone material, re-cut again and filled with cairns of flint nodules. Mercer has suggested that such repetition of events reflects a commonality of purpose between the monuments, involving shared funerary practices, perhaps involving the transferral of selected skeletonised body parts from the enclosure to the barrow.

The final example of an excavated long barrow from Dorset comprises a much disturbed and badly eroded feature on the south-eastern outskirts of Dorchester, discovered in 1984/5. The excavations at Alington Avenue, Fordington (Davies *et al.* 1985) revealed a pair of parallel ditches with hooked ends (**13**). The ditches

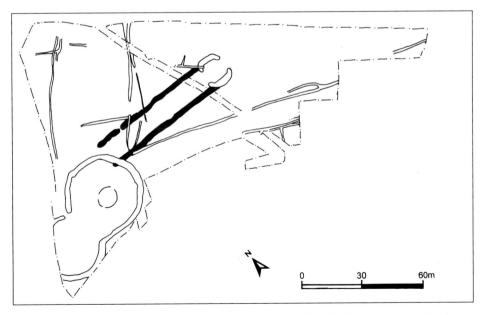

13 *Fordington long barrow: surrounded by later features are a pair of parallel ditches which probably belonged to a long barrow.* Redrawn with amendments from Davies *et al.* 1985

appear to have been constructed by conjoined oval pits totalling 75m in length; the hooked ends seem to have been added after these ditches had almost silted up, and have been interpreted as a later mortuary enclosure or round barrow. Because of the level of post-depositional disturbance to the site, very few material remains were recovered from the excavation although the tradition of structured deposits within ditches seems to be maintained with the finding of an ox skull which had been deliberately placed on the base of the ditch.

Closely associated with the funerary tradition of long barrows is the erection of mortuary enclosures. The example at Fordington is thought to have post-dated the construction of a long barrow but mortuary enclosures are often associated with activity that precedes the construction of long barrow mounds. The form of these monuments is quite diverse throughout the British Isles and definition is therefore somewhat problematic. However, there are some common elements which help justify their isolation as a sub-division of funerary monuments. They generally consist of a rectangular mortuary area bounded by either ditch, kerb or timber posts, which sometimes contain a structure (once again constructed of timber, stone or sometimes turf) which is erected around or over human remains. The human remains are occasionally cremated but in any case are usually fragmentary.

By their nature such monuments leave but little trace in the archaeological record and, until relatively recently, were only associated with long barrows which had been excavated. In Dorset, the best known example of this is Pitt-Rivers' excavation of Wor Barrow in 1893. Underneath the long barrow was found a rectangular trench, with a porch-like extension at its southern end (the enclosure was aligned north-south, as was its later mound). Within this bounded enclosure traces of a funereal area were found, defined by pits and traces of a stone bank which lay either side of human remains. The excavation records refer to three articulated male skeletons and the further disarticulated remains of three more. The bones seem to have been covered as an act of closure by the erection of a small earth mound, with the whole enclosure later sealed by a 46m long barrow. This style and order of funerary tradition is not dissimilar to the sequence of events found at the Holdenhurst barrow excavated by Piggott, described above, and is also mirrored by examples found elsewhere in southern England. It would seem that the funerary and ceremonial traditions associated with at least part of contemporary earlier Neolithic society involved the creation of defined spaces in which bodies were placed in whole or in part, which were then later sealed. There has been much speculation as to the detail and associations of this type of funerary rite over the years, usually involving overlapping themes of excarnation, ancestral cults and links to associated monuments (causewayed enclosures). Unfortunately, however, as perfectly feasible as many of these interpretations are, they at best stretch the data so far recovered from the excavated examples.

In addition to those examples of mortuary enclosures found under later earth mounds, there are increasing numbers of similar ditched enclosures of rectangular form being identified by aerial photography. One such example located at Handley Down on Cranborne Chase (**14**) has recently been investigated by Stephen Burrow and consists of a rectangular ditched enclosure (75m by 32m), aligned approximately north–south, with a causeway on its western flank. A small excavation through the ditch revealed a 2m deep ditch, which contained a sherd of pottery similar to the plain bowl wares associated with the earlier Neolithic. There are several similar forms of monument found throughout the chalklands of Dorset that have yet to be investigated and which may indicate a more common and widespread practice of burial rite.

As we have seen, there is a degree of diversity within the forms of long barrows, but there is none more marked than that concerning a small group of monuments which appear to be restricted to the confines of Dorset – the bank barrow. The bank barrow is defined simply as an elongated variant of the long barrow tradition which has parallel sides and whose latitudinal profile remains constant along its whole length. Only three confirmed examples are known (at Broadmayne, Martin's Down and Maiden Castle), although Bradley (1983, 15-20) has suggested that two long barrows located at Pentridge near to the Dorset Cursus could be interpreted as a further singular example. Whilst their definition is a little vague, their acceptance in the archaeological community as a variant form is well established. The only one of these monuments to have been excavated is that within the bounds of the Iron Age hillfort of Maiden Castle. Excavations during Wheeler's campaigns in the 1930s and then again by Sharples in 1985-6 have defined an earthen mound 546m long and 17.5m wide, which consisted of three different segments, all of which have separate alignments. The monument was clearly constructed some centuries after the causewayed enclosure went out of use, but its purpose remains unclear. None of the excavations have revealed any evidence for a funerary purpose to the monument, a fact which no doubt led

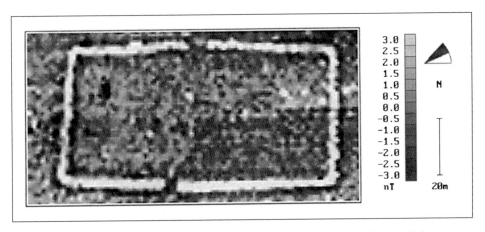

14 *Handley Down mortuary enclosure: geophysical survey (fluxgate gradiometer) of this ploughed-out monument clearly shows the preservation of the enclosure ditch*

Sharples to suggest that the monument may have been constructed as a symbolic barrier. This barrier may have demarcated parts of the landscape separating defined territories that held different meanings to the communities at the time. This interpretation of the Maiden Castle example along with its triple axial alignment does, however, suggest that its function and tradition may be at odds with the little that we do know about the other Dorset examples. The Broadmayne (**15** & **16**) and Martin's Down (**colour plate 1**) barrows each have a singular axial orientation and are both substantially shorter, neither exceeding 230m. If we wish to find a parallel with the Maiden Castle long mound, we have to cast our net further afield. At Crickley Hill in Gloucestershire there is a long mound which is similarly constructed following a period of activity associated with a causewayed enclosure. As with the Dorset example, excavation suggests that there was little evidence for the monument's function being primarily funereal. It is possible that long mounds are a variant form of linear monuments, whose origins are separate from the long barrow and bank barrow tradition, but which nonetheless, may share aspects of commonality of purpose, without necessarily having been constructed for a unitary function.

In addition to the earthen long barrows, as we have already observed, there is a parallel tradition of funerary monuments, which although rare in Dorset, find expression in the south of the county. Chambered tombs are also found quite widely throughout the British Isles, although greater concentrations occur in the west of the country. Within the general title of chambered tombs there are a host of variant forms, which perhaps demonstrate a rich regional diversity focused around the central theme of funerary tradition. The distribution of such monuments is, of course, partly defined by the availability of suitable building stone, and it is no doubt because of this that such diversity appears to be lacking in the related archaeological monuments of Dorset. The problem is perhaps further compounded when we

15 *Broadmayne bank barrow (aerial photograph): this bank barrow forms part of a greater funerary landscape as can be evidenced by the clustering of round barrows (on a linear alignment).*
© Francesca Radcliffe

16 *Broadmayne bank barrow viewed from the round barrow at its eastern end. The bank has been fired to manage the scrub which invades it; note the later round barrows which can be seen on the bank barrow's northern flankpart of a linear barrow allignment. © Julie Gale*

17 *Cursus terminal and long barrow on Thickthorn Down: the barrow excavated by Drew and Piggott is located just off the top of the picture.* © Francesca Radcliffe

compare the records of such monuments, viewed from the perspective of relative antiquity, with the preservation of the monuments today. Grinsell's concordance of long barrows includes reference to seven sites which he found were previously observed as having been associated with large stones in various antiquarian records dating from the eighteenth and nineteenth centuries. Of those records only two sites can now be confirmed as having been part of a chambered tomb tradition (Grey Mare and her Colts and the Hell Stone). In both cases, however, the original form and articulation of the chambers as well as the accompanying earthworks have been obscured by neglect, and in the case of the Hell Stone by some over-zealous and ill-informed reconstruction (**colour plates 2** & **3**).

18 *Valley of Stones: this dry valley is thought by many to be the source of a lot of the sarsens used in the construction of the chambered tombs and stone circles in south Dorset. In the background can be seen the earthworks of 'Celtic fields' which probably date to the Iron Age.* © Julie Gale

19 *Grey Mare and Her Colts (from the south).* © Julie Gale

The Grey Mare and her Colts (**19** & **20**) is located in the south of the county, close to the village of Portesham, at the head of a small valley. The monument consists of an elongated mound with the remains of a megalithic chamber constructed at its south-eastern end. The axis of the complete monument is orien- tated north-west/south-east, similar to the great majority of earthen long barrows discussed above. Piggott described the monument in some detail in 1945 and the site's current condition is largely unchanged. The chamber and its façade is constructed from sarsen stones of a local limestone and flint conglomerate which outcrops 1.5km to the east in an area known as the Valley of Stones. The chamber has been exposed to the elements for some considerable time although originally the main part of the chamber was likely to have been covered by the cairn of the mound. The chamber, formed from vertically set sarsens, was originally roofed by a single slab of sarsen, but this stone has slipped, obscuring the north-eastern side of the chamber. The south-eastern end of the chamber is blocked by a large sarsen

20 *Grey Mare and Her Colts (a sarsen from the south-eastern façade).* © Julie Gale

boulder, which forms part of an elaborate crescentic façade that has now largely disappeared. The line of stones that would have formed and defined the forecourt appears to have been extended around the base of the mound forming a peristalith. The form of this monument shares a number of characteristics with other monuments found outside Dorset, and there has been some discussion as to the monument's pedigree (Piggott 1945, 31: Daniel 1950, 93). Whilst the barrow does indeed share a number of characteristics with monuments in the west of the British Isles, there is no direct parallel linking it to any particular previously defined group. It therefore must be seen as part of a rich diversity of monument types, which inhabit the western seaboard as a whole. There are no surviving records of the monument having been deliberately dug into, although it is hard to imagine that the scale of disturbance to the chambered end has been entirely due to natural causes. Consequently, one can only assume that the chamber originally held human remains, probably in disarticulated form.

The only other comparable monument in Dorset that survives is that of the Hell Stone, which is located only 3km south-east of Grey Mare. Unfortunately the Hell Stone seems to have been almost entirely rebuilt in about 1866 (Oliver, 1922). The circumstances surrounding the rebuilding are not well known but it appears that it was accomplished without any clear understanding of its original form. The surviving monument has the remnants of a cairn or mound around the chamber, which both Daniel (1950, 235) and Grinsell (1959, 81) consider to be of long barrow form.

Cursus monuments

It is a strange irony that the largest of all Neolithic monuments found in the British Isles is at the same time the least well known and also the least well studied. Cursus monuments are typically defined as comprising long linear paired ditches which commonly join at their terminals, and which usually contain internal banks. The length of these monuments varies quite considerably from as little as 170m to 9.8km. Their banks and ditches are extremely small when compared with the overall size of the ground area that they enclose, and over time most of them have been denuded to such an extent that they are only visible when they show up on aerial photographic surveys.

In Dorset there are three confirmed examples of this enigmatic type of enclosure which includes the largest of all the known monuments of this type, the Dorset Cursus. The date of these monuments was for some time considered to be associated with the later Neolithic period, but recent work has, with the aid of radiocarbon dating, established that they tend to be generally older. Their dates tend to cluster in the second half of the fourth millennium BC (Barclay & Bayliss, 1999, 11-29).

Probably the best known of them all is the largest, the Dorset Cursus. With a total length of 9.8km, this is the largest known Neolithic earthwork in western Europe. Unfortunately for the present-day observer, the physical presence of the monument as it survives today is singularly unimpressive, as the visible elements are limited to its southern terminal (**17**), with occasional less substantial fragments surviving elsewhere along its length. The structure is in fact two Cursus monuments, which conjoin very approximately in the middle on Wyke Down. The earlier Cursus is generally ascribed to be the southern section which begins with the well-preserved terminal on Thickthorn Down, where close by there are two long barrows on which the terminal end of the Cursus appears to be aligned (see long barrows above). The paired ditches (approximately 90m apart) of the Cursus extend north-east from this point to a terminal on Gussage Hill. From there the extension to the Cursus begins with a small change in direction, taking it along a slightly more northerly route for a short stretch, before changing direction again, an alignment it more or less maintains before reaching its final destination close to the later earthwork monument of Bokerley Dyke. It is possible that these deviations in alignment are the result of sections being constructed simultaneously by different gangs of workers who were using markers erected upon hilltops. Because it is impossible to see the whole length of the monument from any single vantage point, the builders may not have been able to keep the whole of the monument to an intended alignment.

Assessing the function of any monument of this scale is archaeologically and logistically extremely difficult, particularly when little of the superstructure remains. Limited excavation has taken place on the Cursus, most recently in 1984 when Richard Bradley investigated a small transect across the later northern half of the Cursus at Down Farm (Barrett, *et al.* 1990). The initial fills of the Cursus ditch contained fragments of Peterborough Ware pottery and flint waste, and radiocarbon dates were determined by animal bones which cluster around 3300 BC. Interpretations as to the function of such a massive investment in the contemporary landscape are still, for the moment, understandably vague, but there are some important factors which provide tantalising clues. The Cursus is undeniably closely associated with a number of long barrows and it has been suggested that the Cursus design was deliberately engineered to link these already existing monuments. Both terminals (Thickthorn Down and Bokerly) have long barrows located close by and two other long barrows are incorporated into its structure. It would seem perfectly possible, therefore, to envisage that the avenue created by the Cursus was linked to the belief system of the community, in which a physical representation of their ancestors played an important part. It is not difficult to visualise the Cursus as an elaborate ceremonial monument, an interpretation strengthened by awareness that the alignment of the Cursus coincides with the setting of the sun at the mid-winter solstice when viewed from its northern terminal at Bottlebush Down. If it was used in this way, it is interesting to note that no formal causeways are known to have crossed the ditch at any point, which may suggest that the interior of the monument was in some way special or restricted.

Of the remaining Cursus monuments in Dorset, both are located on Martin's Down to the west of Dorchester and both are spatially related to the bank barrow previously described and may share a similar function to that postulated for the Dorset Cursus. Very little is known of the west Dorset examples as they survive merely as silted-up ditches, visible only with the benefit of aerial photography. The length and full extent of both of these Cursus monuments is unknown, but their width is more in tune with examples identified elsewhere in the country (Springfield, Essex), and certainly much smaller than the Dorset Cursus itself.

All of the above monuments have been dated to the earlier Neolithic period, either directly or by association, and demonstrate quite clearly that the contemporary society that constructed them was fundamentally different from the preceding period. Many of the monuments have clear evidence of long utility and activity suggesting not only a period of innovation but also perhaps of later consolidation. Certainly the complex of monuments at Hambledon Hill were expanded and repaired over many generations.

The later Neolithic – consolidation and new for old

Any structural division of time in prehistory is fraught with conceptual problems and this is certainly the case for the Neolithic. Whilst events naturally have a beginning, a middle and an end, when we wish to examine general trends in disparate data sets of multi-events we start to run into difficulties. This is especially so when we consider regional variation, which can often have a negative influence on our ability to structure developments over time. Julian Thomas amongst others has pointed out that our ability to construct effective stages in artefactual chronology is compromised by the coarseness of the available archaeological data (1999, 32). My use of an artificial partition between the earlier and later Neolithic, whilst conventional, is here used merely to mark a subtle but important movement away from the domination of the linear use of space in monument construction to that of concentric spaces. That this also coincides with other events or trends, such as the introduction of new pottery styles (Grooved ware) may have significant meaning but once again we are hog-tied by the limited chronological resolution of a very limited data set.

The importance of the monuments described above to the communities of the region during the later third millennium BC should not be underestimated. Many of the monuments already described display evidence of continued use into the Early Bronze Age. This is especially true of funerary monuments, but can also be applied to those monuments whose function is more complex. The Dorset Cursus, although conceived and constructed towards the end of the earlier Neolithic, continued to exert an intense influence on the use of its surrounding landscape for many hundreds of years. Much of the evidence for later settlement related use of the Cursus, has been determined via the spatial distribution of lithic materials on, or adjacent to, the monument. That there were demonstrably higher concentrations of flintwork contained within the area bounded by the Cursus ditches compared with that outside, is a subtle but nonetheless significant indicator of use during this period. Some of these artefacts also exhibited characteristics associated with manufacture, use and repair more typically associated with domestic activity (Barrett *et al.* 1991, 75).

Some monuments do, however, appear to go out of use. The causewayed enclosures at Maiden Castle and Hambledon Hill appear to be abandoned, with only minimal evidence of later Neolithic activity. The reasons for this are unclear but they do reflect events observable at other causewayed enclosures across southern England at around this time. The demise of at least some of these enclosures may well have been rather abrupt. Hambledon Hill's Steepleton enclosure seems to have suffered a conflagration, which has been frequently associated with clearer evidence of warfare at such sites as Crickley Hill in Gloucestershire and Carn Brea in Cornwall. Such examples are often cited as forming a coherent pattern of evidence to substantiate the view that later Neolithic society was under extreme pressure, which brought about fundamental changes in society, ultimately visible in the archaeological record as a shift in the use of the landscape. However, it is equally plausible to fit any number of scenarios onto the present archaeological data without recourse to catastrophic events.

What does appear to be clear is that no new monuments of the types previously mentioned (causewayed enclosures, long barrows, etc.) appear to have been built, much after *c*.2800 BC. Whilst certain monuments show continuity of use such as the enclosures at Hambledon Hill, certain monuments are gradually introduced which perhaps indicate changes not only reflective of social behaviour, but perhaps also of the relationship between society, the individual and the landscape itself.

Neolithic round barrows?

As we have already seen, amongst the most visible structures surviving from the Neolithic period are the funerary monuments. During the later Neolithic, emphasis moves away from the construction of linear mounds to those of a circular form – round barrows. Traditionally round barrows are always associated with the following Bronze Age period but their origin is now firmly attested to the later Neolithic period. Two examples of such early round barrows in Dorset are found in close association with the Wor barrow long barrow discussed above. The barrows in question are known as Handley 26 and 27 and both are located in close proximity to the long barrow excavated by Pitt-Rivers (**21**). Pitt-Rivers

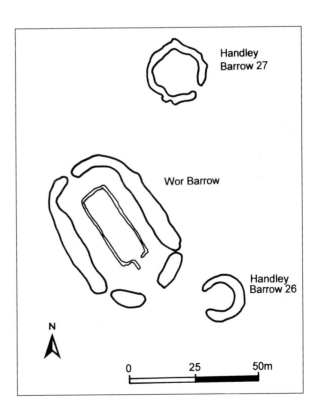

21 Wor barrow complex: close to a long barrow are two round barrows which are also Neolithic in origin. Redrawn with amendments from Barrett et al. 1991

Handley
Barrow 27

Wor Barrow

Handley
Barrow 26

N

0   25   50m

investigated the whole complex of three barrows, but the significance of the two round barrows has long been overshadowed by their linear companion. Handley 26 was located approximately 12m to the south-east of the long barrow and consisted of a circular mound created from an encircling quarry ditch 13m in diameter. The ditch had a relatively wide causeway which faced the long barrow, and located on the old ground surface underneath the mound were two separate inhumations, one of which was centrally placed. The barrow has been dated by reference to the ceramic material contained within the ditch which consisted of Mortlake ware, a sub-style of Peterborough wares which are broadly consistent (but almost certainly slightly younger) with the radiocarbon determinations for the long barrow (3790–3100 BC). The second larger round barrow (Handley 27) is located 80m to the north of the long barrow and had been partially investigated by Sir Richard Colt-Hoare, 80 years before Pitt-Rivers' more detailed excavation. The ditch which delimited the barrow and which probably provided the material for a central mound, was unusual in that it appears to have been created in sections, possibly with narrow causeways which were later breached (Barrett et al. 1991, 85). The ditch retained a single causeway at its south-east, although Pitt-Rivers considered that a later pit was inserted into this entranceway, effectively blocking it. The date of this barrow was thought to be Bronze Age by Pitt-Rivers but Mortlake ware recovered from the lower fills suggests that it is likely to be contemporary with its more southerly neighbour. Information on the number and type of interments contained within the barrow is compromised by the limited recording of the earlier excavations, but Colt-Hoare did note the presence of disturbed remains (1812 cited Barrett et al. 1991, 85). What is significant about the circumstances of burial within this deposit is the articulated nature of the skeletal remains. The general character of the burial rite throughout the Neolithic with regard to inhumation is, as we have seen, largely preceded by a process of excarnation with the later inhumation of skeletal material in disarticulated form. Certainly, the Wor barrow complex presents a marked move away from this form of burial rite, with cadavers being interred prior to significant decomposition of the body, and of course within a new monument form. Interestingly the Wor barrow complex highlights what could be described as the monumental expression of a cultural group undergoing a period of transition in their burial traditions.

Quantification of the extent of the introduction of these 'new ideas' of burial is largely limited to those sites where excavation has taken place and where appropriate dating techniques have been possible. However, there are some round barrows which, by association, are also thought to be potentially later Neolithic in date. Amongst the most prominent of these are large round barrows associated with some of the larger henge monuments found in southern England. As we shall see below, Dorset has a number of such henges and both Mount Pleasant near Dorchester, and Knowlton (southern circle) near Wimborne have very large round barrows associated with them (Conquer barrow and the Great barrow respectively – 22). In neither case have they been excavated but taken together with further occurrences at Marden (Hatfield barrow) and Avebury (Silbury Hill) in Wiltshire, there is a repeating pattern which is hard to resist. Continuity in use of the sites (Mount Pleasant and Knowlton southern circle), which although later than the construction and initial use of the henge monuments, probably suggests that these round barrows are amongst the earliest of a tradition rooted in the Neolithic which later dominates the Early Bronze Age.

Henge monuments

It is an interesting and much discussed observation that the introduction of henge monuments into the landscape of England broadly coincides with the abandonment of the causewayed enclosures that formed such a prominent part of the earlier Neolithic landscape. Between 2700 and 2400 BC, many of the causewayed enclosures appear to have been abandoned with the ditches becoming silted up. It is during this time that we see the appearance of a new circular monument type called a henge, a term that deceptively encompasses a wide variety of forms which confound a single classification. It would be a mistake to assume that the tradition and purpose of causewayed enclosures and henges is a simple chronological progression. As we have seen, the function of the constructional form of causewayed enclosures contains evidence of differing usages, and to a large extent henges must be viewed in the same manner.

The term henge is ultimately derived from the best-known henge of all, Stonehenge in Wiltshire. Stonehenge literally means 'hanging stones' which refers

22 *The Great Barrow at Knowlton seen from the south.* © Julie Gale

to the lintels, which hang on the great trilithons of the sarsen stone circles that dominate the site. Henge, used to classify certain types of Neolithic circular enclosures, has had a somewhat organic development from its first use in 1932. Richard Atkinson's study of Neolithic monuments around Dorchester (Oxfordshire), which was published in 1951, provided a review of henge forms which affords the basis of the definition which is used by archaeologists today. A henge is generally defined as an enclosed circular area which is bounded by a bank and ditch where the ditch is normally located on the inside of the bank, and is pierced by one or more entrances. Within this general definition there exists a wide variety of monuments, which vary in both size and constructional elements, some of which are represented in the Dorset landscape.

In recent years, evidence has begun to emerge of a small number of sites that may be transitional forms of monument which bridge the constructional elements of the causewayed enclosure and henge traditions (Thomas 1999, 173). In themselves, there is a variety of form but they are unified by their chronology, which might be regarded as 'middle Neolithic', c.3000-2500 BC. The initial phase of Stonehenge (Stonehenge 1) could be regarded as one of the best known of these intermediary constructional forms; the bank – ditch – counterscarp bank arrangement of the enclosure which contained the so-called Aubrey holes which may or may not have held wooden posts. The ditch was constructed in segments which conjoined, reminiscent of the techniques employed on causewayed enclosures, for the creation of the ditches (see above). Unlike the majority of causewayed enclosures however, the material cultural assemblage from this phase of the monument is relatively poor.

In Dorset, a site of similar date with a number of common elements has recently been discovered close to the large henge enclosure at Mount Pleasant. The site at Flagstones was discovered during excavations prior to the construction of a by-pass to the east of the town in 1987 (**23**). During the excavation approximately half of a circular enclosure, consisting of unevenly spaced segmented pits with a projected diameter of 100m, was exposed and excavated (Smith, R.J.C. *et al.* 1997, 27-39). The site was dated using the application of radiocarbon dating techniques, which suggest a late fourth to early third millennium BC date for the construction of the pits. The chalk walls of some of the pits contained engravings of unknown purpose, as well as marks from antler picks used to lever away the blocks of chalk during the excavation of the ditch. The excavators concluded that the segments were not left open for very long and were subsequently back-filled with chalk rubble. Some of the segmented pits contained inhumations of both articulated and disarticulated form, as well as fragments of sarsen, limestone and sandstone. The monument therefore, would appear to have had some funerary purpose but little more can be determined.

A smaller but contemporary monument, which also has some funerary associations, has been recently excavated on Cranborne Chase by Martin Green, and has provided some fascinating insights into ritual activity in a landscape which would

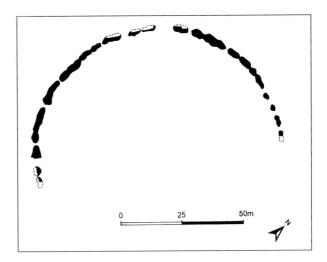

23 *Segmented ditch enclosure at Flagstones: an unusual Neolithic feature partially excavated in 1987.* Redrawn with amendments from R.J.C. Smith *et al.* 1997

0   25   50m

have been dominated by the Dorset Cursus. The site at Monkton Up Wimborne was excavated in 1997 following its discovery as a crop mark of a ring of pits some 35m in diameter. Excavation revealed 14 oval pits that were unevenly spaced. Very few artefacts were recovered from this ring of pits and it was apparent that they had never held posts. Indeed, following their initial excavation they appear to have silted up naturally. At the centre of this ring of pits was a huge central pit approximately 10m wide, which had been cut 1.5m into the chalk. Into this well-cut pit, a multiple burial within an oval pit was placed, at the extreme northern edge of the larger pit. The multiple burial contained the remains of one adult and three children. Extensive scientific evaluation determined that the group had spent a significant period of time in a lead-rich landscape, probably the Mendips in Somerset, and had lived on a high protein diet derived probably from diary products rather than meat (Green 2000, 79). The circumstance of death was not determined but may have been sacrificial and could have occurred around the end of the fourth millennium BC. Following the insertion of the burial deposits, a deep shaft, 7m deep and over 1m in diameter at its base, was excavated in the east of the pit. The purpose of the shaft is unclear but a series of carefully placed deposits within its fills suggest that offerings were being made, perhaps to the cthonic spirits.

The henge monuments proper in Dorset can be broadly divided into two groups, the larger henge monuments, and the smaller, more varied, forms sometimes referred to as hengi-form types. The county contains a number of examples of both of these groups, all of which are located on the chalk downlands in both east and west Dorset.

The larger henge monuments

The largest of these henge monuments are found mostly within the confines of Wessex (here defined as the modern counties of Wiltshire, Dorset, Hampshire and eastern Somerset). A campaign of excavations undertaken in the early 1970s by

Professor Geoffrey Wainwright led to the partial excavation of three of them (Marden and Durrington Walls in Wiltshire, and Mount Pleasant in Dorset). The excavations revealed evidence of large timber-built circular structures within all the enclosures, reminiscent of that found at Woodhenge (only 60m south of Durrington Walls) by Maud Cunnington in 1926.

The example at Mount Pleasant was the last of the three to be excavated by Wainwright and his campaign of excavation undertaken in 1970 and 1971 (Wainwright 1979) benefited from the accumulated knowledge and experiences of the previous excavations. The archaeological investigation of the site by excavation, as is typical with such large areas, was restricted to targeted sample areas to address specific objectives. In this case, the sampling was designed not only to date and examine the cultural affinities of the monument, but also to examine its commonality of purpose with the morphologically similar sites in Wiltshire (Wainwright 1979, 70).

Arguably Mount Pleasant (**24** & **25**) was the least well preserved of the three sites, having suffered particularly from centuries of plough activity. Agricultural attrition of the monument's upstanding earthworks had resulted in the virtual destruction of the enclosure bank which was barely visible at ground level for most of its circuit.

24 *Mount Pleasant henge and palisaded enclosure: viewed from the air and under favourable conditions the outline of both the henge and the later palisaded enclosure can be clearly seen.* © Crown copyright, NMR

25 *Mount Pleasant: This aerial view of the henge and palisaded enclosure is taken at a slightly lower elevation than* **24** *and under conditions which highlight the archaeological features in the southern half of the site. As well as the henge bank and ditch, the internal ring ditch that contained the timber structure* **27** *and the later stone and pit enlosure* **33** *can be quite clearly seen.* © Francesca Radcliffe

Excavation revealed that the bank had been reduced (at best) to a chalk rubble spread 1.5m high and 16-18m broad. The accompanying ditch, as expected, found inside the bank, had completely silted up over time but was approximately 17m wide at the surface. The enclosure is a enormous structure enclosing 4.8ha of chalk hill-top (**26**). The bank and ditch which define the enclosure could be seen to have four entrances and within the enclosed area a timber structure surrounded by a circular ditch was found (probably with an external bank long since ploughed away) which was located close to the highest point on the hill. The monument appears to have had a long period of use, beginning with the construction of the encircling bank and ditch around 2000 BC. The dating of the monument was attained with the application of radiocarbon techniques, using organic material recovered from the ditch fills. During this initial phase of activity at the monument a timber-built structure was erected, consisting of five concentric circles of post-holes with axially arranged corridors, creating four quadrants which have an almost perfect symmetry to their plan (**27**). This structure was clearly no crude hut, its overall size (outer ring of post-holes had a diameter of 38m) and complexity of design single it out as a structure of great contemporary importance. The problem of its interpretation begins with the deceptively difficult question of whether the structure was ever roofed. The outwardly similar structures at Durrington Walls and Woodhenge have all posed the same basic question, which still remains unsolved. Wainwright believed that the Mount Pleasant example was likely to have been roofed, and probably

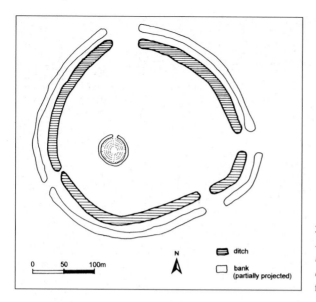

ditch

bank
(partially projected)

26 *Plan of Neolithic features at Mount Pleasant including henge and timber post structure with its encircling ditch.* Redrawn with amendments from Wainwright 1989

27 *Plan of timber structure at Mount Pleasant: this plan of concentric circles of post-holes is paralleled by examples at Woodhenge and Durrington Walls in Wiltshire.* Redrawn with amendments from Wainwright 1989

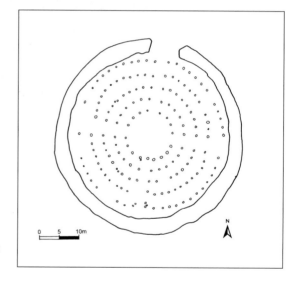

served as a communal structure for social or religious purposes. A bank and ditch surrounded the timber structure, probably with the bank external to the ditch, and from this ditch cultural material was recovered. Amongst this material were fragments of ceramic pots of a form and fabric which are commonly associated with henge monuments – Grooved ware.

Close by Mount Pleasant is a second henge of the classic form, consisting of an earthen bank with internal ditch, albeit smaller in scale – Maumbury Rings. The earthwork, located close to the centre of the busy market town of Dorchester, is today hemmed into a small public park surrounded by busy roads and a railway line which was almost the cause of its total destruction in the late nineteenth century

28 *Maumbury Rings henge: a vertical aerial photograph where the earth bank of the amphitheatre **A** (initially a Neolithic henge) can be seen fighting for survival in an otherwise developed landscape.*
© Dorset County Council

(**28**). The monument lay in the path of the projected line of the London and South Western Railway, which was finally diverted due to a public campaign that represents one of the earliest successful conservation protests on a heritage issue involving development in the British Isles. However, for our purposes a much earlier civil engineering development severely damaged the henge to such an extent that its present form barely testifies to its Neolithic origins. During the Roman period (probably during the Claudian or Neronian periods) the then extant but abandoned henge was reworked to form an amphitheatre. This involved lowering the interior platform and the heightening of the banks. This activity effectively removed much of the internal ditch and the reworking of the banks created not only a more substantial bank but almost certainly one which was more oval in plan. The site was extensively excavated between 1908-13 by Harold St George Gray, but the results were not fully published until 1976 (Bradley).

The interpretative sequence of the construction of the henge was not only compromised by the disturbance caused by its Roman successor but was also limited by the technical limitations of the early twentieth-century excavators (Bradley, 1976, 4-6). However, it is possible to define something of the monument's original form. The earth bank enclosed an area of approximately 0.5 acres (2,100m²) and originally stood to a height of about 3.7m. The bank had a single entrance located in the north-east, and the internal ditch would have been in the region of 5.7m wide and 3.7m deep. Cut into the base of the ditch are an estimated 45 shafts which have an average diameter of 0.9m and an average depth of 6.4m (below the bottom of the ditch cut). It was not possible to determine the chronological relationship between the ditch and the shafts, although it is clear that both sets of features were ultimately open and in use at the same time in the monument's final phase (Bradley 1976, 32). The shafts seem to have contained sealed deposits of a variety of items including animal bone, pottery fragments, human bone and carved chalk, which do not appear to be domestic in character, but rather suggest a ritual deposit of unknown meaning. The use of pits and in some cases ditches to contain sealed offerings is not unusual and spans both the earlier and later Neolithic. As we have already seen, the early Neolithic cause-wayed enclosure at Hambledon Hill was marked by the carefully deposited remains of human bone and flint in the ditches of the enclosure and the weight of evidence nationally testifies to such widely practised activity throughout the period. The Neolithic pottery recovered from the excavations at Maumbury was extremely limited in quantity, with only one sherd reported on by Bradley. The sherd, recovered from the fill of one of the shafts, is almost certainly Grooved ware.

The final example of the larger form of henges consists not of a single monument but of a complex of shared forms known variously as Knowlton Circles or Knowlton Rings (**5** & **29**). Unlike the previous examples which all reside in the south-western part of the county, Knowlton is located on the edge of Cranborne Chase to the east. The site consists of a large number of circular earthworks, which for the most part consist of ploughed-out ring ditches that probably date to the early Bronze Age (see chapter 3). At the centre of these remains is a number of larger features which have frequently been grouped together as a complex or cluster of henge-like monuments, a determination largely based on aerial photographic evidence. Recent work by the author has begun to look at this complex more closely, particularly with regard to its affini-ties with the wider landscape of the Allen valley in which it is situated.

There are five large circular monuments at the heart of the complex, most of which can be tentatively classified as henges or having traits common to henge monuments. The most well-preserved of all of the monuments is the so-called Church henge, whose survival as an upstanding earthwork is largely due to its later adoption for the location and construction of a twelfth-century church. The church, although abandoned in the eighteenth century, continued to provide protection to the earthworks which today represents one of the best preserved monuments of its type in Britain. The Church henge consists of a bank, oval in plan, that survives to a maximum height of 2m. On the inside of the bank lies an irregularly cut ditch, which is likely to have been used as a later quarry. Although there are three current gaps in the earthworks it is unclear which of these is original. Certainly the southerly bank terminal of the south-western entrance shows signs of having been reduced, probably during the period of the church's

29 *Knowlton southern henge during excavation in 1994. The remains of the bank can just be seen in the section edge as can the dark stain of the buried soil underneath it.* © Author

use. The maximum diameter of the enclosure is approximately 110m. As imposing as this monument is, it is only half the size of the Southern Circle, which lies 200m to the south. The Southern Circle has not been afforded the same degree of respect as its close neighbour over the centuries and it has been largely destroyed by agricultural activity over time. The best preserved section of the monument lies in its north-western quadrant, where the bank has been incorporated into a field boundary which separates the farm land from the farm buildings and farm yard of New Barn Farm. Here the bank survives to a height of approximately 1.4m, although the internal ditch is no longer visible at this point. The remainder of the bank is very poorly preserved and survives to its greatest extent in the north-east, to a height of approximately 0.5m.

A small trench was excavated across the bank and ditch of the Southern Circle in the summer of 1994 by the author and Stephen Burrow (Burrow and Gale forthcoming). The excavation was undertaken in the south-western quadrant and revealed a substantial ditch, which would have been over 4.5m deep. Only a few centimetres of the external bank had survived at this point but parallel gullies were discovered at the edges of the bank which suggest that it had been redressed and/or redefined after its original construction (**29**). A cow scapula recovered from the primary fills of the ditch was radiocarbon dated to 2570-2190 BC.

To the north-east of the Church henge lie two further ploughed-out circular earthworks which are often referred to as Henges. The Northern Circle, more of a 'D' shape, has a characteristic relict bank with traces of an internal ditch which has recently been confirmed by geophysical analysis. However, its southern end is open with no trace of bank or ditch and the oval form of the monument is more reminiscent of the plans of oval barrows and mortuary enclosures than henges. A few metres south of the Northern Circle is the 'Old Churchyard'. Its name is likely to be of comparatively recent origin and probably arose through the perception that the Church henge had limited space for burial, and that this enclosure was a cemetery annexe. Geophysical analysis has confirmed that the bank and ditch arrangement of this monument is reversed to that of the henge tradition and therefore is not of the same form. However, this does not preclude the fact that the earthwork may still be contemporary with the complex.

The fifth monument in the group is the 'Great Barrow', a 30m diameter barrow, thought by many to be the largest round barrow in Dorset, which is surrounded by two concentric ditches, which are completely filled up. The outer ditch creates a monument with a diameter of around 120m. As was discussed earlier, it is suspected that a number of these large round barrows which are often found closely associated with henge enclosures in Wessex may be of late Neolithic date and therefore mark a movement away from older traditions and rituals. If we look at the wider environs of the Knowlton landscape we see that that there is little monumental evidence for earlier Neolithic activity, which is somewhat surprising given the intense activity only a few miles to the west. Perhaps the Allen valley represents new beginnings for a society which needed a new canvas upon which to demonstrate or enact its ritual personality.

During excavations in the heart of Dorchester (Greyhound Yard) in 1984 an arc of 21 pits that originally held timber uprightst was discovered there. If the pits represent a section of a continuous arc of similar pits they would form a circle of approximately 380m, that would enclose 11.4ha (Woodward et al. 1993, 351). The site can broadly be compared to the large henge monuments described above, particularly in area and date, although any further comparisons are limited by the fragmentary nature of the remains so far uncovered. The date of the pits revealed by radiocarbon determination suggests that the monument was constructed at some time between 2920-2340 BC. The date of this monument would enable it to be seen as possibly contemporary with that of both Mount Pleasant and Maumbury henges located nearby. It is difficult to imagine them as anything else but interrelated ceremonial sites in a landscape that was clearly of great importance to the communities that built and used them.

Pit-circle henges

As we have already seen, there are a variety of types of monuments associated with the term henge which perhaps incorrectly implies a commonality of function or purpose. In addition to the large henge monuments, there is a smaller class of monuments often described as hengi-form, which are even less well defined. In Dorset these monuments most commonly appear as pit-circles. As earthworks they are far less imposing structures and consequently no upstanding trace of them usually survives in the modern landscape. It has only been in recent years, through the use of improving archaeological field techniques, that such structures have come to light. A number of such hybrid forms of monument have been discovered by Martin Green, all located close to the Dorset Cursus on Bottlebush and Wyke Down.

Two of these monuments are especially worthy of note – Wyke Down 1 and 2 (**30**), both of which have been excavated by Martin Green in recent years and provide an insight into the character of such monuments (Green 2000, 85-89). Wyke Down 1 consisted of a ring of closely spaced pits, 20m in diameter, each separated by a narrow causeway with a 3m entrance gap to the south. The pits were all ovoid in plan and varied in depth from about 1.35-2m. A number of the pits contained objects such as animal bone, antler, flintwork and carved chalk. The pits had been left open and had silted up naturally to approximately half-way, at which time the fills had small pits cut into them, into which ritual offerings were placed. Amongst these offerings were sherds of Grooved ware and fragments of human bone. Sherds of Grooved ware from the same vessel were also found in association with the entrance. Wyke Down 2, whilst smaller and more irregular in plan, appears to have been broadly contemporary with its larger companion. Grooved ware pottery is once again represented, here a substantially complete vessel of a unique form, which had traces of food residues adhering to the inside. Both of these monuments are thought to have had an external bank, created from the initial fills of the pits, although no trace of such a bank survived.

In the south of Dorset close to the county town of Dorchester two further pit-rings were excavated in 1987 (Smith *et al.* 1997, 48-52) which bear some similarity to those described above. The pit-rings were located at the foot of Conygar Hill (**30**) and were discovered during top-soil stripping of the site in preparation for construction work associated with the building of the Dorchester by pass. Pit-ring 52118 consisted of seven oval pits with two further elongated pits which formed a circle of 17m diameter. Within the primary fills of one of the pits were recovered fragments of Grooved ware probably from a single vessel. The second pit-ring (52100) was located 225m east of 52118 and consisted of eight pits but here with an internal arrangement of post-holes.

As we have seen, the Neolithic occupants of Dorset created a complex array of monuments within a period of less than 2,000 years, which demonstrates their ability to model their environment to reflect their way of life and ritual/religious perceptions. The monuments they built are for the most part undertakings that reflect well-developed social and political structures, which enabled communities to come together for the construction of monuments of previously unimagined scale. Several commentators have, in the past, attempted to determine the effort required to construct some of the types of monuments discussed above in meaningful terms which we can understand today. The henge enclosure of Durrington Walls has variously been calculated as having taken anything between ½ million and 1½ million hours to construct. The larger of the henges at Knowlton on

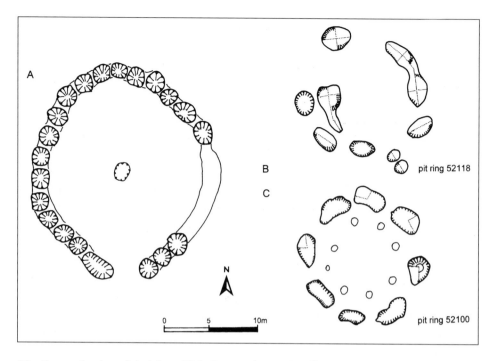

30 *Comparative plans of pit circles at Wyke Down and Conygar Hill: such pit circles are also frequently called hengi-form monuments. It is very unclear as to their function – they may of course have a variety of functions! A – Wyke Down 1, B – Conygar Hill 52118, C – Conygar Hill 52100.* Redrawn with amendments from Smith R.J.C. *et al.* 1997 and Barrett *et al.* 1991

Cranborne Chase whilst only two thirds the size of its Wiltshire counterpart, is likely to have represented a similar investment of time and effort. The question remains, why did the Neolithic inhabitants of Dorset invest so much energy in the creation of such massive earthworks? For the moment the answer remains somewhat elusive, although it is abundantly clear that ever since our Neolithic ancestors demonstrated a need to create large monuments, we have continued the tradition. Although the specific utility of the structures may change (in both space and time) it would appear that the impulse behind them is as strong as ever. Construction of large, often public monuments, if not undertaken for economic gain, is generally about expressions of communal celebration or statements of devotional belief (or of course a mixture of some or all of these!).

What is so fascinating about the Neolithic period in general and particularly the surviving traces of it in the Dorset countryside, is that it represents the coming together of various aspects of the evolutionary process. The right conditions needed to be in place or the monuments at which we marvel today would not have been either possible or even necessary. The ability to control the means of production that allowed significant numbers of the population to take time to participate in such undertakings could not have happened until the social, economic, technological and political systems within a society were sufficiently evolved.

However, we should not get carried away in thinking that Neolithic society was continuously engaged in mammoth building projects. Much of everyday existence was probably as humdrum as any other time, and we certainly see elements of that reflected in the archaeological detail from many of the sites discussed above.

The most difficult and challenging aspect of the period is the detail of settlement activity. Whilst the evidence from Dorset and elsewhere provides testament to the habitation of places, that evidence is chiefly reflective of ceremonial and funerary monuments. Our understanding of domestic settlement is very much compromised by a lack of data. What data there is for places of settlement with discernible dwellings can only be counted nationally by the score rather than in the hundreds. However, this picture is almost certainly distorted not only by the poor survival of structural evidence (which for the most part was probably quite insubstantial), but also by it not being recognised or even looked for in the research agendas of the last two generations of archaeologists. The emphasis has often concentrated upon the better-preserved monuments, which generally were never used for domestic settlement. The less tangible evidence such as scatters of domestic rubbish (flints and pottery) are of course much less conclusive but may, in many cases, be all that survives after several millennia of surface erosion and disturbance. In recent years archaeologists have started to look for much less tangible signs of Neolithic occupation. Martin Green's and John Arnold's work on Cranborne Chase is fairly typical of this sort of approach and has revealed increased activity during the later Neolithic period which at least suggests that areas were being exploited and almost certainly settled in (Green 2000, 64).

3

THE BRONZE AGE
A GAME OF TWO HALVES?

An artificial horizon

The division of archaeological time, as we have seen in the previous chapter, is nothing more than an academic device based on technological advancement, for the classification and subsequent explanation of the progression of human relations and actions, within a linear sequence. The Bronze Age of Dorset occurs in this sequence around 2000 BC, marked by the identification of changes in the archaeological record, only a small proportion of which are directly associated with the introduction of bronze technology. The substitution of metal for stone in the manufacture of tools was not universally adopted overnight, and even its use in the creation of high status decorative artefacts was only marginally more rapidly realised. The introduction of bronze artefacts alongside numerous other examples of changes to material culture, and the increasing adoption of round barrows in the burial rite, have led to the identification of what is variously described as the Beaker tradition or the Beaker culture. However, as we shall see, much of this new material and activity takes place within a landscape which is demonstrably older, and illustrates that the division between the Late Neolithic and the Early Bronze Age is essentially an artificial horizon. Before we can progress further in the examination of the evidence for Bronze Age activity in the Dorset landscape, we need to understand the background to the Beakers more widely, and reflect on how this might affect our interpretation of the material evidence associated with them.

The Beakers

The Beaker culture is named after the drinking vessel that was placed in the grave of individuals, part of a distinctive burial rite recognisable in many parts of western Europe at around this time. Alongside the placement of a Beaker (not all Beaker burials contain a Beaker) other grave goods are frequently found which collectively constitute a 'grave kit'. The components of the 'grave kit', when present, tend to cluster into three distinctive groups:

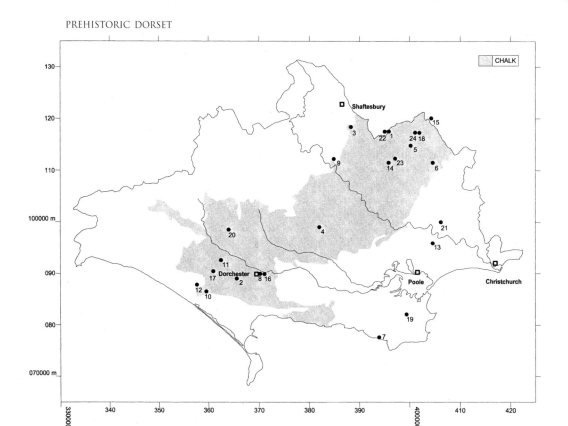

31 *Map of Bronze Age sites mentioned in chapter 3. 1 – Barrow pleck, 2 – Clandon barrow, 3 – Clubmen's Down (cross-ridge dyke), 4 – Deverel barrow, 5 – Down Farm, 6 – Edmonsham barrow, 7 – Eldon's Seat, 8 – Flagstones, 9 – Hambledon Hill, 10 – Hampton stone circle, 11 – Hog Cliff Hill, 12 – Kingston Russell stone circle, 13 – Knighton Heath, 14 – Launceston Down (barrows), 15 – Martin Down, 16 – Mount Pleasant, 17 – Nine Stones, 18 – Oakley Down, 19 – Rempstone stone circle, 20 – Shearplace Hill, 21 – Simon's Ground, 22 – South Lodge, 23 – Thickthorn Down, 24 – Wor barrow*

- Weapons – consisting of archery equipment (wristguards, barbed and tanged arrowheads) and daggers or knives. The inhumations are exclusively male.
- Personal/dress adornment – consisting of buttons, pins and beads, belt rings etc. The inhumations can be male or female.
- Craft tools – bronze or bone tools thought to be associated with the individual. The inhumations can be male or female. (Darvill 1987, 90)

The Beakers themselves are, for the period, a very distinctive form of pottery. The pots are generally thin-walled, finely finished vessels, usually highly decorated with impressions of twisted cord, comb or stamp, and in later examples with incised decoration. The shape of the Beakers, whilst generally bell- or S-shaped in profile, with either short or long necks in the earlier examples, does evolve into biconical forms. The grave goods (when present) would be associated with an individual crouched inhumation which was usually placed in a grave or cist under a small round barrow.

Beakers have been one of the most intensely studied of pottery types from the prehistoric period, which has enabled a detailed analysis of their typological progression to be constructed across their geographical distribution. Such studies have demonstrated that whilst the earliest forms of these vessels (AOC – All Over Corded and Maritime types) were imported, probably from the Low Countries and the Rhineland, they were quickly copied and were then developed in an insular manner (Burgess 1980, 62-64).

The idea that the earliest of Beakers, contained within such burials were the product of a culture located outside the British Isles raises an issue we have discussed before (see chapter 2). The issue in this instance is whether the introduction of the Beaker burial rite was the product of folk migration or alternatively the migration of the cultural ideal to a receptive indigenous population. For a long time it was believed that the introduction of Beaker pottery into the British Isles was the direct result of colonisation by populations from Continental Europe, and the archaeological literature before the 1960s reflects this view. This fact, supported by the change in burial rite and furthered by a belief that the skeletal remains of those burials in Britain were anatomically different from the indigenous population, seemed to provide ample evidence for the colonisation/invasion theory. Closer examination of the data in more recent times, whilst not completely and unambiguously refuting the possibility of invasion, does indicate that the initial Beaker phase of activity could be a product of the migration of cultural identity; in other words the movement of ideas not people (Case 1977, 71-101). For the moment we will have to consider both possibilities, as the body of evidence is insufficient to warrant refutation of either hypothesis in favour of the other. In either case the end result was the same – the new ideas manifest in the cultural package linked to the burial rite were largely adopted by the indigenous population.

So what impact did the cultural manifestation of the Beakers leave on the landscape of Dorset? Well, their cultural identity did not exclude them from an involvement with the indigenous culture already present in the landscape. Evidence for the use of essentially Neolithic monuments by individuals who at least ended their lives associated with Beaker ritual beliefs is not particularly rare in Britain, and in this regard Dorset monuments are no exception. The main enclosure within the Neolithic complex on Hambledon Hill near Blandford Forum in the Stour Valley had a deliberate deposit of flint nodules placed in the enclosure ditch following a final episode of its recutting and almost immediate backfilling (Mercer 1980, 37). Contained within the deposit of flint nodules were fragments of Beaker pottery of a relatively late form (Lanting and Van der Waals step 6/7). It is a matter of speculation as to the purpose of the deposit, but it certainly indicates that by around 1700 BC the monument (which was by then over 1,500 years old) was still attracting attention and activity.

Another monument that is traditionally linked to the preceding period, which frequently shows evidence for Beaker and Early Bronze Age activity is that of the henge. Henge monuments, as we have already seen, appear to date from the end of the Neolithic period and we consequently should not be surprised to see them in use at the turn of the second millennium BC, nor in association with Beaker activity. The final major phase of activity at the Mount Pleasant henge involved the construction of a massive timber-palisaded enclosure within, and mirrorin, the earlier henge enclosure ditch (**32**). The palisade enclosed an area of 4.5ha and consisted of a continuous palisade trench, which originally contained over 1,600 oak posts closely set together, the average diameter of which was approximately 0.45m. It is only possible to estimate the original height of the posts, but the excavator estimates that they may have been as much as 9m long with a third of the length embedded into the ground. The enclosure had two entrances, and the excavation of the eastern entrance revealed that the timbers on each side of a narrow (0.7m) entrance consisted of even larger oak timbers, probably around 1.5m in diameter. Pottery found that was associated with the enclosure was largely comprised of fragments of Beaker. It is also likely that the site of the concentric timber circle located within the enclosure was replaced at around this time with a stone monument, which

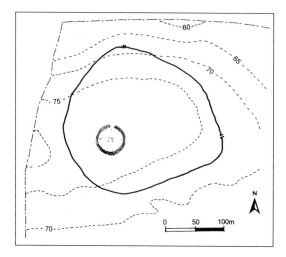

32 *Mount Pleasant palisaded enclosure: it is estimated that the construction of this palisade involved the use of 1,600 oak posts, each approximately 0.45m in diameter.* Redrawn with amendments from Wainwright 1989

33 *Plan of stone and pit enclosure at Mount Pleasant: the earlier timber circle on the interior of the enclosure was replaced by a setting of stones and pits. The function is unclear but seems to be connected to ritual rather than domestic activity.* Redrawn with amendments from Wainwright 1989

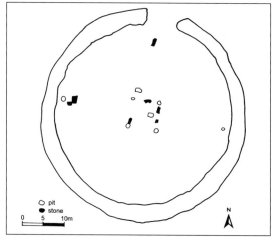

34 *Beaker burial at Thickthorn Down: this Neolithic barrow which contained no primary interments was used by the Beakers to bury their dead. This photograph from the excavation of the monument in 1936 reveals the partially exposed skull of an adult accompanied by a beaker vessel.* Courtesy of Dorchester County Museum

consisted of pits and sarsen stones arranged on three sides around a rectangle (**33**). As with the palisade, this structure was associated with Beaker pottery although there were few material clues to suggest a use for the feature. Whatever its function it is clear that the interior of the palisaded area would have been hidden from view creating a degree of exclusivity which would have required an enormous amount of social organisation to achieve.

Slightly clearer behaviour can be determined through the identification of Beaker burial activity at extant Neolithic monuments. The most obvious expression of the reuse of older funerary monuments is found at Thickthorn Down. The long barrow excavated by Drew and Piggott was described in chapter 2 and during the excavation the only recorded burials encountered were those inserted into the body of the mound after it had been raised (1936, 77-96). Three secondary interments were located along the spine of the mound, two of which were associated with Beakers. Interment 1 consisted of a crouched inhumation probably of a young woman of about 20 years of age that lay over the remains of a child who was approximately 1-2 years of age. It was unclear as to whether the two interments were made at the same time although it would seem that the child was interred first. Accompanying the adult female was a Beaker (**34**). In interment 2, an adult male of about 17-18 years of age was interred in the crouched position, laying on his right side. Accompanying this burial was a Beaker and also a bronze awl. The awl may be broadly associated with the craft/tool type of burial indicated earlier although clearly the awl could have been utilised in a wide variety of crafts. The final interment, which stratigraphically could be determined as having post-dated interment 2, consisted of a 17 to 18-year-old adult female in the usual crouched position, although no grave goods were found with her. The upper fills of the barrow's ditch also contained fragments of Beaker pottery, all of which highlights that the barrow was not only a feature within the landscape occupied by people aligned to the Beaker culture but that it maintained a utility which was far from redundant.

That monuments were reused or adopted by later Beaker communities can be further demonstrated by the large pit ring enclosure at Flagstones near Dorchester (Smith *et al.* 1997, 27). This middle Neolithic enclosure was reused during the beginning of the Bronze Age when an oval pit was excavated into the centre of the monument, into which was placed a crouched inhumation of an adult male (**35**). Although no Beaker was recovered from the excavation, a copper alloy rivet was found and a radiocarbon date of 2010-1830 BC was determined from the skeletal remains, all of which would suggest a deposit of Beaker type. The inhumation had been covered by the placement of a large sarsen (measuring 1.8 by 1.4 by 0.65m) over it, which was probably rolled or levered into place and the whole was surrounded by a concentrically placed ring ditch 28m in diameter. Because of post-depositional disturbance and later activity on the site it was impossible to determine if a barrow had been raised over the burial area.

Several other sites of Neolithic origin have contained fragmentary remains of Beaker pottery in their upper levels. Wor barrow, Handley barrows 26 and 27, Wyke Down henge and the Dorset Cursus all located within a few miles of each other on Cranbourne Chase can be included in such a list (Cleal in Barrett *et al.* 1991, 114). This would appear to demonstrate not only continuity in landscape use but also the rather transient nature of the Neolithic – Early Bronze Age divide.

As we have seen, the occurrence of Beaker burial in monuments of an earlier period is not particularly unusual, however, they are more commonly associated with round barrows. A number of such sites in Dorset have been excavated in the past and the barrows are usually of the smaller and lower varieties of bowl barrow with the mound created from the encircling quarry ditch. As an example one can cite a low mound on Launceston Down in the parish of Tarrant Launceston which was one of several barrows excavated by Stuart Piggott in 1938 (Piggott

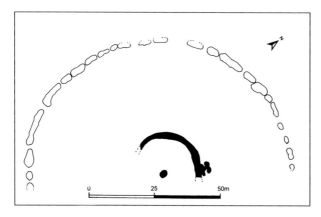

35 *Beaker inhumation at Flagstones: the Neolithic segmented ditch enclosure on the outskirts of Dorchester was selected for the later insertion of a Beaker inhumation in a pit. The pit was covered by a sarsen boulder and surrounded by a quarry ditch that suggests that the burial may have had at one time a mound raised above it.* Redrawn with amendments from Smith R.J.C. *et al.* 1997

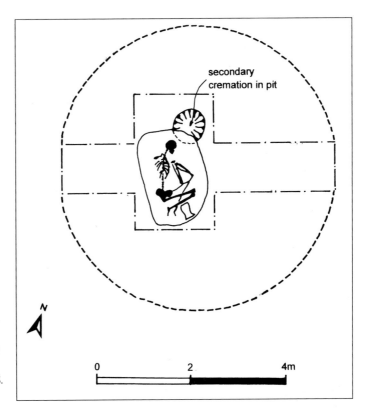

36 *Crichel Down Early Bronze Age inhumation: plan of the central deposit excavated by Piggott in 1938.* Redrawn from S. and C.M.Piggott 1944

1944, 75-6). The barrow recorded by Piggott as Crichel Down barrow 14 (Grinsell no. 5) was at the time of the excavation approximately 5m in diameter and less than 0.2m high. Upon excavation a D-shaped grave pit measuring 2 by 1.5m was discovered which had been cut into the chalk to a depth of approximately 0.8m. On the floor of the grave cut lay the crouched inhumation of an adult lying on its left side with a Beaker placed at its feet (**36**). Interestingly the skull had been trepanned in the left occipital region and the bone roundel had been replaced prior to burial. As no healing had occurred it may be assumed that the individual did not survive the operation. The only grave good recovered in addition to the Beaker was a single flint flake, although a flint pick was found in the rubble filling of the grave.

The stone circles of Dorset

One of the most enduring symbols of prehistoric activity in Britain is that of Stonehenge, the magnificent stone circle located on Salisbury Plain in Wiltshire. Alongside over 900 other identified stone circles, no other prehistoric monuments have captured the public imagination in quite the same way or are as easily recognisable. However, their distribution in the landscape is variable, and in many parts of the south and east of England, they are totally absent. The dating of stone circles is, as with most monuments, determined by excavation and for those sites not excavated (at least in modern times) dating is often by association to those of similar form that have been. Generally speaking, stone circles appear to have been constructed in the British Isles from the Late Neolithic through to the late stages of the Bronze Age (Burl 1976, 8).

In Dorset there are a small but significant group of such monuments all located close to the coast with a cluster in south Dorset. A characteristic of all the Dorset examples is their small diameter, none exceed 28m, and all the surviving examples are oval in shape (1976, 297), although in most cases this may not be a true reflection of their original form. Burl records the presence of nine possible examples in the county. The most westerly of these sites located at Litton Cheney which in the 1930s consisted of an earth bank with an external ditch (Piggott 1939, 143-6). It was excavated in the early 1970s and appears to be prehistoric, but sadly not a stone circle (Catherhall, 1974). Additional circles located at Little Mayne to the south of Dorchester and at a site between the villages of East Lulworth and Povington were noted by the Antiquarian Charles Warne (1872, 121 & 136), but no trace of either site survives today.

The main concentration of surviving sites found within the county are all located within a few kilometres of the village of Portesham to the south-west of Dorchester (**37**). This cluster consists of three surviving circles (Kingston Russell, Nine Stones and Hampton) and originally may have also included the example of Little Mayne and a second site close to the Nine Stones at Winterbourne Abbas. All of the surviving monuments have issues concerning the integrity of the position of stones located within them, and only one of the sites has been excavated. Geoffrey Wainwright excavated Hampton in 1965 because of concerns

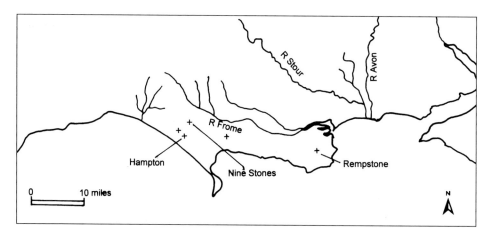

37 *Distribution of stone circles in Dorset: in addition to those sites named on the map are those at Kingston Russell (the cross to the north-west of Hampton) and the destroyed site of Little Mayne (to the east of Hampton)*

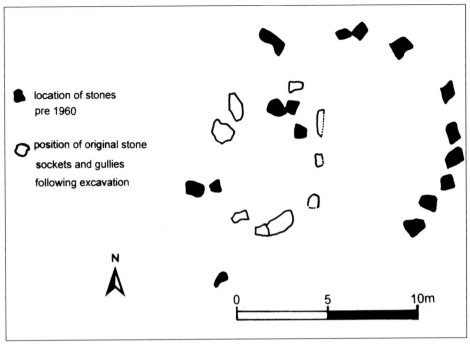

38 *Plan of Hampton stone circle: this stone circle is an excellent example of the misleading nature of some archaeological monuments. Prior to excavation in the 1960s, the plan of the stone circle was approximated to be that of the stone positions. The excavation demonstrated that the original monument was significantly different.* Compiled after S. and C.M.Piggott 1939 and Wainwright 1966

related to the disturbance of the monument by agricultural operations (Wainwright 1966, 122-127). The site is located on high downland to the west of Portesham and if the extent of the contemporary vegetation was limited its location would have afforded extensive panoramic views of the south coast. The monument had been visited and recorded thirty years earlier by Stuart Piggott, who produced a plan of the surviving 16 irregularly spaced sarsen stones (Piggott S. & C.M., 1939, 142). This record suggested that the eastern half of the stone settings were the better preserved and indicated that the original diameter of the circle was in the region of 11-12m (**38**). A survey of the stones prior to the excavation, however, revealed that a total of 28 stones were present, some of which had recently been moved to the site after ploughing of the field to the east in 1964. The fieldwork and excavation of 1965 revealed that the articulation of the stones was entirely fallacious, but fortuitously the settings of an original stone circle were discovered a few feet to the west underneath a hedge bank. It is likely that it was during the construction of the hedge bank that the original articulation of the monument was finally destroyed probably some time during the seventeenth century. The original stone circle seems to have consisted of eight or nine stone sockets in an oval shape with the perimeter of the circle additionally defined by V-shaped ditches. The maximum axis of the circle was approximately 6.5m making it considerable smaller than the reconstruction recorded by Piggott. Following the excavation, stones were placed in the original sockets thereby returning the sites integrity to that of the original construction, although it was of course impossible to remarry the original stones to the correct sockets.

Comparable in size (maximum axis 9m) but not in location, is the site known as Nine Stones located on the western edge of the village of Winterbourne Abbas in west Dorset (**39** & **colour plate 5**). The circle is located, rather unusually, in a valley bottom close to the course of a winterbourne. The articulation of the nine stone settings is probably the most well documented of all those surviving in the county, and it would appear that the stone positioning that visitors to the site see today is probably little changed from that seen by Stukely in 1723. Charles Warne, in describing the site at the end of the nineteenth century, records the possibility of a tenth stone but this has never been substantiated. Alongside the unusual setting, two of the stones within the ring are out of proportion to the remaining seven in terms of their size. The two stones are located to the west and north-west and are more than twice the height of the remaining seven (1.2 and 2.1m high). Circles with pairs of large stones are known elsewhere in Britain although their distribution is limited to south-western Scotland. The example interestingly but coincidentally known as Ninestone Rigg in Roxburgh, is of similar size and also has two large stone pillars, but with over 300 miles separating the two areas there is unlikely to be any contemporary association between the respective populations

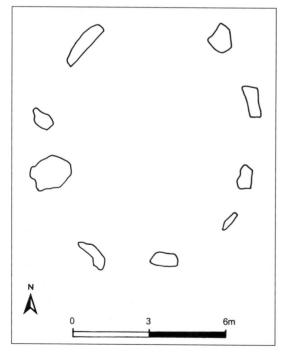

39 *Plan of The Nine Stones: this stone circle is located on the edge of the village of Winterbourne Abbas in southern Dorset. Its siting is somewhat unusual in that it is found in a sheltered valley bottom by the side of a winterbourne. Redrawn from Piggott S and C.M. 1939*

40 *Kingston Russell stone circle seen from the south.* © Julie Gale

which the monuments served. The presence of a second circle at Winterbourne Abbas is suggested by the account of John Aubrey's visit to the area in 1773, which is supposed to have been located about half a mile from the Nine Stones (Piggott 1939, 150). Support for this may be found in Warne's account of a standing stone called the Broad Stone located near Winterbourne Abbas in the late nineteenth century:

> . . . a somewhat larger and better proportioned stone, now lies prostrate by the side of the turnpike road (now the A35), one mile west of the Stone Circle. It measures about 10 feet in length six and a half in breadth and two feet in thickness. (Warne 1872, 134).

It is possible that this second circle was a group of outlying stones or perhaps even the remains of a chambered tomb, but as nothing remains it is at the moment impossible to resolve.

The largest of the Dorset circles is Kingston Russell, which sits upon the chalk ridge west of Portesham. All of the stones, which trace a flattened circle, are now recumbent (**40**), although at least one of them was upright when recorded by the historian John Hutchins in the middle of the nineteenth century. There are 18 stones in the circle (maximum diameter 27.7m) which in common with those from the Nine Stones and Hampton are all constructed from a sarsen conglomerate, which was almost certainly obtained from a nearby outcrop at a place called the Valley of the Stones. As discussed in chapter 2, all of the known local megalithic tombs in the area were also constructed using boulders from this site. It is surely therefore, entirely likely that the distribution of megalithic remains within the county is linked to the availability of suitable building stone rather than a culturally derived preference. In those areas in which no suitable stone was available, or it was too difficult to recover, the functional or ceremonial utility of the stone circles was probably met through similar constructions in less permanent materials – wood and earth. Certainly the pit rings described in chapter 2 may represent more than a passing resemblance in plan form. The utility of the great timber circles located within henge monuments (Woodhenge, Durrington Walls and Mount Pleasant) are often discussed as wooden counterparts to stone circles although in some cases this is probably unlikely.

The last of the stone circles to be considered is a geographical outlier to the cluster of sites around Dorchester. The site at Rempstone is the most easterly of the Dorset stone circles, located on the Isle of Purbeck 4km east of Corfe Castle. The site has clearly been much disturbed and now consists of eight sandstone boulders, only five of which are erect, with further stones presumably part of the circle lying displaced nearby. The curvature of the arc would indicate that the original diameter of the circle may have been as much as 26m in diameter making it comparable in size to that at Kingston Russell. The type of sandstone represented by the boulders is likely to be of local origin. In 1957 Bernard Calkin visited the site to examine a report of additional stones found approximately 1km west of the circle following a period of ploughing. As a result of some rapidly convened fieldwork, a total of 26 stones were revealed averaging 2ft 6in by 1ft 6in (0.85m by 0.5m). Some of the stones seem to form pairs approximately 3m apart which suggested to Calkin they may form part of an avenue of stones linked to the stone circle (Calkin 1959, 114-116). Whilst avenues of stones are known to be associated with stone circles (Avebury, Wiltshire is amongst the best known of examples) this group is quite a distance from the circle and as Calkin himself pointed out the stones themselves are extremely small. Thoughts that the stones were part of an earlier field wall were only partially reduced by the lack of evidence of a field division on the tithe map of 1844 or the 2in (1:25000) 1805-6 Ordnance Survey map. The afore mentioned destroyed site at Little Mayne is similarly conjectured to have been associated with a stone avenue, which was recorded as being present in 1728 by Roger Gale (no relation as far as I am aware – author). However, in this case there were two avenues leading to the circle, one from the south, the other from the north. In neither case has their presence been confirmed.

As to the purpose and date of these megalithic monuments there is little firm local evidence to build upon. The excavation of Hampton revealed no dateable or associated finds to help us answer either of these questions and consequently we must rely on generalisations drawn from excavated stone circles around the British Isles. All of the Dorset examples fit into the general open site classification promoted by Burl (1976, 36-39) and consequently appear to have little direct association with burial practices. All of the sites are, however, located close to burial monuments which may indicate that they were associated with the ritual/ceremonial beliefs of the local communities, but the picture is far from clear. That some of the monuments may have other features such as avenues associated with them may suggest that the circles were part of a more complex monument, of which only the more lasting elements survive. Other places within such a landscape of significance might be natural places (springs, specific or revered trees, streams, etc.) which combined to create places where ceremonies were enacted and rituals undertaken. In essence the stone circles may represent therefore, a place of focus for a community where interaction with the world (spiritual or real) was controlled through the ordering of the landscape. Such control of the landscape might require points of access in which elements of the natural landscape could be amplified or defined by the construction of monuments. The difficulty in the mapping of such a process today is the identification of the elements within the landscape that our ancestors chose which marked out such locations as special. If such elements were organic (such as a grove of trees perhaps) then we are clearly going to be unable to detect them today.

The evolution of the round barrow and 'The Wessex Culture' in Dorset

Based upon current evidence, the practice of interring a Beaker alongside an inhumation within a round barrow appears not to extend beyond about 1600 BC. However, the raising of round barrows in the landscape to cover funerary deposits and, perhaps more importantly, the continued use of such monuments via secondary interments inserted into them continues for some considerable time. The form of the round barrow linked with the earlier Beaker burials was usually associated with a generally low mound. Whilst such mounds can be found in great numbers around Dorset even the casual observer cannot fail to notice the great diversity that there appears to be in size, shape and clustering of round barrows. In 1982 Lesley Grinsell published a supplement to his mammoth survey of barrows in the county which lists the existence of at least 2,233 round barrows (Grinsell, 1959 & 1982). Of this number, the largest proportion by far (94 per cent) is that attributable to the form known as the bowl barrow, from which there appears to be a number of derivative types (**41**). The bowl barrow simply consists of a round mound of piled earth and rock, usually but not exclusively derived from a surrounding quarry ditch. The quarry ditch would in this case be immediately adjacent to the edge of the mound, and occasionally an outer-bank was constructed (Tarrant Hinton – Grinsell no 3a). The presence of minor fluctuations in barrow components such as an external bank, and their subsequent recognition some three and a half thousand years later is a matter of debate. The presence of an outer bank, in bowl barrow design appears to be extremely rare in Wessex generally and specifically in Dorset. Although Grinsell considered this to be a probable honest reflection of the original population, his interpretation contrasts with that of Charles Warne's observation in his late nineteenth-century publication, where he records that the barrows were frequently accompanied by a ditch with an external bank which was 'slightly raised' (Warne 1866, 8). Such slight features can leave little trace in the archaeological record, particularly in landscapes that have been subjected to continuous ploughing and

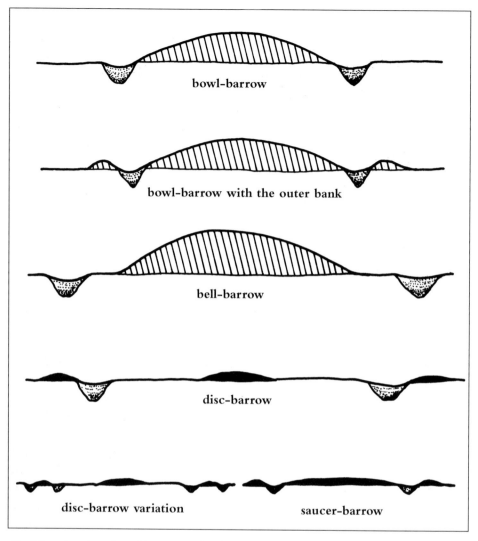

41 *Schematic sections of round barrow types found in Dorset.* Redrawn with amendments from Grinsell 1959

associated agricultural tillage of the soil over considerable periods of time. Their numbers consequently may have been larger, particularly when we consider the derivative forms of barrows associated with the landscape of Dorset which also frequently contain an external ditch. Disc and saucer forms of round barrow also have an external bank, as do pond barrows which in most cases rarely survive as observable features in the landscape.

The presence of so-called 'fancy barrows' in Dorset has long been associated with the activities of a cultural group which seem to appear in the archaeological record during the Early Bronze Age period. In 1938 Stuart Piggott published a paper on his examination of a discrete number of Wessex funerary deposits (approximately 100) which had been excavated mainly in the eighteenth and nineteenth centuries. The material examined largely consisted of grave goods which seemed to display a characteristic 'richness' highlighted by the occurrence of weapons, and personal ornamentation not usually seen in burials of the period (1938, 52-106). Piggott's original hypothesis led him to conclude that the artefacts were of a culturally diverse and elite group, whose origin could be linked to stylistic affinities with material found in Brittany in northern France. Within his hypothesis, Piggott not only established a commonality of material remains but also noted an association with barrow types (bell and disc types) and concluded that they must 'represent the Wessex Culture'. In more recent studies whilst the identification of a distinctive tradition within the region is generally accepted, some of the interpretations and inferences made by Piggott have been questioned. The principal issues have been summarised recently by Anne Woodward in her overview of British barrows (Woodward 2000, 101-108). In essence Piggott may have overstated the hierarchical and militaristic model for Early Bronze Age society proposed to explain the rich burials associated with the Wessex Culture. He was after all conducting his analysis against the backdrop of a world under-going the preliminary steps of a Second World War, and in an academic climate which would have been sympathetic to an interpretation whereby the rationale for change was based upon ideas involving a colonising foreign elite.

Amongst the finest examples of a rich burial in the tradition of the Wessex culture is that excavated by Edward Cunnington in 1882 at the site of the Clandon barrow located close to the Iron Age hillfort at Maiden Castle. Along with the more famous example from Bush barrow in Wiltshire, the grave goods exemplify the stereotypical image of a Wessex culture burial. At Clandon barrow, within the body of a very large bowl barrow, Cunnington discovered a low stone cairn on whose surface had been placed an incised gold lozenge, a shale macehead embellished with five gold bosses, an amber cup and nearby a dagger complete with its wooden sheath and an incense cup. Unfortunately Cunnington was unable to identify a primary interment at the barrow and consequently the rich deposit is likely to be associated with a secondary interment or rite separate from the primary deposit, which presumably remains undisturbed deeper within the mound.

Many other examples of burial attributable to the period have been excavated in Dorset but unfortunately, as elsewhere in the region, the majority were unearthed by antiquarian diggings in the last two centuries. Frequently, therefore, whilst artefacts often remain, the context and even the individual provenance of the deposits were insufficiently recorded. However, Grinsell lists between 15 and 24 excavated bowl barrows that contain cultural elements that link them to 'Wessex' grave groups. Smaller numbers of associations can also be made for the much smaller populations of fancy barrows, but frequently it appears that this relates to the second phase of the Wessex tradition, commonly referred to as Wessex II which is chiefly characterised by a switch to cremation from inhumation.

One of the best examples of a Wessex II burial was excavated in 1959 close to the village of Edmonsham in east Dorset (Proudfoot 1963, 395-425). Here a small bell barrow, which had been badly eroded through plough damage, was found to contain a single grave located in the north-east quadrant of the mound, having been dug into the contemporary ground surface to a depth of approximately 0.5m (**42**). The cremated remains of an adult male had been placed into the grave, on top of which a number of grave goods had been placed, including a dagger which had been sheathed in leather and a perforated whetstone made from a micaceous calcareous sandstone. Also within the grave, but slightly displaced from the cremation deposit, were a pair of bone tweezers and a bone pin over 10cm long. Alongside the rite of cremation which is a characteristic of Wessex II burials, the dagger recovered from the grave deposit could also be dated to the period. Its form consisted of a grooved ogival blade whose handle was secured via three large bronze rivets, which is of a type that are collectively referred to as Camerton-Snowshill daggers.

An area of burnt soil, heap of ash and small burnt bone demonstrated evidence for an *in situ* cremation pyre at the site which the excavator suggested may have been originally as much as 4m in diameter. An unusual feature of this burial however, is the size of the grave pit which was large enough to contain an

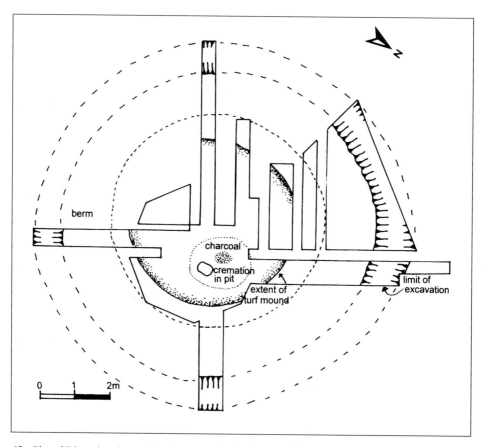

42 *Plan of Edmonsham barrow following excavation.* Redrawn with amendments from Proudfoot 1963

inhumation. This may suggest that both rites were practised at the time, which may in turn suggest that the burial is early in the Wessex II sequence.

As with the Beaker burials the Wessex Culture burials often exhibit differences in gender and wealth via the grave contents. Males are frequently associated with daggers, battle axes and similar weaponry whilst female deposits are often accompanied by necklaces, beads and other types of personal decoration as well as occasional small knives. The quantity and quality of such grave goods can vary considerably from the wealth associated with deposits like those found at the Clandon barrow (see above) with its gold items, to much more simple materials such as the bronze awl and bead found in a bell barrow on Oakley Down in 1950-1 (Parke 1953, 36-44).

The nature of the burial record by around 1500 BC is highly diverse with no single burial rite or tradition being universally adopted in Dorset, or for that matter in Britain generally. Previously held ideas that the multiple interments common during the Neolithic period, were replaced in the Bronze Age by a burial rite essentially marked by a single grave tradition, do not stand up to scrutiny. We have already seen that barrows frequently contain multiple deposits, many of which are inserted into an already extant funerary area (a barrow). What does, however, appear to be developing is the concept of a funereal area rather than a funereal monument, which we would recognise as a cemetery. It is likely that the burial rite is reflective of social structure at the time, and if this is the case it would suggest that society in Early Bronze Age Dorset was more overtly structured, with greater emphasis on the formal recognition of kinship groups. The likely kinship association of burials within round barrows is often suggested by the mix of gender and age groups within barrows but this is by no means constant as there are numerous examples of single interments in barrows. Barrows, whilst occurring within the landscape as singletons or in small groups of two or three, are very commonly found in groups of more than six. Nowhere is this more noticeable than within the county of Dorset. These groups of barrows have long been recognised as forming two distinct forms; those that cluster together with no apparent order, generally referred to as nucleated cemeteries and those that defined through a clear spatial association in lines, which are generally classed as linear cemeteries (**43**). A number of studies have refined this basic division of cemetery layout (Fleming 1971; Woodward 2000) and included further subdivisions, such as Row cemeteries and Dispersed cemeteries, all of which can be seen within the Dorset landscape.

Alongside the general trend of a change in burial rite, which focuses upon a preference for cremation as time progresses, we also witness changes in the form of pottery accompanying the funerary deposits. Although so-called food vessels are more readily associated with highland geographical zones, particularly in northern Britain, they do occur in Dorset barrows albeit in small numbers, with examples found at Sturminster Marshall (Calkin 1966, 138) and at Launceston Down (Green et al., 1982, 48). Whilst Food Vessels usually accompanied inhumation

43 *Winterbourne Poor Lot barrow group: the tell-tale signs of Antiquarian disturbance can be seen in the tops of many of the barrows.* © Crown copyright, NMR

burial as with the contemporaneous Beakers which we examined earlier, larger forms, referred to unsurprisingly as Enlarged Food Vessels, often contain the cremated remains of the individual, as was the case with an example discovered at Hampreston (Grinsell 1959, 31).

An excellent example of the intermixing of pottery forms within barrows of the Early Bronze Age can be seen in the excavation of two round barrows on Launceston Down to the north of Blandford Forum (Green *et al.* 1982, 39-58). The excavation of two barrows (a bell and a bowl) within a larger cemetery group in 1959-60 revealed a series of complex deposits in both instances, which demonstrated that both barrows had been utilised over a period of many centuries. The bowl barrow (Long Crichell 5) began as a small mound which covered a centrally placed grave, into which a classic crouched inhumation was placed, accompanied by a bell-shaped Beaker placed at the feet of the individual. After the insertion of a secondary Beaker burial, the centre of the barrow was partially removed along with part of the central grave fill and into this the flexed body of a child was placed, accompanied by a Food Vessel. The grave was then backfilled with chalk and the barrow extended, but was later disturbed again to take a third series of burials, mainly cremations (**44**). Within the second barrow (Long Crichell 7) to be excavated, a similarly complex series of deposits was discovered, which this time revealed the existence of other funerary urns that are more commonly found in Dorset and throughout the British Isles. Once again a barrow whose origin was associated with Beaker deposits, was later reused and re-defined at an early stage of its history, to include cremated burial underneath up-turned Collared urns, and later still Biconical urns of Deverel-Rimbury form.

Urns, Urnfields and the Deverel-Rimbury tradition

As we have seen thus far, the evidence for Early to Middle Bronze occupation of Dorset is dominated by the funerary remains associated with the great barrow cemeteries found chiefly, but not exclusively on Cranborne Chase and the chalk downs and associated areas of the South Dorset Ridgeway. After about 1500 BC, the construction of round barrows of whatever form, whilst still an important funerary feature within the landscape, seems to decline. The insertion of burials into pre-existing barrows, typically cremations associated with funerary urns of collared types, begins to dominate the burial rite. However, by about 1400 BC we also see an extension of this process with the establishment of cemeteries which contain significant numbers of burials in what prehistorians recognise as Urnfield cemeteries. In these cemeteries the generally adopted receptacle for cremated remains comes in the form of an urn, either of collared or Deverel-Rimbury type. Deverel-Rimbury urns are named after two sites in Dorset where the ceramic style was initially recognised. The Deverel-Rimbury style of pottery was long thought to be derived from the continent but has, since the late 1960s, been recognised as

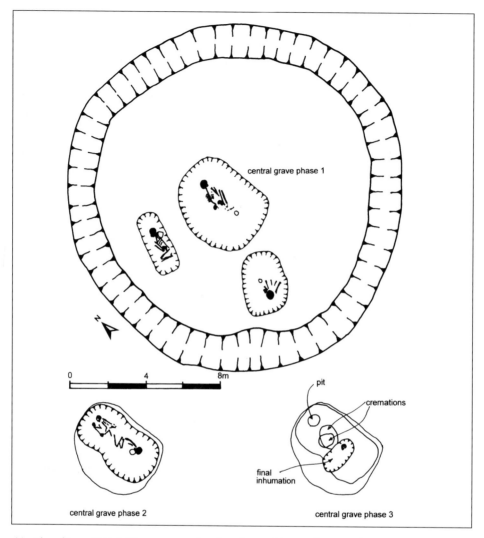

central grave phase 1

0   4   8m

pit

cremations

final
inhumation

central grave phase 2

central grave phase 3

44 *Plan of Long Crichel 5 barrow: a complex plan of a round barrow that received several interments including inhumations and cremations during the Bronze Age.* Redrawn with amendments from Green *et al.* 1982

being of indigenous origin, probably having its roots in the Late Neolithic pottery forms of Grooved ware. Collared urns are also considered to have derived from indigenous pottery types, possibly the later forms of Peterborough ware, but are primarily funereal in function, whereas Deverel-Rimbury pottery can also be found in settlement contexts.

At the site of Deverel barrow near the village of Milborne St Andrew, W.A. Miles excavated and discovered the remains of a round barrow, which contained a primary or initial cremation interred within a collared urn, which was followed by more than 20 other cremations. Sixteen of the cremations were contained within upright urns that lay underneath red sandstone stones that were laid out in a semi-circular pattern.

It would appear that all of the burials were interred before the mound was thrown up over them but as the site was excavated in 1824 a lot of detail is unrecoverable. A number of more recently excavated sites in Dorset do, nonetheless, give us a clearer picture of these Middle Bronze Age cemeteries

Two sites excavated within a few years of each other both ably demonstrate the form of burial tradition adopted by the contemporary populations of the area during the Middle – Late Bronze Age period. The first site of Simon's Ground located at Hampreston near Wimborne, consisted of four separate excavations which revealed about 300 cremation urns within 15 identifiable clusters, dating from the period 1200-550 BC. All four excavated areas at Simon's Ground were excavated between 1967-69 by David White, and the overall site still represents the largest Bronze Age Urnfield complex yet discovered in Britain. All of the excavated areas were examined in relation to low surviving mounds of barrows which appear to pre-date the main sequence of cremations in each case. Although some of the barrows had urns inserted into the barrow mounds most of the urns were located in clusters outside the barrow area (**45**). There appears to have been a good deal of variation in relation to the burial rite enacted at the site and

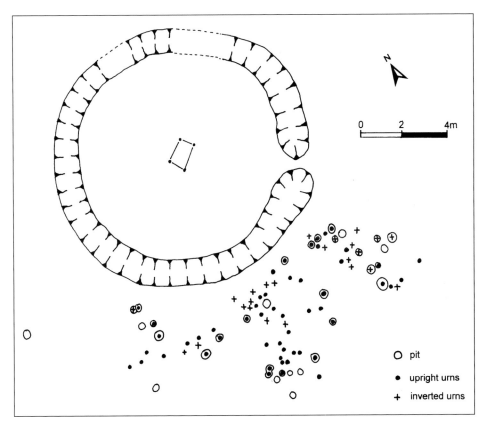

45 *Plan of Simon's Ground urn cemetery: the urnfield cemetery at Site B.* Redrawn with amendments from White 1982

although cremation was universally adopted, no evidence for cremation pyres was discovered during the excavation. Some urns were buried upright, whilst others were inverted; others were covered with a capstone, and in some cases urns contained no trace of cremated bone at all. Interestingly it would appear that at least some of the urns were only partially buried, leaving the remainder above ground presumably as a form of grave marker.

The second site at Knighton Heath on the outskirts of Poole, excavated by Frederic Petersen in 1971 highlighted another cemetery associated with a large number of Deverel-Rimbury Urns, but in this case the great majority of burials were undertaken within the confines of a round barrow (**46**). The excavation, prompted by encroaching gravel extraction, revealed the presence of 60 urns, most of which had been interred at the site after it had been cleared by fire and before the subsequent mound was constructed over them (Petersen 1981, 176-7). It would appear that some urns were inserted after the mound had been constructed, suggesting that although the burial area had been symbolically closed, its impor-

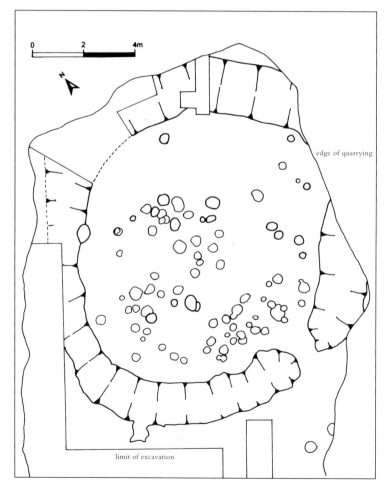

46 *Plan of Knighton Heath urn cemetery: this urnfield cemetery excavated prior to the sites destruction revealed a dense concentration of Middle Bronze Age burials bounded by a ring ditch. Redrawn with amendments from Petersen 1981*

tance and significance as a funerary/spiritual place was such that later populations were compelled to reuse it. As with the burials at Simon's Ground there was variation in the burial record and examples of all the three principal types of urns were represented (Bucket, Barrel and Globular).

The distribution of the larger Deverel-Rimbury cemeteries in the county appears to be concentrated in the heathlands of the Poole basin, and the fluvial terraces of the Avon, Stour and Frome rivers. However, other parts of Dorset also contain cemeteries associated with the tradition, and on Cranborne Chase Deverel-Rimbury style cremations in urns have been found at the Down Farm Ring Ditch (Barrett *et al.*, 1991, 211-214), as well as those examined by Pitt-Rivers in the late nineteenth century at South Lodge, and at Handley barrow 24.

Landscapes of the living?

So far in this chapter there has been little description or discussion of places of habitation. Activity at the great palisaded enclosure at Mount Pleasant, or the possible reuse of the Neolithic monuments at the Hambledon and Knowlton complexes, hardly constitute extensive evidence with which to characterise the nature of settlement for the period. As with the Neolithic period it is likely that the form of settlement, particularly in the first few centuries of the Bronze Age, was likely to have been dispersed within the landscape. The physical characteristics of the structures associated with the settlement of the time may have also been of a type that leaves a minimal footprint, which is now only likely to survive in the rarest of circumstance.

In contrast to this, by around 1500 BC we start to see evidence for the existence of a planned landscape, which contains not only areas which can be clearly defined as places that were occupied, but also their incorporation into landscapes which were more formally divided up. The division of the landscape takes the form of the establishment of blocks of extensive field systems and in some areas (particularly noticeable on the Chalk Downs of Dorset) the creation of formal territorial boundaries as long linear boundaries constructed of earth banks with accompanying ditches.

A number of sites have been discovered over the last century within Dorset that provide an effective insight into the nature of at least part of the organised landscape that existed in the Later Bronze Age. Some of the best evidence for settlement activity of the period is derived from the pioneering excavations of General Pitt-Rivers at the end of the nineteenth century on a number of sites located on Cranborne Chase – South Lodge, Martin Down and The Angle Ditch, (Pitt-Rivers, 1898). The work of Pitt-Rivers on these sites has been revised and enhanced in recent years through the efforts of a number of archaeologists working together, whose work was largely published in the volume *Landscape monuments and society* in 1991 (Barrett *et al.*).

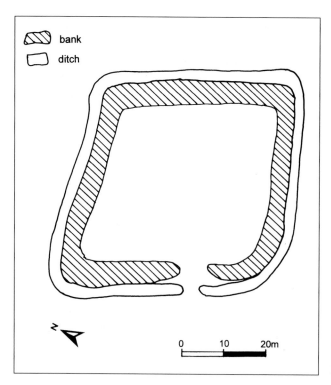

47 *Plan of South Lodge enclosure: a Middle Bronze Age enclosure initially excavated by General Pitt-Rivers at the end of the nineteenth century but later re-examined by Richard Bradley in 1977. Redrawn from Barrett et al. 1991*

The site of South Lodge is located within Rushmore Park north of the village of Farnham in the heart of Cranborne Chase. The site consists of a number of lynchets which to some extent pre-date the construction of a rectangular enclosure comprising a bank with an external ditch (**47**). The interior of the enclosure contained two circular post-built structures, one of which has been dated by radio-carbon dating to 1630-1050 BC. Most of the pottery recovered from the interior of the enclosure is consistent with Deverel-Rimbury urn types, illustrating that the vessels were clearly not singularly associated with funereal deposits. Located 100m to the north of the enclosure, a small barrow cemetery of five round barrows (known as Barrow Pleck) was found to be broadly contemporary with the enclosure. Several cremations were recovered from the barrows, some of them associated with pots of Deverel-Rimbury form. The barrow cemetery appears to have been longer-lived than the enclosure with elements of it possibly pre-dating the construction of the enclosure when there could have been an open settlement at the site. The enclosure is likely to have functioned as a small farmstead although, probably not as originally pictured by Pitt-Rivers, whose pioneering excavation technique was not sufficiently robust to identify post-holes, which were subsequently identified when the site was re-excavated by Richard Bradley in 1977.

A more detailed picture of a similar settlement was recovered from the nearby enclosure at Down Farm, which was excavated between 1977-9 (Barrett, *et al.* 1991, 183-214). As with South Lodge, settlement at Down Farm appears to begin with an open settlement consisting of two structures defined by post-holes. The two structures have noticeably different plans and may represent a residential structure accompanied by an ancillary building located within a field system. Fragments of loomweights were recovered from the outer ring of post-holes of one of the structures from this phase, an association not uncommon on sites in southern England. This is usually interpreted as evidence not only for the production of woven cloth, but also that sheep were likely to have formed part of the agricultural basis of the farming practised by the occupants of the settlement. After a period of abandonment, a partially ditched enclosure was built comprising a low bank and ditch constructed to the east and south. On the inside of the bank and enclosing a total area of 750m², a perimeter palisade was erected with opposed entrances located at the north-east and the south-west. Within this second phase of the site's occupation there appears to be a similar arrangement of residential and ancillary structures to that discovered in the earlier phase, but with two possible ancillary structures attendant to the residential round house with what appears to be an entrance porch (48). Both of the ancillary structures contained storage pits probably for the storage of grain. The latest stage of construction within the enclosure sees the erection of an unusual rectangular building nearly 20m long in the lee of the eastern enclosure bank. The function of this structure has been difficult to determine partly due to

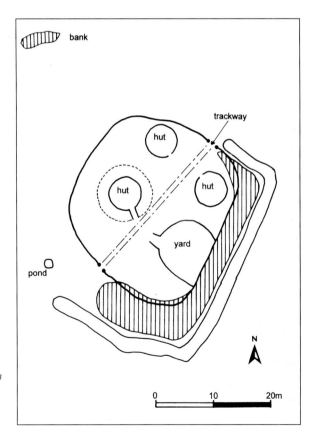

48 *Plan of Down Farm enclosure: phase 2 of this Middle Bronze Age enclosure reflects different ways to enclose space in a unified enclosure. Whilst the whole of the farmstead is enclosed in a palisade, only the eastern half has a bank and ditch. Redrawn with amendments from Barrett, et al. 1991*

modern plough damage, but it has been suggested that the structure could have been used as a storage barn or alternatively, as a longhouse combining both storage and residential use, which is extremely unusual for the period.

Amongst the most well known of sites dating to the Later Bronze Age in southern Britain is that of Shearplace Hill located near the village of Sydling St Nicholas in west Dorset. As with South Lodge the site is unusual as it has survived reasonably well as an upstanding earthwork, complete with enclosure banks and ditches. In addition, earthworks in the form of platforms on which were located the trace remains of post-built structures also survive, as do the inter-linking earth-works identified as field banks and holloways. In one of the most influential studies of landscape development undertaken in the last thirty years, Christopher Taylor has correctly suggested that many sites which fulfil this basic description can also be identified in various parts of Britain, particularly on the chalk downs (Taylor 1983, 56). Taylor goes on to indicate that many of these sites have been arbitrarily dated to the Iron Age or the Romano-British period without confirmation by excavation, and that subsequently many of them could be Bronze Age in date.

The enclosure at Shearplace Hill was excavated by Philip Rahtz in 1958. Rahtz identified the site as a small defended farmstead of Middle Bronze Age date, occupied by a community linked to the Deverel-Rimbury tradition by way of the ceramic material recovered from the main enclosure (Rahtz 1962, 289-328).

The farmstead consisted of two sub-circular houses, contained within an embanked D-shaped enclosure but separated from each other by a further low bank projecting from the northern circuit of the main enclosing bank (**49**). The more substantial of the two houses consisted of a post-built roughly circular structure, approximately 9m in diameter. A rectangular porch located at its southern end defines the entrance to the house which opened out onto a courtyard. Many of the post-holes of this structure had been replaced at least twice, indicated by the cutting of new, and re-cutting of old, post-holes. Within the house further post-hole settings were discovered, some of which are likely to be structural but others probably functioned as internal features, possibly looms. Support for this interpreta-tion was found by the presence of a complete loom weight within one of the post-holes from the interior of the house. The second structure in the main enclosure was a smaller less well-defined post-built structure, approximately 5m in diameter. The excavator considered this structure to be of lesser importance and therefore possibly used as a barn for storage or even for the housing of servants. There is little direct evidence to support either function, although studies of contemporary sites such as Down Farm (see above) would tend to support the former.

In the courtyard directly in front of both houses was an area that contained numerous post-holes and small pits that seem to belong to a number of discrete small structures, possibly drying racks or granaries, rather than larger roofed struc-tures. A shallow depression in the south-east corner of the enclosure that contained a sump was interpreted as a working hollow on the basis of similar examples found at sites of later date elsewhere. However, there was little evidence

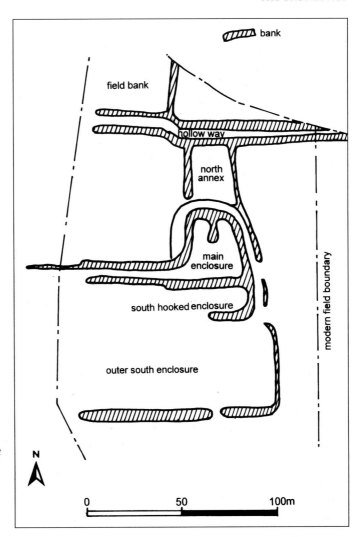

49 *Plan of enclosures at Shearplace Hill: an integrated complex of earthworks which mark out a small farmstead with supporting enclosures and hollow ways.* Redrawn with amendments from Rahtz 1962

to suggest what activity the feature was connected to, although it was positioned close to a pond, the proximity of which may have been significant.

The main enclosure at Shearplace Hill was linked to a complex of earthworks, which alongside the artefacts recovered from the site, present some detail as to the economic basis of the settlement. To the north and west of the main enclosure hollow ways, relict field banks and a possible stock-enclosure surviving as earthworks suggest that at least part of the farming activity was pastoral, an interpretation bolstered by the finding of quantities of animal bone including ox, sheep and pig.

The management of livestock appears to have become a major consideration for the occupants of many of the settlements that we have examined so far. Many of them have exhibited evidence for the exploitation of livestock, either directly through the recovery of animal bones, many of which carry distinctive 'butchery' marks, or indirectly via stock enclosures and hollow ways. In addition to earthworks at the site of settlements, much of Dorset has considerable numbers of linear boundaries surviving as earth banks and ditches (occasionally ditches only), which seem to act as land divisions mainly in the upland areas of the chalk downs. Many, if not all, of these land divisions are interpreted as a type of ranch boundary, which could have acted as territorial markers as well as obstacles to restrict the movement of stock. Several of these features cut across spurs and are frequently referred to as cross-ridge dykes and whilst common in Dorset, are to be found over many parts of downland throughout Britain. However, as with many features of the agricultural landscape, their dating is frequently poorly defined and much has been assumed or generalised without recourse to extensive investigation. In some instances these linear boundaries appear to have been constructed over more ancient field systems as is the case at Martin Down on Cranborne Chase (**50**), where a 'ranch boundary', possibly associated with a rectangular enclosure can be clearly seen to post-date quite an extensive field system. The date of the enclosure is certainly Middle Bronze Age although neither the field system nor the later linear boundary is dated. Interestingly the axial alignment of the fields, the linear boundary and the enclosure are all similarly arranged which may suggest that they all share a common origin.

An excellent example of a surviving cross-ridge dyke is to be seen close to Melbury Beacon to the south of Compton Abbas. The double ditch and bank located on Clubmens Down at the eastern end of Fontmell Down, runs for approximately 250m and is one of a number in the area which divide up the downs. Not all of the dykes are necessarily contemporary with each other but all would have been significant undertakings in terms of labour. Such elaborate

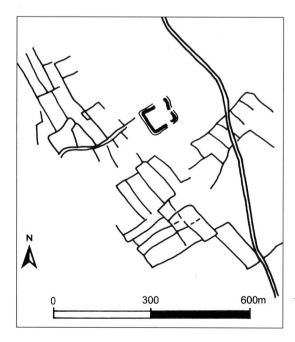

N

0   300   600m

50 *Plan of Martin Down enclosure and related earthworks: this Middle Bronze Age enclosure is seen surrounded by relict field systems which are overlain by a ranch boundary.* Redrawn with amendments from Burgess 1980

measures hint that their function was not necessarily limited to preventing the straying of animals alone. The establishment of such visible and costly (in terms of labour) land divisions are a significant expression of power, demonstrating territorial control and ownership in no uncertain terms. That such measures were necessary would seem to suggest that they were being undertaken in a period when society was under particular pressure or stress, possibly at a time of expansion into areas that had been previously less densely occupied or the land less intensively exploited.

As we shall see in the next chapter the form of settlement in our study area appears to change very little between approximately 1500-500 BC. The settlement pattern seems to be largely of a dispersed nature and more often than not enclosed in some way. The form of such enclosures can vary considerably, however, the utility of the enclosing boundary is not straightforward to determine. The large banks and ditches present at Shearplace Hill, where the earthworks might have served as a serious protective barrier against intruders of whatever species, could equally be a statement of prestige. The broadly contemporary farmstead enclosure at Down Farm on the other hand, with its combination bank and fence boundary, could never have functioned as a serious defensive barrier against a human foe. It should, therefore, be seen as an observable boundary, probably marking family or group space in much the same way that similar groups have done for millennia.

Two settlement sites that begin late in the Bronze Age period, which ultimately are utilised and developed into the Iron Age are those at Eldons Seat and Hog Cliff Hill. The former is located on the Kimmeridge clays of Purbeck in the parish of Encombe and was partially excavated by Barry Cunliffe between 1963-6 (Cunliffe 1968, 191-237). At around 700 BC the site is likely to have consisted of small palisaded enclosures which surrounded an undefined number of post-built round houses, interpreted by Cunliffe to be reminiscent of the site at Itford Hill in Sussex. Four houses of this period were investigated by Cunliffe but it was impossible to deduce whether more than two were in use at the same time, and of course, others may have been constructed in un-excavated parts of the site. Several huts provided evidence that they had been rebuilt, although little cultural material associated with the buildings beyond pottery sherds and fire hearths survived to indicate the finer detail of activity associated with the structures. The pottery associated with this phase of occupation of the site was of a developed form of Deverel-Rimbury consisting of plain bucket vessels with occasional finger-tip decoration.

The second site at Hog Cliff Hill (near Maiden Newton), whilst similar in some respects, may have been significantly larger in terms of area and population and may represent potential evidence for nucleated settlement during the period. In the excavated area three round houses were discovered, that were possibly constructed within a bank and ditched enclosure. The enclosure probably consisted of a 5.6ha ellipse-shaped enclosure, with the ditch of the enclosure being unusually located on the inside of the bank, rather in the manner of henges as we saw in chapter 2. Enclosures such as that found at Hog Cliff Hill may be early attempts at nucleated settlement, possibly linked to specialist activities within landscapes, where at times people would need to congregate.

The Bronze Age is, as one would expect, a period within which the revolutionary landscape of the preceding Neolithic period is at first consolidated, prior to the establishment of more evolved economic and social systems that become manifest in the following Iron Age. However, the identification of this process within the archaeological record is at best patchy, hampered as it is by partial survival of evidence and our limited abilities to locate, identify and interpret what evidence there is.

As we have seen, the nature of the evidence that is available to us for the period is marked by an imbalance. This imbalance, generally speaking, divides the period into two, with the earlier Bronze Age being dominated by sites that have traditionally been seen as funerary or ceremonial. At the same time there are only limited amounts of corresponding evidence for settlement. As time progresses the balance of the archaeological record for the Bronze Age period shifts with settlement data becoming much more apparent, and consequently it is easier to present a more balanced picture. For the moment therefore, we must accept the gaps that exist in the archaeological record and work around them, whilst also endeavouring to fill them.

4

THE IRON AGE

THAT IS THE LAND OF LOST CONTENT

The last stop on our sojourn through the monumental landscapes of the later prehistoric period not surprisingly provides a greater number of albeit partially surviving sites, from which to examine how the inhabitants of Dorset lived at this time. Such a quantity of evidence, however, does not necessarily clarify our interpretation of life during this period. As we shall see many of the sites illustrate some aspects of human activity exceptionally well but other aspects of cultural behaviour are less well evidenced in the archaeological record.

The Iron Age is of course principally defined as a technological epoch in which tools manufactured from iron came into use, replacing copper alloys as the material of choice. However, as we have seen in the preceding periods, change in technology is often part of an evolutionary package, which comprises associated areas of economics as well as political and social structures. As usual, this change manifests itself in the actions of the community that lives through it, and fortunately for us it is mirrored in the monuments and the portable artefacts that they made, used and ultimately abandoned. In addition to the gradual replacement of bronze with iron, the archaeological evidence also provides increasing evidence of contact with continental Europe, which undoubtedly provided a massive stimulus to the economic basis of many areas, most notably in those bordering the coastal zones of southern England. In addition to economic change, contact with the European mainland would assuredly also have stimulated cultural diversity within the population, a factor that has provided succeeding generations of archaeologists with ammunition for a vigorous debate on the vehicles of change. A perusal through the archaeological literature published before the 1960s is littered with references to invasion and colonisation. To understand the context of such change and how it affects our understanding of the genesis of the Iron Age habitation of Dorset we must have a brief look at the history of Iron Age studies.

Following a period of archaeological discovery in the second half of the nineteenth century by such notable archaeologists as General Pitt-Rivers, Harold St George Gray, Arthur Bulleid, J.P. Bushe-Fox and Arthur Evans, much new information was recovered from Iron Age sites in southern England. Evans published an account of his investigations at the Late Iron Age cemetery site at Aylesford in Kent in 1890, which introduced a theme which was to dominate the study of the period for the next quarter of a century. In his discussion of the site he presented an hypoth-

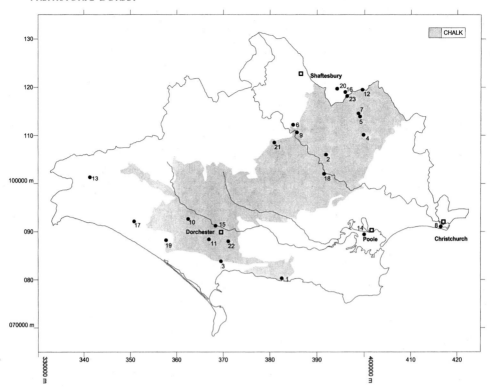

51 *Map of Iron Age sites mentioned in chapter 4. 1 – Bindon Hill, 2 – Buzbury Rings, 3 – Chalbury, 4 – Gussage All Saints, 5 – Gussage Cow Down, 6 – Hambledon Hill, 7 – Handley I.A. barrow, 8 – Hengistbury Head, 9 – Hod Hill, 10 – Hog Cliff Hill, 11 – Maiden Castle, 12 – Mistleberry hillfort, 13 – Pilsdon Pen, 14 – Poole harbour, 15 – Poundbury, 16 – Rotherley, 17 – Shipton Hill, 18 – Spetisbury, 19 – Tennants Hill, 20 – Tollard Royal, 21 – Ringmoor (Turnworth Down), 22 – Whitcombe, 23 –Woodcuts*

esis which characterised the site as comprising of a culturally unique people without precedent in the British Isles, whose immediate origins could be traced (via similar material culture) to the Belgic cultural material in northern Gaul (present-day Belgium). He dated the Aylesford site, principally upon the style of the excavated metalwork, to the period after 150 BC. Evans also linked the site to a reference in Julius Caesar's account of his Gallic Wars (*De Bello Gallico* 5, 12), which refers to the maritime tribes of Britain having crossed from the Belgic tribal areas into Britain in search of plunder. Conventionally this event is attributed to the period *c.*75 BC, just twenty years before Caesar's own limited invasion of the south coast of Britain.

With this account begins a long period of association between cultural change manifest in the typological progression identifiable in portable artefacts, and the processes of invasion and colonisation as an explanation for such progression within defined geographical areas. Evans's work in Kent was further expanded by J.P. Bushe-Fox's discovery and excavation of a second major 'Belgic' cemetery in Swarling, also in Kent, which confirmed the 'intrusive' nature of the material culture found there.

1 *Long Bredy (Martin's Down) bank barrow: both the bank and ditches of this monument can clearly be seen, as can the damage through the middle of the bank. A number of round barrows also exist in the vicinity.* © English Heritage, NMR

2 *The Hell Stone (from the south).* © Julie Gale

3 *The Hell Stone (from the north).* © Julie Gale

4 *Round barrow on Portesham Hill. Located only metres away from the Hell Stone, this round barrow shows a quite common later incorporation into a boundary.* © Julie Gale

5 *The Nine Stones (from the north).* © Julie Gale

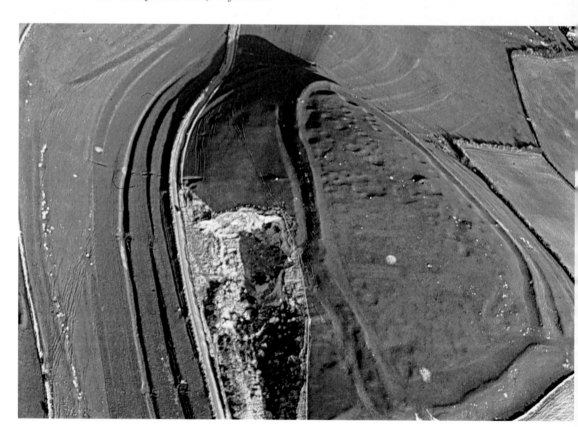

6 *Chalbury Hill hillfort. Too close for comfort! Quarrying came very close to damaging this hillfort; fortunately the threat has now receded.* © Francesca Radcliffe

7 *Flowers Barrow hillfort. Nature is doing its worst to this hillfort. Little by little it is slipping into the sea.*
© Francesca Radcliffe

8 *Pilsdon Pen hillfort. Located on the highest point of Dorset this hillfort in west Dorset was partially excavated by Peter Gelling between 1964-71.*
© Francesca Radcliffe

9 *Rawlsbury hillfort.*
© Francesca Radcliffe

10 *Buzbury Rings hill-slope enclosure. A rare form of defended enclosure whose closest parallels are to be found in Devon and Cornwall. It has suffered from the incursions of a golf course but is otherwise well preserved.* © Crown copyright, NMR

11 *Ringmoor settlement. Located on Turnworth Down in the north of the county this is one of the best preserved integrated collection of enclosures, fields and trackways in the south of England. It is probably Late Iron Age in date although it could be earlier.* © Crown copyright, NMR

12 *Iron Age settlement reconstruction (Butser Hill). This overview of the centre of the reconstructed settlement shows the main roundhouse, the plan of which was based upon an excavated example from Pimperne Down in Dorset.* © Author

13 *Iron Age settlement reconstruction (inside a round house at Butser Hill).* © Author

14 *Maiden Castle (from the west).* © Crown copyright, NMR

In the early decades of the twentieth century, Iron Age studies were to become dominated by this 'Invasionist' explanation for change observed in the archaeological record. Increasing archaeological fieldwork throughout the British Isles on Iron Age sites demanded a chronological framework into which sites and their cultural assemblages could be incorporated. The evolution of an A B C framework based upon 'Celtic' metalwork and art styles from *Halstatt* and *La Tène*, was promulgated by C.F.C. Hawkes in 1931 and considerably revised in 1959. This framework, which at various times was adjusted and developed by other scholars, survived in usage into the late 1960s and early 1970s. Simplistically, the Early Iron Age (A) was associated with *Halstatt* styles and covered most of the British Isles up to *c.*150 BC. Iron Age B and C are associated with the later *La Tène* styles, with B being generally restricted to the south-west of Britain (*La Tène I* and *II*), and C forming the latest incarnation of *La Tène III*, generally only associated with the Belgic invasion in the south-east around 75 BC. It is important to realise that the framework was designed and used as a cultural framework linking aspects of cultural association, which only very crudely could be used as a chronological framework.

In essence the changes formalised in this framework are based upon an inherent 'invasion hypothesis' which not only used the Belgic invasion associated with the Aylesford–Swarling culture of the south-east, but also utilised additional invasions to rationalise change in material culture throughout the British Isles. The evolution of the 'A B C' system during the middle of the twentieth century was dominated by the emphasis on the extensive pottery typologies resulting from increased fieldwork activity. These sequences were highly regionalised and ultimately, it could be suggested, led to the downfall of the 'A B C' framework. By the 1960s the framework was becoming so unwieldy and academically restrictive that it began to ring alarm bells in sections of the academic community. It was becoming apparent that much of the now highly regionalised cultural affinities of the material assemblages (largely pottery and metalwork) were explicable in terms of indigenous development and consequently need not involve the direct movement of populations, or for that matter the importation of artefacts. Much could be rationalised by changes in manufacturing and economic systems within cultural and geographical zones as a response to ideological and technological advancement, either internal or external in origin.

In addition to this theoretical shift in explanation for culture change, the 1960s also heralded developments in archaeological dating through the application of absolute techniques (primarily radiocarbon) which reduced the need to rely on relative dating techniques on which the 'A B C' framework had been developed. It is these developments that have ultimately tempered archaeological interpretations away from an invasion-dominated rationale to one in which change is explained in more diversified forms involving a combination of invasion, colonisation, interactive trade and communication as well as indigenous development. An excellent summary of the development of this process is contained within Barry Cunliffe's definitive account of the Iron Age (1991).

Today, the frameworks that we use to describe and define archaeological sites from the Iron Age landscape are very much based on regional artefact affiliations, particularly in the pre-tribal regions which pre-date the proto-historic establishment of tribal areas during the Later Iron Age (Cunliffe 1991, 60-106). These affiliations, often based upon ceramic styles, are subsequently refined with recourse to absolute dating techniques and do allow for a meaningful, if necessarily simplistic, framework.

For our purpose, with regard to the landscape of Dorset during this period, there appears to be a general uniformity of development throughout the Iron Age, culminating in the well-defined territorial tribal group called the Durotriges in the first century BC. This is not to say that the Durotriges were not a distinct grouping prior to the first century BC but that this is the period in which we find the earliest reference to them.

Prior to the historical references which refer to the tribal communities that lived in the region which we now know as Dorset, there is a wealth of archaeological evidence, particularly in the form of monuments, which testifies to the presence of extensive occupation, and it is to this evidence that we must now look.

The Earlier Iron Age – continuity and strife?

To all intents and purposes the landscape of 1200 BC is no different from that of 700 BC and as we have seen in previous chapters, the division of time into ages is somewhat blurred. The adoption of iron as the material of choice for tools and weaponry did not happen overnight any more than computers did to modern-day society (when did the computer age begin, 1940, 1950, 1960, 1970?). It of course depends on what you mean by a computer and to what level it permeates society. The same can be said for the Iron Age, but the problem is compounded by a lack of evidence. We do not know (and will never know!) what was the first iron tool or weapon to be used in Dorset and we certainly only have a general impression of when iron became the material of choice for use in a wide variety of circumstances. What we know more about, however, are the monuments associated with people that were using such materials. When we begin to examine sites which have characteristically Iron Age attributes we notice that they appear to continue traditions begun in the Middle and Later Bronze Age, and in many ways appear to be little changed from their earlier counterparts.

The form of rural settlement which appeared in the Middle to Late Bronze Age discussed in chapter 3 is to be found with little substantive change in the landscape of the Iron Age. The examples of Shearplace Hill and South Lodge Camp are in many ways similar to excavated examples whose material assemblages can be securely dated to the Iron Age. During the last 40 years a number of these sites have been excavated which, along with examples from the Sussex and Hampshire Downs, have characterised the variety of forms of settlement for the downland economy of much of southern Britain.

Dispersed rural settlement

Few of the monuments typical of the dispersed rural settlement pattern of Dorset in the Early Iron Age survive today as extant earthworks. However, the application of aerial photographic techniques has greatly enhanced our understanding of the fragile remains that do survive. It is with the investigation of such sites that archaeologists have been able to piece together often quite detailed accounts of the nature and extent of the constructional elements of individual settlements. The analysis of materials found in association with the structural remains (artefacts, environmental remains etc.) frequently combine to provide information on economy, technology and social activity.

There is a degree of morphological variation in the sites in question which, when coupled with data from outside the region, allows for a rudimentary list of site types (not all of which have been identified in Dorset): (Cunliffe 1991, 215-223.)

- Earthwork enclosed settlement
- Banjo enclosure
- Palisaded enclosure (not yet found within the Dorset Iron Age landscape)
- Open settlement

Earthwork-enclosed settlement

The unifying theme behind many earthwork-enclosed settlement sites is primarily that they consist of small farmsteads for the support of a family or extended family group within a landscape. Many of them show signs of being located within ancient field systems, with which they are thought to be economically linked. The oft-quoted type-site is that of Little Woodbury, in southern Wiltshire, excavated by the German archaeologist Gerhard Bersu and published in 1940. Whilst this site established a model for an Iron Age enclosed farmstead it should not be viewed as universally representative of the complete picture of downland settlement in the Early Iron Age. However, parallels to Little Woodbury do exist in Dorset and probably the best understood of all is the site of Gussage All Saints in Cranborne Chase, which was totally excavated by Geoffrey Wainwright in 1972 (1979b). This site dominates our understanding of Iron Age settlement in the county through the quantity, diversity and quality of data that was recovered from the excavation.

By the time of excavation the site had been completely levelled by centuries of agricultural activity, and its presence was only discernible through aerial photography. The objectives of the 1972 excavation took this factor into account and the ensuing report indicates that the excavation had to take place before any surviving structural evidence was completely destroyed. It is a sad fact that many sites in a similar condition at the time, and since, have lost much structural detail due to the activity of the plough. At Gussage All Saints, aerial photographs had revealed the presence of an enclosing boundary ditch complete with 'antennae' ditches emanating from the main entrance and evidence for internal features similar to those found at Little Woodbury, and the site thus provided excellent comparative data for investigation.

The first phase of occupation at Gussage All Saints consisted of a 1.2ha enclosure surrounded by a ditch, which was 1.2m wide and 0.8m deep. Although the accompanying bank had long since been ploughed away, the ditch silts suggested that it had lain on the outside of the ditch and therefore was unlikely to have been contrived as defensive. The antennae ditches, which emanate out from a main entrance on the eastern arc of the enclosure ditch, also appear to originate from this primary phase, which has been dated to the fifth century BC. In addition to the main entrance there were a number of secondary or ancillary entrances, which the excavator presumed to have led directly onto the surrounding fields with no surviving evidence for substantial gateways. Within the enclosure, evidence was discovered of a palimpsest of pits, post-holes and working hollows which appear to have a non-random structure indicative of a planned interior. Largely restricted to the central zone of the interior were 17 four-post structures, a feature not uncommon on sites of this period throughout southern Britain. The four-post structures are square or rectangular in plan and several of them showed signs of having had their posts replaced, hinting at the intended relative permanency of their construction. The purpose of these 'four-post' structures has been variously attributed to dwellings, granaries, excarnation platforms and watchtowers, to name but a few, and clearly such a simple constructional form would be suitable for any of these uses. Firmer evidence on utility is usually provided by analysis of the archaeological surfaces in the vicinity of the features. One might reasonably expect domestic structures, for example to exhibit evidence of flooring, hearths and distributions of domestic artefacts such as pottery. However, domestic areas might be swept and kept clean compared to surrounding areas. Granaries, on the other hand, are typically raised off the ground and consequently would have unworn ground underneath them, with little or no domestic debris in their immediate vicinity.

Unfortunately, at Gussage All Saints the upper levels of the Iron Age surfaces have been eroded away by plough action, which has obviously all but destroyed contemporary surfaces. This, of course, compromises the effective interpretation of many of the features found at the site, necessitating the establishment of parallels from contemporary sites elsewhere. In this first phase of activity it is likely that some of the many post-holes found are to be related to huts used for dwellings but it is not possible to determine their form, number or size. Parallels with sites like Little Woodbury suggest that one or two huts were contemporary as part of a small family or extended family group. The date of this first phase of occupation has been determined by radiocarbon dating and also through an examination of artefactual material. The radiocarbon determination from animal bone recovered from the enclosure ditch's primary deposits suggest a date of 750-430 BC. The ceramic material associated with this first phase would appear to have been locally made, of forms generally attributable to the Early Iron Age, and compatible with variants of the All Cannings Cross type of pottery found throughout central southern Britain at this time. Further confirmation of date was found in the form of a *La*

Tène brooch from a pit from phase 1, which on stylistic grounds could be dated to around 400 BC.

During the second phase of activity at the site (**52**) the enclosing ditch was replaced with a wider and generally deeper ditch which followed the alignment of the previous ditch. However, recutting of the ditch was not undertaken uniformly over the whole circuit; in parts of the north and west it was done only intermittently. The main entrance to the east was remodelled, with a stronger gateway and a realignment of the projecting antennae ditches. The internal features of this phase were largely determined through examination of styles of pottery, where a change in the ceramic record could be isolated to some features, notably pits and post-holes. It is in the structural record of this phase of the site's occupation that we see more substantial evidence for the construction of huts. The presence of circular gullies (strictly speaking segments of them) close to the western boundary of the enclosure ditch seem to indicate the presence of huts approximately 9m in diameter. It is possible that these gullies represent the construction of two huts, although the more northerly of the two is the better preserved, and also shows signs of having been rebuilt. As in phase 1, the succeeding phase of occupation also evidences a number of pits, largely confined to the eastern half of the enclosure, but they are fewer in number.

The identification of two phases of occupation should not be seen as evidence of a discontinuity in the life of the settlement. In fact, as the excavator points out, the re-modelling of the enclosure is suggestive of continuity, as is the continued usage of pottery forms from phase 1 into phase 2 (Wainwright, 1979b 184). Dating of this second phase of activity is once again achieved through a combination of relative and absolute dating techniques mainly through stratified material contained within the pits of the interior of the enclosure, thus pit 437

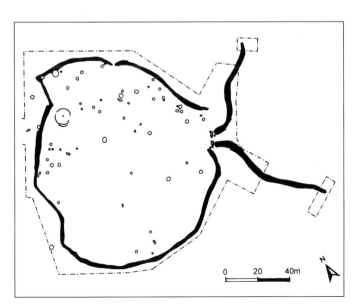

52 *Plan of Gussage All Saints: phase 2 of the enclosure showing the presence of numerous pits (69) which seem to be largely clustered in north of the enclosure. A small round house can also be found opposite the entrance.* Redrawn with amendments from Wainwright 1979b

0   20   40m

within the enclosure produced charcoal, radiocarbon dated between 410-140 BC. This date is consistent with the ceramic styles found at the site and conventionally attributed to the third and first centuries BC. These pots are part of a tradition characterised by the so-called vertical-sided 'saucepan pots' and jars with rounded shoulders and beaded rims found throughout southern Britain.

The economic basis for both Earlier Iron Age phases of the settlement is that of a farmstead apparently based on both arable and pastoral regimes. This can be demonstrated both through the examination of the structural features from the site and the artefactual and environmental material recovered during the excavation. Evidence supporting the arable basis for the settlement is in the form of carbonised grain, iron tips or shoes for ards, the presence of possible storage structures for harvested grain – granaries and/or storage pits – and ultimately corn grinding equipment represented by both saddle and rotary querns. In addition, there are traces of possible contemporary field systems to the north and east of the enclosure.

The carbonised grain in some of the pits on the site does not prove that the grain was placed in them for storage; it could have been thrown in as refuse. However, support for the principle of storage pits has been demonstrated through experimental work in recent years, where harvested grain has been effectively stored within reconstructed structures with surprisingly little wastage (Reynolds 1979, 71-82). It has also been demonstrated that effective sterilisation of pits could be undertaken, following emptying, by firing them. This might partially explain why pits from a number of sites contain varying quantities of burnt grain - the last vestiges of caches of grain which were not recovered before the pit was prepared for reuse. The type of grain recovered is entirely consistent with the known types of domesticates of the period. Wheat in the form of spelt (*Triticum spelta*) is the most commonly found type on the site with lesser quantities of barley and oats.

The faunal assemblage from the site points to a pastoral element in the site's economy, with significant quantities of a range of animal domesticates, dominated by sheep, cattle and pigs. The nature of the assemblage suggests that the husbanding of animals was not purely for the provision of meat but may have been part of a much more expansive, integrated and diversified economy, involving the production of wool, hides, dairy products and traction. The use of wool within the economy of the site is further suggested by the presence of loomweights, spindle whorls and bone weaving combs. The finding of such materials associated with spinning and weaving is a common occurrence on settlements throughout the British Isles during the Later Bronze Age and Iron Age.

In addition to weaving, the enclosure at Gussage All Saints provides some of the best evidence yet recovered in the south of Britain for metalworking. Whilst this points to such activity taking place during both phase 2 and 3 of the site's occupation, there is sufficient information to indicate that there was a foundry at the site, contemporary with the ceramic sequence attributable to the Middle Iron Age period, possible as early as 250 BC (Wainwright and Switsur 1976, 32-39). Amongst the metalwork being produced on the site were horse and cart fittings, including bridle bits, lynch-pins and terrets similar to types discovered in the Arras burials of Yorkshire, which are broadly contemporary.

A number of other sites thought to be consistent with this model can be observed elsewhere in Dorset, all of them to be found on the chalk downs which dominate the archaeological landscape of the county, but none have been excavated. Without recourse to excavation the dating of such sites is extremely difficult with little to distinguish between Later Bronze Age farmsteads and those associated with Durotrigan occupation during the Late Iron Age – Romano-British period. Some of these as yet undated sites survive as earthworks in areas that have, for varying reasons, escaped the attention of intensive ploughing and agricultural attrition. One of the most complete examples of such is that in northern Dorset located upon Turnworth Down (**colour plate 11**).

This site is generally known as Ringmoor and comprises an extensive complex of earthworks that appear to be contemporaneous. The foci for the complex consist of three earthwork enclosures, only one of which survives in plan as a complete earthwork. The enclosures are inter-linked by a track or drove-way, all of which are integral with a surrounding complex of fields, which in part is defined by surviving earthen field banks. The surviving earthwork enclosure, which is oval in plan, consists of a low earthen bank with an external ditch that encloses an area approximately 48m by 36m. The entrance to the enclosure is located to the north and is protected by an outwork of curving bank, in the manner of entrances to some hillforts of the Iron Age. Whilst there is no direct evidence for an internal structure, the limited size of the enclosure would suggest that the presence of more than one or two huts is unlikely. The site is clearly a farmstead located within a network of fields. The absence of an antennae ditch and the relatively small size of the enclosure might suggest that the economic system displayed in the surviving monument is different from that at Gussage All Saints, but this may just be a variation borne out of lesser reliance on pastoral farming. Certainly the track leading through the site and visible on the photograph (**colour plate 11**) could be seen as an animal drove-way, especially as the field banks which border the track-way are generally higher and more substantial than elsewhere in the complex. This perhaps suggests that animals were herded through the settlement and field complex at various times. The close proximity of the three enclosures on the site (the maximum distance from enclosure to enclosure is little more than 400m) may be indicative of a greatly increased population at the time. Whilst it is perfectly feasible for the enclosures to have been occupied at different times, the observable integration between them through the trackway suggests that they are likely to be contemporaneous. Christopher Taylor and others have elsewhere made the observation that settlement density during the Iron Age appears to be at its maximum for the prehistoric period. In Hampshire, settlement evidence in some areas during the Later Iron Age indicates a density whereby sites are as little as 800m apart (Taylor 1983. 63-4). As we shall see below, evidence for an enlarged population is not only suggested by the intensity of the settlement pattern, but is also evident in other aspects of social behaviour reflected in the archaeological record.

Another similar but less well-preserved site can be found in the west of Dorset on Tenant's Hill, close to the village of Little Bredy. Here the traces of the associated field systems are less extensive but the ring-work of the earth bank survives well. Interestingly, the site is located close to the earlier prehistoric stone circle of Kingston Russell (see chapter 3). Although there is no direct association between the two monuments, the Iron Age inhabitants of the hilltop must have been familiar with the earlier site, and it may have influenced the location of the later one. A noticeable feature of The Tenant's Hill enclosure is the substantial nature of the enclosing ringwork. The bank survives to a height of approximately 1m, which is over twice the height of the Ringmoor example. The reasons for this are unlikely to have been due to differential erosion, particularly as Tenants Hill is located in a more exposed situation. Whilst the more substantial earthwork may be the product of an outward display of ostentation it could equally be a more determined attempt at defence at a time when there was increasing pressure for land and instability in the population.

Within the tradition of earthwork-enclosed settlement are a number of monuments that are less well understood and which are generally larger in area. A number of such monuments are found on the open downland to the north of Blandford Forum on Cranborne Chase. None of these enclosures survive as visible earthwork features today, but typically have shown up on aerial photographs, where the enclosing ditch survives as a crop or soil mark. One such site located on Pimperne Down was examined by excavation between 1960 and 1963 (Harding and Blake, 1963; Harding 1974, 24-5). Its form, an oval enclosure of over 4.5ha in area, defined by a bank with an external ditch perhaps suggests that its inhabitants were involved in a more pastoral-focused agricultural system. The original dimensions of the bank are unknown but the ditch was only approximately 2m in depth and would have afforded only minimal defensive capabilities. Within the interior of the enclosure the remains of a large roundhouse 15m in diameter were found, somewhat larger than the slight traces of a hut found at Gussage All Saints. The recovered plan of this structure was used by Peter Reynolds and his team at the Iron Age experimental farm at Butser Hill in Hampshire as the basis for their reconstruction of a dwelling of the period (**colour plates 12 & 13**).

With the exception of the large roundhouse there was little compelling evidence for additional dwellings within the enclosure, which is surprising, given its overall size. The roundhouse was approached from the eastern side of the enclosure evidenced by an avenue of timber posts leading to the hut's entrance. Within the packing material, the fragmentary remains of human crania were set around some of the posts, which would seem to represent deliberate foundation offerings. The enclosure itself was also linked to a smaller enclosure (1.5ha) to the south, by a small stretch of ditch (referred to by the excavator as an antennae ditch). The inferred purpose of this secondary enclosure would seem to be associated with the management of livestock, perhaps being transferred from one enclosure to the other, or perhaps from the grazing lands to the south into the enclosure for over-wintering. To the north of both these enclosures are extensive remains of ancient fields, which are likely to be contemporary and form part of an arable component to the site's economic basis.

Banjo enclosures

Banjo enclosures are a form of earthwork enclosure which have been singled out because of a general uniformity of size and form, which in itself is relatively unusual for Iron Age settlement types. Although they are a relatively common feature within the landscape of Wessex they are few in number in Dorset, and those that do exist seem to be restricted to Cranborne Chase and none of these have been excavated in modern times. Amongst the best examples are those located within the greater settlement complex on Gussage Cow Down and although fragmentary earthworks still survive, ploughing over the last century has for the most part destroyed them. As the name implies, banjo enclosures have a distinctive plan which consists of a circular ditched and banked enclosure usually not greater than 0.4ha in extent. The single entrance to the enclosure is formed through the extension of the bank and ditch forming a funnelled passage, which usually open out to form a wide neck, similar to the antennae ditches of enclosures like Gussage All Saints and Little Woodbury. Occasionally, as we see with the Dorset examples, these antennae ditches extend and double back behind the circular enclosure to form larger enclosures. As is the case on Gussage Cow Down this construction can incorporate one or more units to form even larger enclosures (**53**). Probably the best understood example of this type of monument is that excavated at Milcheldever Wood in Hampshire, which throws some light on the likely purpose and date of the Dorset examples. In general the enclosures appear no earlier than the middle of the Iron Age period and are usually associated with the saucepan pots that we have seen from phase 2 of the occupation at Gussage All Saints. The interiors usually contain evidence of the ubiquitous pits found on settlements of the period, but they have a tendency to be located on the periphery of the enclosure, leaving the central space relatively clear of structures. As with the previous enclosures the banjo types display evidence of a mixed farming economy, although few of them exhibit any signs of dwellings inside them. The pits themselves frequently contain occupational debris not unlike examples already quoted, but this material could have been brought in for disposal from outside. These monument types, therefore, may represent a later introduction of a subsidiary form of monument, which supported already established settlement nearby, as part of a reorganisation and expansion of agrarian land use. As Cunliffe points out (1991, 223) the detail of how these monuments functioned can only be provided by further large-scale excavation.

As we have seen, within this general classification of earthwork-enclosed settlement, a variety of sub-types exist, which actually display many common elements,

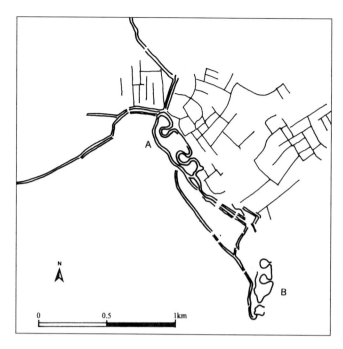

53 *Iron Age earthworks on Gussage Cow Down: A and B are 'banjo' type enclosures.* Redrawn with amendments from Green, M. 2000

generally located within a geographically dispersed settlement pattern mainly on the chalk downs of the county.

Evidence for nucleated settlement?

Whilst the evidence for settlement in Earlier Iron Age Dorset is in part dominated by relatively small agricultural units dispersed within the chalk lands, there are other forms of settlement within the county which testify to an even greater diversity of behaviour and activity.

Amongst the earliest of such sites so far identified in the county is that of Hog Cliff Hill, located near Maiden Newton in west Dorset, and excavated by Phillip Rahtz in 1959 (Ellison and Rahtz 1987). As we have seen (chapter 3) the site was originally occupied during the Later Bronze Age (around the ninth century BC). The basic form of this settlement consisted of at least seven circular buildings (not all contemporary) contained within an earthen-banked enclosure whose area may have exceeded 5ha. The general form of the settlement would appear to have continued in use into what we would conventionally call the Earliest Iron Age, *c.*800-550 BC. The number and distribution of huts contained within the enclosure are unknown although the authors of the report believed that it was likely to have been densely occupied. The huts, which belong to the Early Iron Age settlement, are primarily semi-circular in plan and may not be dwellings but ancillary structures, and may have served as working or processing areas. The enclosure may therefore have a planned interior with working, storage and living areas separated out to form discrete zones. Without further excavation, the answer to this question is unlikely to be forthcoming particularly as the form of settlement represented here is for the present almost unique. Following the construction and use of this 5ha enclosure the site was redeveloped some time during the Early Iron Age. A larger enclosure was constructed with a minimum internal area of over 10ha, utilising part of the alignment of the earlier one. Contained within it were the remains of a number of stone-built penannular structures. Four of these were completely excavated with a further two being sampled. The excavator believed that the six structures were the total number present in the enclosure but their interpretation has remained somewhat prob-lematical. The structures each comprised a penannular bank of loose flint and chert, with an average internal diameter of 5.5m. The banks of stone were, of course, found in their collapsed state and consequently the original internal area is likely to have been substantially larger. Large quantities of pottery (Maiden Castle-Marnhull types) were recovered from the structures, which date them to c.600-300 BC, whilst flint and chert rubbers (used with querns to grind corn or other vegetable matter) as well as fire-cracked flints were also common. All of the structures contained pits which seem to have been associated with burning, and the weight of evidence suggests that they were used for cooking. Few if any parallels exist for this type of activity in the Early Iron Age but may be similar to that associated with the so-called Bronze Age 'burnt mounds' found throughout the British Isles, but more common to the Highland Zone and Ireland. If so, these structures may be evidence for the conspicuous consumption of food for feasting or the rendering down of animals during seasonal culls.

However, irrespective of the last phase of activity at Hog Cliff Hill, the earlier settlement does point to a degree of nucleation within the settlement pattern of Dorset. There is little evidence yet for the open settlements that are to be found elsewhere in southern Britain. Large unenclosed settlements of the type known at Potterne and Boscombe Down in Wiltshire and Little Waltham in Essex have still to be found in Dorset. However, such sites are difficult to detect and are usually only discovered by chance. We have already seen that the enclosed farmsteads rarely survive as visible earthworks in the modern landscape, and are usually iden-tified through their enclosing banks and ditches via aerial photography. It is therefore unsurprising that open settlements, which left little evidence of perma-nency by way of above ground remains, are even less easily recognised within the landscape over two millennia later.

A picture seems to emerge where perhaps significant proportions of the Iron Age population were dispersed within the landscape, working the land intensively, and taking advantage of its potential by proportional adoption of both arable and pastoral farming dependent upon local conditions. During this earlier period of the Iron Age (c.800-200 BC) such dispersed farmsteads would have required a second tier of settlement with which to trade and exchange surpluses for materials that they were unable to produce themselves. Whilst the evidence for this in the form of open settlement is restricted to examples like Hog Cliff Hill, it is likely that further similar settlements did exist, and are awaiting discovery. Such sites as

Hog Cliff Hill are clearly comparable with what we should today recognise as a village, and presumably acted economically and socially as central places, where farmers would come to barter and trade, as well as maintain, renew and establish social bonds. This economic scenario is probably little changed from that operating four or five centuries earlier and does present a picture of relative stability. However, also contained within the settlement pattern of the early Iron Age is a monumental feature of such power and significance that many of them survive today and are amongst the most well-known of archaeological monuments in the Dorset landscape – the hillfort.

The early hillforts of Dorset

Dorset is very much part of what is generally referred to as the 'Hillfort Dominated Zone', which includes many of the counties of western Britain. For England and Wales this zone extends west of a line drawn approximately between East Sussex and the Dee estuary in north Wales. In this zone the construction of hillforts began as early as the Late Bronze Age and continued until the Roman invasion of AD 43. However, it should be noted from the outset that the term hillfort is in many ways an unfortunate term, which can infer a commonality of utility for what in reality is a much more complex and diverse group of monuments. It is a common misconception to view hillforts as wholly defensive earthworks, whose size is merely reflective of the power of the group that built or occupied them. There is much more to them than this, and their function over time can be seen to change, providing a clearer picture of Iron Age society, particularly when examined in relation to regional and contemporary patterns of settlement and land use.

Dorset has a total of 34 surviving enclosures which can be loosely classified as hillforts. Most of them are to be found on the chalk downlands but others are found on the limestone of Purbeck and in the extreme west of Dorset as well as those on the gravels of Poole basin. Within this broadly based classification there is a rich diversity of forms, from small barely defended hilltop sites such as Mistleberry, which encloses less than a hectare, to the elaborate giants of the genre typified by the magnificent Maiden Castle which encloses a massive 17ha (**colour plate 14**). Of these 34 sites, more than a third of them have been the subject of some form of excavation but only five of these could be claimed to have been significantly sampled (Chalbury, Hengistbury Head, Hod Hill, Maiden Castle and Pilsdon Pen). The problem is not that the sites are especially difficult to excavate but rather it is a question of scale. As we saw with some of the large Neolithic monuments in chapter 2, our understanding of such sites is compromised by their sheer size. To understand complex earthworks it would of course be preferable to excavate them completely but generally, large-scale sampling should be sufficient. However, how large is large? This is a matter which can only be defined on a case by case basis, but certainly it is likely to be greater than 25 per cent of the whole. Only two hillforts in the whole of England and Wales have achieved such attention, Crickley Hill in Gloucestershire (Dixon 1996) and Danebury in Hampshire (Cunliffe 1984) each with more than 50 per cent of their interiors excavated. The most closely and extensively studied of the Dorset sites is that of Maiden Castle, which has been the subject of two major excavation campaigns, Sir Mortimer Wheeler in the 1930s (Wheeler 1943) and Niall Sharples in the mid 1980s (Sharples 1991). Neither of these excavations sampled more than a fraction of the enclosed area (in both cases less than 1 per cent) but in both cases, as we shall see, the recovered evidence presents a detailed picture of life within the hillfort spanning almost the whole of the Iron Age.

The introduction of hillforts into the landscape of the British Isles is not synonymous with the beginnings of what we now call the Iron Age, but it is certainly a period when hillforts appeared to dominate certain areas. The reason for the emergence of hillforts is still unclear and various possible theories have been proffered in the last three decades as a global rationale for their introduction. These theories range from a reaction to the introduction of iron which may have caused conflict within society at the time (Bradley 1984, 132), to the formation of élite centres in a redistribution network to facilitate expanding agricultural and industrial economies (Cunliffe 1984, 30-1). Other theories have been advanced which consider hillforts as religious centres or the fiefs of tribal chiefs, where the hillfort represents an expression of oligarchic or religious power. In truth the answer may include all or part of these theories, and it is only through more detailed research that a clearer picture will emerge. Certainly, within Dorset there is little evidence of any of our hillforts having their origins in the Later Bronze Age, but the results from excavation do demonstrate that some of them were occupied during the first centuries of the Iron Age.

The hillfort at Chalbury (**54** & **colour plate 6**), overlooking the modern town of Weymouth, provides some of the best evidence for the early construction and occupation of a hillfort within the county. The site was partially excavated in 1939 by Margaret Whitley (1943). The excavation programme was scheduled to continue beyond 1939, but was unfortunately curtailed by the outbreak of The Second World War, later that same year. This hillfort occupies a dominant position at one end of a limestone ridge, affording it an excellent defensive position on all sides. The relatively steep slopes which form the knoll on which the hillfort was constructed, were enclosed by a single bank and ditch capturing approximately 4ha of the hilltop. The building of the ramparts at Chalbury made use of the natural stone available by a construction method which utilised dry stone walling to create front- and back-revetted walls that were in-filled with limestone rubble (**55**). This type of construction is not very far removed from the so-called timber box ramparts, which are a common design feature of hillfort construction in England and Wales, particularly with early hillforts. Recognising the construc- tional method employed by the Iron Age builders of hillforts from the earthworks that survive in the landscape today is in most cases impossible, without recourse to archaeological excavation. The visitor to any of Dorset's many fine examples of

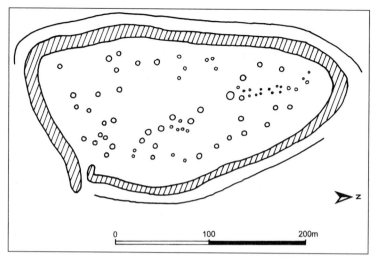

54 *Plan of Chalbury hillfort including round houses and pits defined by survey and excavation.* Redrawn with amendments from Cunliffe 1984

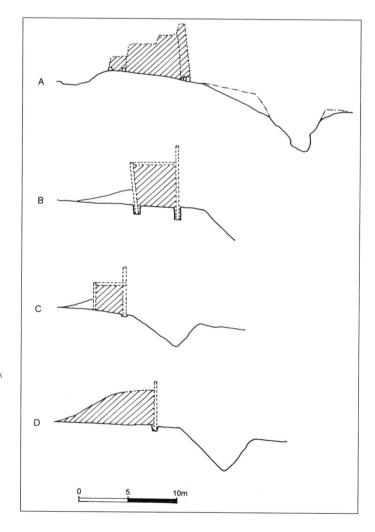

55 *Comparative sections through Early Iron Age ramparts of Dorset hillforts: a – Chalbury, b – Maiden Castle, c – Hod Hill and d – Poundbury.* Redrawn with amendments from Cunliffe 1991

hillforts will be faced with a slumped and eroded rampart, which while usually impressive in terms of scale, collectively tends to look much the same. Quite complex structures are often contained within the earth banks, which in addition will frequently display evidence for repair and quite often major rebuilding.

Whitley excavated two sections through the single rampart and ditch at Chalbury, and both of them displayed the same characteristics of constructional method, as well as indicating that there had been no major rebuilding of the defences after their initial construction. The ramparts probably stood to a height of approximately 2m above the original ground surface, with their earth and stone derived from the external defensive ditch and from a shallow quarry which lay in the lee of the bank on its interior. The hillfort appears to have had only one entrance/exit through this defensive curtain, located in its south-eastern corner. The entrance has not been excavated, but appears to have been a relatively simple breach in the line of the defensive ramparts, approximately 5m wide. Rather unusually the hillfort is approached by a causeway, which runs parallel to the eastern flank of the hillfort. This appears to have been a deliberate design feature of the hillfort's construction, presumably intended to intimidate and/or impress those approaching the site.

Within the interior of the hillfort, the outline of a large number of circular depressions or platforms can be seen quite clearly within the turf sward. Whitley recorded over 70 of these structures. However, it is clear that they are not all of a uniform type. While most appear to conform to a diameter of between 8-10m, there is a spatially isolated group of structures which form a linear cluster in the northern third of the monument which are considerably smaller in diameter (3-4m). The excavations of 1939 only examined four of these internal features, some completely, some only partially. The largest of all these circular platforms was completely excavated and revealed a large round hut, whose diameter was just over 10m and was defined by a foundation wall which survived to a height of 0.5m (**56**). The hut had been constructed within a pre-excavated and levelled scoop and the height of the original wall may have been as much as 1m. Although the excavator detected the likely presence of a floor within the hut (Whitley 1943. 107), there was little surviving evidence for an entrance or indeed an internal hearth. Within the earth fill of the hut's interior there was domestic debris, which included abundant sherds of pottery. The broken pots consisted of mainly small carinated bowls with a haematite slip, similar in style to some of those found at All Cannings Cross in Wiltshire, and they are definitely associated with the early Iron Age period, dating to approximately 600 BC.

Two further circular platforms were excavated in the interior of the hillfort, and whilst evidence for the construction of levelled areas, similar to those of the larger hut, were found, there was no sign of a stone-built foundation wall, in either case. Although Whitley suggested that these features were probably analogous to the working hollows found by Bersu at Little Woodbury in Wiltshire, it is extremely unlikely that they are for the same purpose. The platforms excavated by

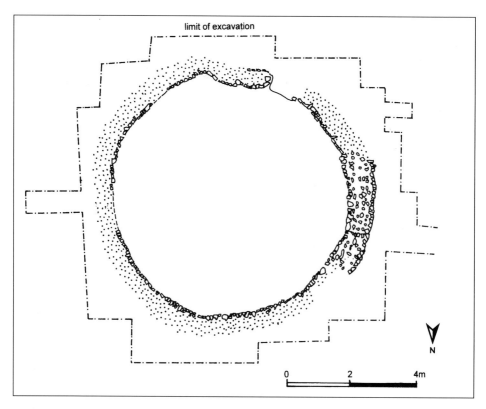

56 *Plan of the large round house at Chalbury hillfort excavated by Whitley in 1939.* Redrawn with amendments from Whitley 1943

Whitley probably were used as sites for the construction of huts, but their constructional form must have been relatively light not to leave a tangible trace. Certainly the use of stone foundations, as evidenced in the larger hut, appears not to have been a universal method of construction on the site, and may indicate that this structure was at least of some special significance.

One of the smaller scoops on the site was also excavated and turned out to be a pit, 1.2m deep, which appears to have silted up naturally. This is probably too shallow to be considered as a storage pit, although the depths of such pits do vary quite considerably. It remains unknown as to whether the linear cluster of pits, of which this was one, are of similar size, and their purpose is still unclear.

Chalbury therefore provides us with a limited but relatively uncluttered picture of a hillfort constructed and occupied during the early years of the Iron Age. We can detect the construction of a well-designed defensible settlement which contained a number of huts carefully constructed and planned. How many of these huts were occupied at any one time is impossible to determine without further excavation, but of the 30-40 platforms which survive it is certainly possible that a significant number may have been contemporaneous. The demise of the hillfort does not appear to have ended abruptly, and there is as yet little evidence to suggest that occupation continued beyond the Middle Iron Age. Certainly the pit excavated by Whitley silted up gradually and contained within its upper fills a few small sherds of pottery which possibly date to the Late Iron Age, but the overwhelming evidence from the pottery found on site suggests a predominantly Early Iron Age occupation.

Whilst Chalbury presents a relatively uncomplicated sequence of archaeological deposits, this cannot be claimed for the second of our hillforts to be examined, Maiden Castle (**57** & **colour plate 14**). The hillfort at Maiden Castle is amongst the best known of archaeological sites in Dorset and Britain as a whole, but the complexity and extended chronology of its occupation suggests that its location and status within the landscape was of a different order from sites like Chalbury. As we have seen in chapter 2, Maiden Castle is located to the south of the county town of Dorchester and was the site of a causewayed enclosure as far back as the fourth millennium BC. The earthworks which defined this Neolithic enclosure have been partially determined by the excavations of Mortimer Wheeler (1943) and Niall Sharples (1991). During the course of their separate excavations they also discovered that the circuit of the first phase of the Iron Age defences probably followed an almost identical plan to that of the earlier enclosure (**57**).

The defences of the first Iron Age hillfort consisted of a single rampart and ditch, enclosing an area of approximately 6ha. The circumstances which led to the coincidence of both the causewayed enclosure and the first hillfort, sharing what is almost certainly a similar articulation of defining boundaries is clouded by the

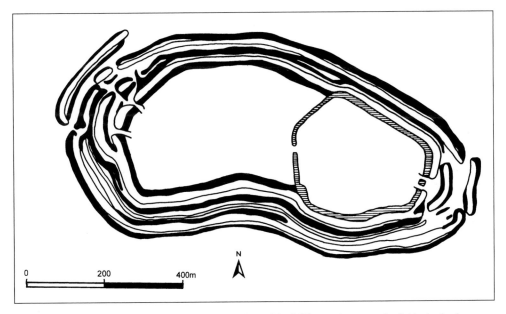

57 *Plan of Maiden Castle hillfort showing the first phase of the hillfort on the eastern knoll (the bank of which has striped shading).* Redrawn with amendments from Cunliffe 1991

complexity of archaeological deposits which are superimposed upon one another. Inter-cutting archaeological features, where earlier deposits are almost entirely destroyed by later occupation, make for a complex sequence of activity, which is often difficult to interpret. It does seem likely, however, that the defining extent of the Neolithic enclosure was sufficiently well-preserved that the Iron Age builders may have decided to adopt them (at least in part) for the circuit of their defensive rampart and ditch. The choice of locale, on the other hand, may reflect a more complex rationale on behalf of the Iron Age builders other than simply that the position of the site lends itself to being defensible. Although there appears to be little monumental activity following the construction of the Neolithic long mound at Maiden Castle, the site appears to have remained a focus for communal gathering. The manifestation of this is, of course, reflected in the earlier earthworks, and whilst the function of the Neolithic monuments may have been lost over time, the symbolic representation of their relative importance as focal places may well have survived and could well have been passed on by word of mouth over many generations and centuries. Whilst the original purpose of the monument may have become irrelevant, the significance and importance of the location could well have been imprinted on succeeding generations.

Wheeler considered the constructional form of the early rampart at Maiden Castle as having been of the box rampart form, but Sharples in his later excavation throws some doubt on this interpretation. It appears that whilst a box rampart may have existed around the eastern entranceway, the remainder of the rampart was probably a much less elaborate affair with earth and chalk piled behind a turf revetment. The eastern entrance appeared to have consisted of a double gateway, and at some stage had an outer earthwork (often referred to as a hornwork) associated with it. It is not entirely clear as to whether the elaboration of the eastern entrance was part of the original design, or a later addition.

Evidence for the occupation of this Early Iron Age hillfort is rather limited, as it had been largely destroyed or corrupted by later activity as noted above. However, a road leading from the eastern entrance had a number of post-holes lying adjacent to it, which could be interpreted as a long house or alternatively could represent a group of four-post structures, possibly granaries (Sharples 1991, 61). The dating for the Early Iron Age hillfort is based exclusively upon the material culture found during the excavation campaigns, with the majority of finds related to this early phase of activity on the site recovered from Wheeler's excavations. Most of this material consisted of large, undecorated situate jars and flared-rim bowls, which correlate well with material found at other sites in Dorset, Chalbury, Gussage All Saints and Eldon's Seat, and suggest a date for initial occupation probably no earlier than the fifth century BC.

Barely 3km north of Maiden Castle, located on the Upper Chalk and overlooking the River Frome, is the hillfort of Poundbury. This site has been subjected to a number of excavations over the last century, during which time it has been established that it too finds its origins in the Early Iron Age (Richardson 1940; Green 1987).

The excavations of 1939 conducted by Katherine Richardson examined the defences in the north-west corner of the site and determined that the largely bivallate hillfort had been constructed in at least two distinct phases. The Earlier Iron Age hillfort seems to have consisted of a single rampart and ditch, which was later remodelled in the Later Iron Age. The inner rampart had been constructed from spoil obtained from its paired outer ditch, coupled with material excavated from a shallow inner quarry similar to that noted at Chalbury. The constructional form of the rampart consisted of an outer revetment built of vertically set posts, which probably braced horizontally laid timbers, and would have presented a vertical wall facing outwards. Behind this revetment, chalk and earth was piled up to form the completed rampart. It is likely that the timber revetment would have been tied into the mass of earth behind it, although no structural evidence has been recorded.

During 1939 a grid of 38 test pits was excavated in the interior of the hillfort, but they revealed little structural or artefactual evidence that would indicate intense occupation. Later excavations at Poundbury undertaken between 1966-82 (Green 1987) re-examined and re-evaluated the phases of the hillfort's defences, and whilst broadly agreeing with the earlier findings, were able to establish a more complex constructional sequence. Excavation to the east of the hillfort's defences also discovered the presence of an enclosure, only partially defined, which would seem to date from the early Iron Age, although it may have been preceded by a Late Bronze Age enclosure constructed on a different alignment. No further excavation has taken place in the interior of the hillfort, and although there are possible traces of hut platforms on the eastern side, their date is unclear. Certainly there would be little evidence at present to indicate a densely populated settlement.

Of the remaining Dorset hillforts only two others have provided any dating evidence which suggests that they may have been constructed during the Early Iron Age period. In both cases the title 'hillfort' may be stretching the definition of a hillfort to its limits. The smaller of the two sites is located upon Shipton Hill in the Bride Valley to the west of Dorchester. The upper slopes of this green sand-topped hill indicates evidence of having been artificially steepened on the northern and southern sides. Further down the hillside there is evidence for the remains of a bank and ditch, but as with the upper slopes, the work does not seem to have extended round all sides of the hill. An as yet unpublished excavation was undertaken in the 1950s which produced sherds of Early Iron Age pottery, but a cache of over 1,000 sling stones also found at the site might suggest that the occupation was slightly later in date (Bailey 1982, 90).

A more convincing case of Early Iron Age activity can be made for the site of Bindon Hill located on the coast close to the village of Lulworth Cove on the Purbeck Hills (**58**). The earthworks at Bindon Hill consist of an earth rampart that is over 2.5km in circuit, which along with the natural barrier of sea cliffs, encloses a massive 160ha. Cunliffe (1991, 346) categorises Bindon as a type of hill-top enclosure which is perhaps more closely related to sites like Hog Cliff Hill (see above), whose enclosure was more of a statement, defining territory rather than a serious attempt to create a defensible barrier. Although there has been no excavation on the interior of Bindon Hill there is little evidence to suggest that it contained intensive occupation. The 'defences' of the site were, however, examined in 1950 when Sir Mortimer Wheeler excavated two trenches through the long northern rampart as well as making some investigations around the only known entrance, also located on the northern rampart (Wheeler 1953). The construction of the rampart would seem to have been similar in design to that engineered by the builders of the first hillfort at Maiden Castle, namely a box rampart. At Bindon the external face of the rampart was probably intended to be faced by a palisade of vertical timbers, set within a continuous slot, which was about 0.75m deep. It is almost certain that this palisade was to have been tied to an inner revetment of vertical posts that had been placed 3m behind the palisade by horizontal timbers which would have been buried within the rampart itself. This inner revetment of posts had been spaced about 1m apart. During the excavation of the two trenches through the ramparts Wheeler also noticed that a low bank, no more than 0.3m high, was present just in front of the inner revetment. His interpretation of this feature, which would have been buried within the body of the rampart, saw this as a marking out of the line of the bank, which the construction teams would have followed. It would appear, however, that during construction, the design was changed or else later destroyed. The palisade slot seems not to have had timbers placed within it; rather it had been filled with packed chalk, and the space between the palisade and the inner revetment had not been filled in. The surviving bank seems to be the remnants of one which had been piled on the inside of the rear revetment. The implication would therefore be that the original design was never completed, possibly as Wheeler himself suggested because the enormity of the scale of the work required was no longer

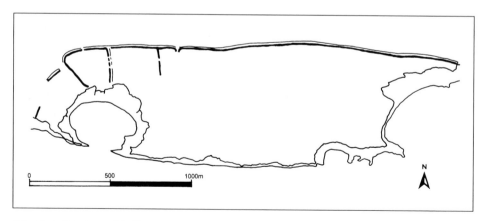

58 *Plan of Bindon Hill hillfort: this hillfort (if it is a hillfort!) is certainly the largest in Dorset in terms of enclosed area. The banks, however, even allowing for erosion, were never massive.* Redrawn with amendments from Wheeler 1953

needed or possible. The date of the earthworks at Bindon has almost exclusively been based upon the ceramic forms discovered during the excavations, which consisted of situlate pots with finger impression decoration on the rim and shoulder. Whilst such wares are similar to those found at Maiden Castle, Eldon's Seat and elsewhere, the absence of a haematite coating may indicate that the material is slightly earlier in date, although this is by no means certain. It is likely that the hill-top enclosure was constructed sometime between 800-600 BC.

The main question which remains to be answered in relation to Bindon Hill is, of course, its purpose. Without further excavation within its interior, that is very difficult to answer. Wheeler himself, perhaps over-reliant on his military back-ground, considered that such a vast area, located adjacent to the safe anchorage at the foot of the cliffs, would have served admirably as a beach-head. His suggestion that the site was a transit camp for Gaulish tribesmen, who then dispersed into the Dorset heartland and beyond, has no collaborative supporting evidence on either side of the English Channel. Its function therefore, remains somewhat of an enigma, particularly as it would seem to have no direct parallels in the archaeological record.

Many of the other hillforts in Dorset may have been constructed within this early period, but evidence is not available. It is possible that Hod Hill (**59**), north of Blandford Forum, may have its origins prior to the fifth century BC, but although this hillfort was the subject of an excavation programme carried out between 1951-8 (Richmond 1968) the first phase of ramparts could not be securely dated (Brailsford 1968, 143).

Funerary practices of the earlier Iron Age in Dorset

The picture emerging so far of the population of Earlier Iron Age Dorset would possibly suggest a landscape which was filling up. Certainly the density of monuments allied to settlement is greater than at any earlier time. If this density is a fair reflection of a growing population, one might also expect to see such growth in the contemporary burial record. As we have seen in the previous two chapters, the landscape pattern had been dominated by monuments and locations set aside for the interment of the dead. These places frequently displayed a variety of forms, but they have a degree of unity in that they infer, at the very least, that elements of the popu-lation were, in death, afforded a great deal of reverence or ritual significance. The reasons behind this could have varied, but essentially the end result is a defined place where the burial rite is enacted in such a way as to leave traces (in addition to the human remains themselves) which testify to the importance of the process.

When we look at the instances of formal burial in the Iron Age, however, we immediately see a general absence of evidence, which appears to be at odds with that for settlement. This state of affairs is particularly acute in the earlier Iron Age (before *c*.600 BC) which to some extent mirrors a similar dearth of evidence for the Later Bronze Age (after *c*.1000 BC). Dateable burial during the period 1000-600 BC is extremely rare and when discovered is not necessarily indicative of what would have been the common practice. Amongst the paucity of human

59 *Aerial photograph of Hod Hill hillfort: this photograph taken in 1924 clearly shows both the Roman fort and a triangle of relatively undisturbed ground, where the traces of huts can be clearly seen.* NMR (Keiller Collection)

remains found on firmly dated Early Iron Age sites is that recovered from the fill of the quarry ditch on the inner sides of the rampart at Chalbury (Whitley 1943, 103). The human remains were mixed with those of animal bone in a deposit, which was sealed by the construction of a hut. It is likely that the remains were disturbed by the construction of the hut and may well have been dispersed at an earlier date. The presence of disarticulated human remains within features such as pits and ditches is certainly attested in other parts of the country for this period (Whimster 1977, 317-9; Russell 2002, 124-5) but the numbers concerned are very small. So for the moment our understanding of burial at this time is inexplicably limited.

We began this examination of the earlier Iron Age with a question – continuity and strife? The use of the question mark implies that the period reflects one or other of these two states, and certainly academic debate has considered both over the last few decades. So which is true? As we have seen, a case can be presented to substantiate both elements in the phrase without excluding either. The breadth and variety of settlement form can certainly trace its origins back to the previous period, implying a strong thread of continuity and growth. However, the increasing demonstration of power and control of landscape displayed by the elaboration of defence suggests that contemporary society was becoming increasingly competitive. As we move into the second half of the Iron Age period we shall observe that such dominant themes continue, but the pace of growth and change appears to accelerate, with greater evidence of influence from mainland Europe.

Later Iron Age Dorset

During the fifth and fourth centuries BC the archaeological record of Dorset demonstrates a number of changes in the settlement record, heralding a period of growth and development sustained until the Roman Invasion of AD 43. None of these changes can be illustrated better than through an examination of the evidence from the hillforts of the region.

Hillfort development
In Wessex generally at this time, there is enough evidence to suggest that by about 400 BC, a number of the early hillforts were being abandoned, whilst others were being significantly expanded with the enclosure of larger areas with newly rebuilt ramparts. Perhaps the best understood example of this in Dorset is that at Maiden Castle. We have already examined the origins of this hillfort earlier in this chapter, where we saw that a relatively modest bank and ditch encircled just under 6.5ha of the hilltop location. This hillfort is in many ways a pale reflection of the hillfort that came to replace it during the early part of the Middle Iron Age, probably at sometime between 400-300 BC. The hillfort that has survived so well today

largely follows the layout that was undertaken at this time, which enlarged the enclosed area to a massive 17.22ha (**57** & **colour plate 14**). The construction of this extended hillfort not only involved the enclosure of a greater area, but eventually it also involved the construction of multiple banks and ditches. The resultant monument was, and is, an immensely imposing structure, which provides us with a clear statement of the abilities of the society that built it. Before we examine what may be inferred about the society that constructed this great hillfort, we should first look in a little more detail at the defences themselves.

In essence the defensive earthworks consisted of three circuits of bank, with ditches on either side of the middle bank. The line of the Early Iron Age fort's bank was extended to the west, followed by the construction of two additional ramparts concentric to the first. A new western entrance was constructed opposite the redesigned eastern gateway, and both entrances had elaborate outworks designed to protect them. Whilst both Wheeler (1943) and Sharples (1991) excavated samples of the defences, the precise dating of the sequence of construction is still not completely understood. Certainly, the works so far described were completed before 100 BC, but the small size of the total sampled area and the limited precision of the dating of the ceramic sequence on the site (on which much of the Iron Age activity is established), leaves a wide degree of latitude in which to anchor the constructional phasing.

It is in the interior of the hillfort that we see a clearer picture of activity and occupation during the Middle Iron Age, defined by a number of features which are commonly found on hillfort interiors. The excavations during the 1930s and the 1980s confirmed for the most part the presence of round huts, four-post structures and pits within the interior, all of which could be assigned to this period. It would seem that following the rebuilding of the defences, the hillfort was only sparsely occupied, with the emphasis being placed upon a number of four-post structures built directly behind the inner rampart. Whilst this can only be positively confirmed in the south-east of the hillfort where excavation has taken place, similar findings on other hillforts in the south (notably Danebury, Cunliffe 2003) suggest that the construction of this form of building is repeatedly found in the lee of the inner rampart. As we observed at the enclosed farmstead at Gussage All Saints, four-posters can be variously interpreted, but Sharples considered that those found at Maiden Castle were likely to have been granaries (Sharples 1991, 97). If they did indeed serve as such, it would seem that they were relatively short-lived, as they appear to have been dismantled before the inner rampart was heightened. The heightening of the inner rampart would seem to have been the last phase of the strengthening of the defences during the Middle Iron Age. In rationalising this sequence of events, Sharples suggests that the construction of granaries may have been to meet the needs of the construction workers involved in the extensive rebuilding programme of the extended hillfort. However, whilst this hypothesis is entirely feasible, there is little evidence to support it at Maiden Castle or elsewhere. Whatever the rationale of this early activity within the hillfort, there is evidence for later occupation, with the presence of a dense cluster of features, including round huts, fences and outside hearths (with, of course, the associated domestic refuse associated with settlement). This initial phase of settlement, however, appears not to demonstrate any signs of internal planning, which may suggest that occupation at this time was limited to discrete clusters, perhaps of extended family units – an interpretation which can only be qualified by further excavation.

The activity clusters represented by the above were replaced after a period of abandonment by a much more regularly planned development of round houses, constructed in a line at the rear of the ramparts. The round houses were constructed approximately 15m behind the rampart and each appeared to have, within its allotted space, a section of it. These allotments seem to have been work areas with traceable remains of metalworking being found in the form of the reworking of bronze scrap (Sharples 1991, 97). A further demonstration of the level of organisation and planning associated with this phase of occupation was demonstrated by the presence of streets which, as a by-product, divide the settlement into 'zones', which subsequently may have been exploited to form distinct social units. This phase of occupation appears to have been replaced by about 100 BC by a return to occupation which is notably lacking in organisation, and is further marked only by limited evidence for any hut building.

Nearly all of the phases of the Middle Iron Age occupation of Maiden Castle contain evidence for the presence of pits, similar to those found in the small settlement at Gussage All Saints. The total number of pits within the hillfort is of course unknown, as only a small percentage of the total interior has been excavated. However, the number of pits found in the excavation campaigns has been estimated at about 289. The extrapolation of this figure over the whole of the hillfort would suggest that the total number of pits could have reached several thousand, which would suggest that they formed a significant function. The common interpretation, as previously noted in relation to Gussage All Saints, is that the pits were utilised for the storage of grain. The presence of such features within hillforts is often used to demonstrate that hillforts formed the function of 'grain banks' in which the accumulated wealth of the community was secured over the short term. The grain was potentially for both consumption and planting the following season (or the season after), but Reynolds (1979) has demonstrated that the pits were more efficient if left undisturbed, with the likely capping clay seal left unbroken. The grain, therefore, would not be exposed to oxygen and the occurrence of biological deterioration would be minimised. However, it should be noted with some caution that there is little evidence to prove that all the pits were used for such a singular purpose, and whilst a case can be made for their final usage as waste dumps this is by no means always the case.

Of the remaining hillforts excavated in Dorset all have evidence of occupation within the Middle to Late Iron Age. Amongst the most celebrated of sites is that of Hod Hill to the north of Blandford Forum (**59**). As indicated in the earlier part of this chapter the origin of the hillfort at Hod Hill is conceivably attributable to the Early Iron Age, particularly as the first phase of the rampart is of the box type construction, but the case is far from proven. The site was partially excavated by Sir Ian Richmond between 1951-8 and posthumously published in 1968. An extensive survey of the hillfort's features undertaken by the Royal Commission on the Historical Monuments of England (now incorporated into English Heritage), revealed within the unploughed part of the site's interior a dense concentration of round houses, yards and fences (**59**), all of which were sampled by Richmond during his excavation campaign. Whilst Richmond's report includes a detailed account of his findings, the precise dating of the remains relied heavily on the ceramics from the site. As with the material recovered from elsewhere, including Maiden Castle, the pottery remains largely unchanged throughout the Middle Iron Age, which makes precise dating problematic. Certainly the evidence provided by the excavation would suggest that the occupation of the hillfort was to some extent continuous, possibly from as early as 400 BC to the time of the Roman assault in the years following AD 43. Unlike the main concentration of settlement at Maiden Castle, which presented a picture of organised planning in the spatial layout of the structures, it is difficult to identify similar organisation at Hod Hill. However, the planned remains are unlikely to be indicative of a single phase; they may even be intercutting or overlapping features, a palimpsest of unrelated chronological layouts of the settlement. Certainly many of the structures excavated by Richmond contained pottery of Durotrigan forms which date to after 100 BC and include several small caches of slingstones. Some of the huts were also contained within their own palisades, which perhaps suggests that they were occupied at a time of great social stress – which would certainly fit with the finding of a number of Roman ballista bolts within the interior.

The excavation of Pilsdon Pen (the highest of Dorset's hillforts at an elevation of 279m) in west Dorset between 1964-71 by Peter Gelling (1977) concentrated mainly on features within the interior. Several round houses were excavated, which were largely defined by a U-shaped penannular gully (**60**). Some of the houses contained post-holes located either within the gullies themselves or inside the area defined by the gullies, which may indicate a variety of constructional techniques and perhaps also that the huts were not necessarily contemporaneous. Dating of the site's occupation was again essentially determined through the associated pottery, which included surprisingly small quantities of abraded and largely undecorated jars and bowls which the excavator suggested were of earlier date than the more heavily decorated types associated with Durotrigan settlement of the first century BC. Interestingly, the excavations at Pilsdon Pen indicated no evidence for four-post structures or indeed for the ubiquitous deep pits that we have encountered on similar sites. It may be that such features are to be found elsewhere on the site, but it is worthy of note that the landscape in this part of Dorset may have been dominated by a pastorally based economy (as it is today),

hut 13

hut 10b

hut 11

hut 12

hut 10a

hut 9

hut 7

hut 8

hut 5

hut 6

hut 4

hut 3

0   5   10m

N

60 *Plan of excavated huts at Pilsdon Pen hillfort.* Redrawn from Gelling 1977

and that consequently the storage of grain was not a significant element of the site's raison d'être.

As with Maiden Castle and Poundbury there was evidence at Pilsdon Pen to suggest some metalworking with the finding of crucible fragments but it would appear that generally speaking the material culture was quite limited.

The remainders of the known hillforts in Dorset are, for the most part, unexcavated, and consequently our understanding of them is restricted to inter-pretations based upon their observable component features. The range of types defined by area, location and the earthworks themselves is nearly as numerous as the numbers of the forts and clearly, therefore, they were monuments created socially and economically in response to localised need, and of course with due reflection of the locale's topography. The date of many of them is of course unknown. Many may have their origin during the initial hillfort construction phase of the earlier Iron Age or alternatively they may have been constructed in response to immediate or prolonged periods of threat or aggression, such as those pertaining at the time of the Roman invasions of 54 BC and AD 43, or even instances of inter-tribal raiding, during the intervening years.

One of the more intriguing questions associated with hillforts concerns the territory to which hillforts were related. The construction of a hillfort represents a huge investment in both time and labour, and would have required a high degree of social organisation to bring people together to undertake the work involved. That this was present is manifestly self-evident, but how geographically extensive these social frameworks were is confused by the close geographical proximity of some hillforts to each other. The pairings of hillforts, separated by little more than a kilometre or so, can be seen at some of the largest sites in the county. Maiden Castle and Poundbury lie within 3km of each other and in north Dorset Hod Hill and Hambledon Hill are even closer neighbours. At both pairings there is suffi-cient evidence to suggest that occupation chronologically overlapped, which would imply that the hillforts were not located at the geographical centre of their respective territories. It is more likely, therefore, that any geographical determina-tion for the choice of site location in these cases is directed towards the periphery of the territorial influence of each unit (hillfort). The periphery would naturally constitute a border or boundary where a point of contact with an adjoining territory perhaps coincided with rich agricultural lands and/or a trading route.

Amongst the rich diversity of hillforts within the county, there is a single rather unusual example of what is commonly referred to as a hill-slope fort. Buzbury Rings (**colour plate 10**) is located on the east facing slope of Keyneston Down, overlooking downland as it stretches away to the River Tarrant. Located as it is on the slope of a hill, it is extremely vulnerable defensively, which of course suggests that the purpose of its defining banks was stimulated by other criteria. To under-stand the possible purpose of Buzbury we must look further afield, with the nearest comparable sites being located to the west on the south-west peninsula is Cornwall and Devon. The lowland areas of Devon and Cornwall contain a form of enclosure which appears to be associated with pastoral communities, probably dating to the fourth or third centuries BC and generically identified as multiple enclosure forts. Characteristically such forts are located on the slopes of hills, frequently overlooking springs or river valleys and are enclosed by earthen banks with corresponding ditches (Cunliffe 1991, 252-6). The inner enclosure at Buzbury (1ha) probably functioned as an enclosed farmstead, containing houses and huts probably related to an extended family group. The outer enclosure of almost 5ha is likely to have afforded protection for cattle or sheep during round-up or at other times when they were not grazing on the open downs. However, the earthen banks of these enclosures, it could be argued, are out of proportion with that required for the corralling of animals. The additional motive therefore for building such elaborate enclosures may be reflective of the stresses within society at the time or alternatively they may simply be a statement of the owner, reflecting his wealth and power in an ostentatious manner.

Rural settlement and the 'Durotrigans'

As we have seen, hillforts increasingly seem to dominate the landscape of Dorset by the fourth century BC. However, whilst this appears to represent the focusing of administrative and economic control into centres with presumed territories, these centres do not generally appear to contain large populations. For the most part the economy was agriculturally based and the mass of the population was still located within farmsteads spread throughout the county.

The nature of the settlement pattern seems little changed from that identified three centuries before, with dispersed farmsteads dominating the landscape, many of them exhibiting the defensive characteristics of their predecessors. Many of the banjo enclosures which probably appear as early as the Middle Iron Age may be more numerous during the Later Iron Age and may be indicative of a more developed pastoral economy in some areas.

The earthwork enclosed farmstead at Gussage All Saints, which had its origins in the Early Iron Age (discussed above), continues to develop and function into the Late Iron Age. The material culture associated with the site indicates that by the first century BC the settlement was occupied by a community whom we conventionally recognise as Durotrigan (**61**).

The Durotriges is a name for the tribal group that occupied the Dorset region during the Late Iron Age and comes to us as a piece of recorded history. It is during the last century BC that we have the first fragmentary documentation which traces events, people and places in time. This documentation not only takes the form of the writings of classical authors such as Caesar, Ptolemy and Strabo, but also, much more importantly at this time, includes tribal names on some of the coinage used in the developing commercial networks of the time. Whilst the tribes were minting their own coinage it becomes possible, through examination of their distribution, to suggest the territories of the tribal units as well as their respective sphere of influence. As far as we are able to determine, the territory of

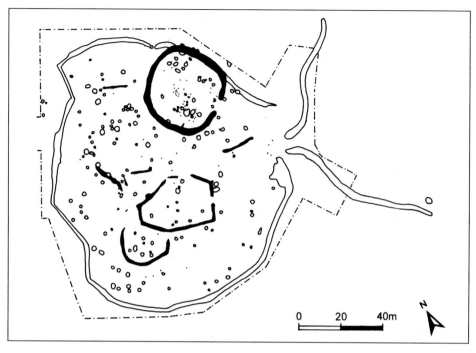

61 *Plan of Gussage All Saints (phase 3): during the late development of this enclosure the interior was sub-divided into separate enclosures. There was also a greater concentration of pits dug into the interior with a more widespread pattern than that seen in phase 2.* Redrawn with amendments from Wainwright 1979b

the Durotriges extended from the River Avon in the east to the River Axe in the west, with the River Brue possibly marking part of the northern boundary (Cunliffe 1991, 159; Putnam 1998, 52-54).

The emergence of an entity, which we recognise as a tribal unit called the Durotriges, is of course not defined solely through associated coinage, nor is it something which imprinted itself in the landscape overnight. Whilst the distinctive character of its material culture is noticeably different from that of a century earlier, this should not be viewed as evidence for the region being colonised. Whilst it is likely that traders and limited numbers of migrants from Gaul would have settled in Dorset at this time, the change in material culture is much more likely to have been in response to the rapidly expanding trading network with the continent at this time. That local culture absorbed many new ideas relatively quickly is not surprising, particularly as communication would have been faster and easier in the developing trading network.

At Gussage All Saints the evidence for continued occupation into the first century BC is demonstrated by the presence of wheel thrown pots of Durotrigan form and also significant reorganisation of the interior. Whilst the interior, as previously, contains large numbers of pits, the construction of secondary enclosures within the main earthwork enclosure takes place, one of which seems to have served as a stock enclosure.

The ultimate form of these settlements is perhaps best viewed in conjunction with a number of excavated sites on Cranborne. Three sites located close to the Wiltshire-Dorset boundary have provided much evidence for the character of farmstead settlement in the Late Iron Age, at around the time of the Roman conquest in AD 43. Whilst this volume is generally unconcerned with developments of the Roman period, these sites do allow an impression of the likely character of settlement during the last century BC.

Two of the sites were excavated at the end of the nineteenth century by General Pitt-Rivers but were reviewed in a synthesis of early settlement of the region by Christopher Hawkes in 1947. The site at Rotherley (Wiltshire) consisted of a number of small enclosures contained within an associated network of fields. The enclosures contained the now recognisable palimpsest of post-holes and pits, indicating the presence of storage and probable round huts of the type seen at Gussage All Saints. The phasing of the site's component parts is now difficult to determine, and certainly post-Roman activity and occupation complicates the picture. However, the presence of more than one enclosure at the site (**62**) appears to mirror the construction of the additional enclosures at Gussage All Saints, indicating perhaps a slight shift in the social relations operating within what may have been an extended family unit. The second site of Woodcuts (**63**) also excavated by Pitt-Rivers (one of the earliest of his excavations in the area), consists of a ditched circular enclosure which contained a large number of pits and possible working hollows (used possibly for winnowing corn). This site is compromised, however, because Pitt-Rivers' techniques of excavation were not sufficiently advanced to recognise surviving post-holes within the archaeological strata. It is likely that the interior of the enclosure would have contained four post structures, and presumably traces of round houses and other less well defined features. The overall picture of the occupation activity may consequently be incomplete. To some extent the failings of Pitt-Rivers' pioneering work on Cranborne Chase in examining these Late Iron Age settlements has been addressed in the excavation of a similar farmstead near Tollard Royal (Wainwright 1968).

The excavation of the kite-shaped enclosure on Berwick Down close to the village of Tollard Royal in 1965 revealed details of a Durotrigan farmstead which appears to date from the period immediately preceding the Roman conquest of AD 43 (**64**). Within the bank and ditched enclosure, the remains of a round house were found, alongside storage pits and granaries. Of the three granaries discovered two had remains of six-rowed barley (*Hordeum hexastichon*) in a number of post-holes. Interestingly, a number of pits found on the site also contained surviving grain within them, but in most cases the grain was wheat (*Triticum spelta* and *Triticum dicoccum*). To the south of the enclosure there are traces of field systems, and to the north there is a further enclosure, possibly contemporary but as yet undated, with hut platforms and nearby indications of unenclosed pits and a round house.

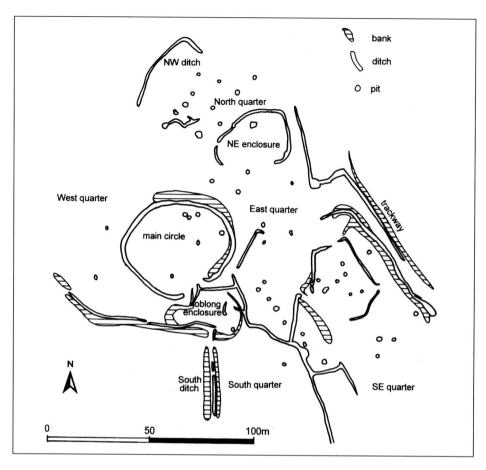

bank

ditch

pit

NW ditch

North quarter

NE enclosure

West quarter

East quarter

main circle

trackway

oblong
enclosure

N

South
ditch

South quarter

SE quarter

0   50   100m

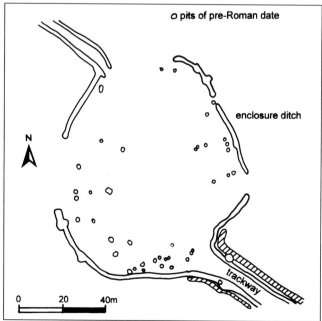

○ pits of pre-Roman date

enclosure ditch

N

trackway

0   20   40m

62 (Above) *Plan of Rotherly during the Late Iron Age. Excavated by Pitt-Rivers in 1886.* Redrawn with amendments from Hawkes 1947

63 (Left) *Plan of Woodcuts: phase 1 Late Iron Age settlement (banjo enclosure?) Excavated by Pitt-Rivers in 1885.* Redrawn with amendments from Hawkes 1947

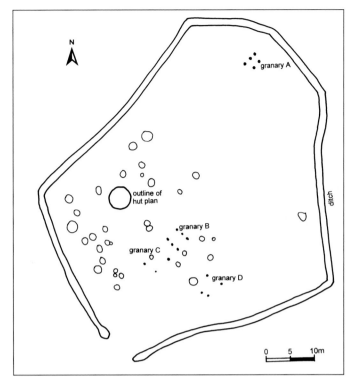

64 *Plan of Tollard Royal: a Late Iron Age settlement. On the plan can be seen a round house, granaries and pits. The basic form of Iron Age farmsteads can be seen to have changed little over the period.* Redrawn with amendments from Wainwright 1968

Developed hillforts, oppida and trading networks

Whilst there is an overriding lack of precision with the dating of sequences of activity within the excavated hillforts of Dorset, the overwhelming impression derived from these summarised findings does suggest a degree of commonality between the sites. During the Middle Iron Age whilst some hillforts like Chalbury were being abandoned, others show evidence of extensive remodelling (Maiden Castle), which has led to the use of the term developed hillforts to describe them. The nature and extent of these forms of hillfort, whilst essentially variable, do tend to indicate that in addition to their often massive refortification there was denser and more overtly planned occupation. The classic example of this process is Danebury (Cunliffe 1984) but elements of the activity demonstrated there can be seen in the evidence outlined above, particularly at Maiden Castle. It is of course a matter of conjecture as to how representative or widespread this pattern of activity is on other sites within the county.

As we approach the Late Iron Age, generally dated from *c*.100 BC, the nucleation of settlement into what we recognise as urban centres can be identified in many parts of England. As with developed hillforts, the form of such centres can vary greatly but many of them share essential characteristics, which has led to the adoption of the term, oppida. The term was initially used by Julius Caesar to describe the centres of settlement. Essentially the term, oppidum, is now given to large nucleated settlement of the final phase of the Iron Age that functions as a centre of production and distribution within a larger network of trade and exchange.

Whilst oppida elsewhere in the country can be associated with tracts of land which are not necessarily enclosed within significant boundaries, such as Silchester in Hampshire, the examples from Dorset so far identified appear to be centred upon hillforts. Whilst there is some evidence to suggest that generally hillforts were being abandoned at around this time, some of the sites in Dorset continued to develop. Evidence to suggest that the sites of Maiden Castle, Hengistbury Head, Hambledon and Hod Hill fulfil the essential criteria for classification as oppida (Cunliffe, 1991, 1660) has been produced in recent years, and for some sites the evidence is compelling.

At Hengistbury Head, located between the modern towns of Bournemouth and Christchurch, a headland protected by a pair of earth ramparts contains the remains of what was a busy trading centre from c.150 BC. It is not surprising that the site was chosen as the location for a major focus for trading at this time if you examine its natural advantages. Safe anchorage for seagoing vessels is afforded through the harbour which lies behind the protecting headland, into which run two of the region's rivers, the Avon and the Stour. These rivers meander into the heartland of Dorset and would have provided excellent conduits for trade. The site has been subject to a number of excavations, although none of them were of significant proportion until those directed by Barry Cunliffe between 1970-1 and 1979-84 (Cunliffe 1987). Although the construction of the defensive ramparts probably belongs to the Earlier Iron Age when there is some evidence for occupation dating from about 800–100 BC, it is with the Late Iron Age that we see evidence of the settlement's wider role and significance. By around 100 BC there appears to have been intensive occupation of the area extending along the coastal strip eastwards from the ramparts for approximately a kilometre. Industrial activity included evidence for bronze and glass working, and possibly iron working, although the latter is likely to date to after 50 BC. However, perhaps the most significant of the results obtained from the excavation programme concerns evidence indicating that overseas trade was of some significance at the time. Amongst a great many artefacts discovered were ceramic materials including Armorican pottery and Italian amphorae (Dressel type 1A), lumps of unworked purple and yellow glass, coinage from Armorica and north-west Gaul, even ecofactual remains of figs, corn and even chamomile, previously unseen in the British Isles.

This sudden burst of trading is likely to have been stimulated by the expansion of the Roman Empire at around this time. The annexation of territory allowed for the opening up of trade routes into north-west Europe which ultimately included Britain (Cunliffe 1987, 340-1). Importantly, alongside the foreign imports already described, materials which were 'imports' from elsewhere in Britain that may have been ultimately intended for export to the Continent were also found at Hengistbury. Lead from the Mendip hills is attested, as is copper and silver ore from Callington on the Devon-Cornwall border. Pottery of the

'Glastonbury style' with heavy curvilinear decoration, also from Cornwall and Devon, has been discovered. An unusually large ratio of cattle bones in the animal bone assemblage, whilst tempting to be interpreted as evidence for export would seem to represent local consumption. All this sits well with the observation by the Roman historian Strabo (commenting on circumstances 50-100 years later) who refers to a number of 'British' products – 'corn, cattle, gold, silver, hides, slaves and clever hunting dogs' (IV.5.2). All the evidence therefore suggests that Hengistbury Head was located at the hub of a trading network where the exploitation of the mineral and agricultural wealth of southern Britain was being tapped. The traders at Hengistbury would appear to have been acting as middle men, probably in association with Armorican traders on the other side of the Channel, who in turn were dealing with markets ultimately linked into the Mediterranean world, which was, of course, dominated at this time by Rome.

Although it is clear that Hengistbury was functioning as a trading port in this period it is likely that the natural harbour at nearby Poole may also have been involved in this trading network. Finds from Hamworthy on the northern coastal strip of Poole Harbour, and also those made at Green Island nearby, are not dissimilar to those found at Hengistbury, and may indicate the presence of a second trading port on the Dorset coastline. Certainly the River Frome, which empties out into Poole Harbour, would have afforded a natural trade route to be developed to the west of the county and beyond.

As for the sites of Maiden Castle and Hod Hill, whilst they may well have functioned as centres of administration and distribution, the excavations at them have thus far revealed little in the way of exported material. Many of the 'exotic' finds which have been recorded at Hengistbury Head and in the region of Poole Harbour, which indicate the presence of continental trade, are absent from these inland sites.

Disposal of the dead in Late Iron Age Dorset

We saw earlier in this chapter that the evidence for the disposal of the dead in the earlier part of the Iron Age was extremely limited, and to some extent the same can be said for the period leading up to the Roman invasion and conquest in AD 43. However, the excavation of a number of settlement sites has revealed a growing body of evidence, which may throw some light on the situation. Several of the sites already described – Gussage All Saints, Tollard Royal, Maiden Castle, and Hod Hill – contain what are known as pit burials where cadavers were placed in pits within settlements (usually in a crouched position) when the pit had gone out of use. It is certainly difficult to quantify how widespread a practice this may have been, or indeed if it was restricted to certain sections of society. It can only account for a very small fraction of the total population, and one must suppose that other burial rites were practised, for which as yet we have only very limited evidence.

Earth mounds, as we have seen in previous chapters, had been a common construction associated with burial ritual and they continued to play a part in the mortuary practices of Iron Age populations in parts of the British Isles, most notably the Yorkshire burials associated with the Arras culture. In Dorset there are a limited number of sites which have characteristic square quarry ditches or banks which are thought to be Iron Age in date. The only example to have been excavated in the county is that near Handley on Gussage Hill in Cranborne Chase (**65**). A layer of cremated human bone, ash and charcoal was covered with a mound of earth and chalk derived from the surrounding area, and from the enclosing square ditch. The cremation layer seems to have been spread thinly (possibly scattered) over an area of approximately 3m². Dating of the deposit was attained through fragments of pottery found both in the old ground surface beneath the barrow and in the deposit itself which appeared to be Late Iron Age in date (White 1970, 26-36). Other possible examples of this form of monument occur on Cranborne Chase (Bowen 1990, 81) and at Winterbourne Steepleton in west Dorset (Whimster 1981, 393) but they have yet to be confirmed through excavation.

Towards the very end of our period there is evidence for the use of defined areas set aside for burial. Unfortunately some of these were only poorly recorded in the

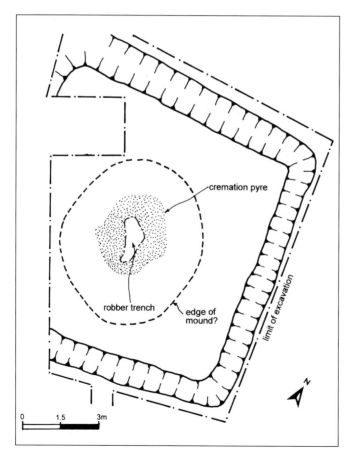

65 *Plan of Handley Down Iron Age barrow: the only example of an Iron Age barrow excavated in Dorset was unfortunately disturbed at its centre when excavations commenced in 1969. However, it was possible to determine that the mound was associated with cremated human remains. Redrawn with amendments from White 1970*

nineteenth century and included sites discovered in Weymouth and Dorchester which contained as many as 80 individuals (Whimster 1977, 319-320). Amongst the most recently excavated of cemeteries definitely dating to the pre-Roman Iron Age is that discovered outside the ramparts of Poundbury hillfort in Dorchester. Although the site was used intensively during the years following the Roman occupation of the region, it did have its origins in the years leading up to AD 43. The burials were located within oval or rectangular grave cuts and were typically crouched, predominantly on the right side (Farwell and Molleson 1993, 6-7).

Even rarer still are the presence of so-called 'warrior burials', which do occur in small numbers throughout England. An example of this type of burial was discovered amongst a small cemetery at Whitcombe, south of Dorchester. The individual was buried in the crouched position, lying on his right side, and was accompanied by an iron sword, an iron hammer head, and a spearhead amongst other items. The date of the burial is thought to be around the first century AD, possibly pre-Roman (Aitken 1990).

All of the inhumations identified within the Late Iron Age share a commonality of burial rite, in that there is a predominance of crouched inhumation on the right side usually with the head orientated to the east. This can be seen as the adoption of a particular burial rite associated with the Durotriges probably originating in the pit burial traditions of the Middle Iron Age.

Much has been made of two cemeteries at the hillforts of Maiden Castle (Wheeler 1943) and Spetisbury (Grisham 1939). In both instances we see the interment of large numbers of individuals, some with wounds, which has promoted the interpretation that they represent war cemeteries associated with clearing up operations following fighting with Roman forces. In both cases the circumstances can be seen to be unusual and therefore unrepresentative of the normal funerary practice of the Late Iron Age.

The overall picture of the burial record for the Later Iron Age is one which demonstrates a variety of form that is compromised by a lack of data for the disposal of the general population of the time. The fact that defined cemeteries such as Poundbury came into use towards the very end of our period, perhaps indicates a move towards a more formalised method of disposing of the dead that previously had been undertaken within the small dispersed communities spread throughout the county.

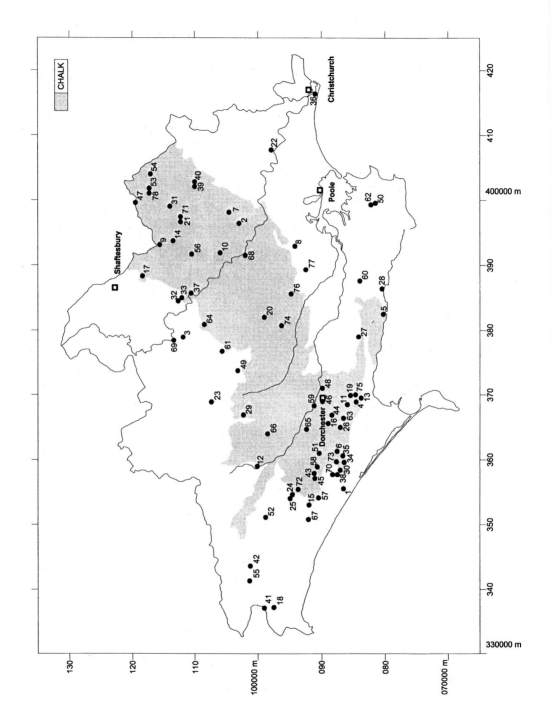

66 *Map of archaeological sites listed in Gazetteer*

GAZETTEER OF PREHISTORIC SITES IN DORSET (*c.*4000-50 BC)

The sites chosen for this gazetteer represent a cross-section of the major monuments and places in the county spanning the Neolithic – Iron Age periods. For the most part the sites retain a portion of their structural past through surviving earthworks and therefore a sense of ancestral presence is maintained which is plain for the visitor to see. A few other sites are included where there is little in the way of obvious remains, but are nonetheless important places where archaeologists have been able to establish activity.

The great majority of the following sites are on private land and access to them should not be assumed. All, however, can at least be viewed effectively from public footpaths, which either pass over, around or very close to them.

The use of Ordnance Survey national grid references (NGR) has been used throughout and in all cases the full reference is given without the use of the prefix codes that indicate 100km tiles. The NGR can accordingly be used with figure (**66**) and any Ordnance Survey mapping on which full figure references are given.

1 Abbotsbury Castle

Type Hillfort

Period Iron Age

Description
A predominantly bivallate hillfort enclosing approximately 1.8ha overlooking Chesil beach and Portland. The defences consist of two banks separated by a ditch in a triangular plan form, with additional strengthening in the south-east where the banks have been increased to four with external ditches. This additional strengthening has clearly been designed to address the levelling out of the natural topography at this point. The principal entrance to the hillfort is also located in the south-east where access to the enclosure would have been more straightforward (see also Eggardon hillfort). It has been suggested elsewhere that the additional strengthening of the defences undertaken after the original construction of the hillfort. This is based on the observations around the south-east entrance where the ditch appears to be have been partly filled in with material from the innermost bank. If this is the case it may suggest that the first phase of the hillfort's defences consisted of a single bank and ditch. Evidence for occupation is limited to the presence of a number of circular hollows in the south-east sector. All of the hollows are of similar size (approximately 6-7m in diameter) and are consistent with

circular hut platforms observed and excavated on other hillforts elsewhere. The observable earthworks in the south-west angle of the inner rampart, which form an almost rectangular earthwork, would appear to be an additional phase of activity. Certainly rectangular earthworks are not consistent with our understanding of Iron Age constructional techniques and it would therefore seem that the feature is of a later date. This interpretation is further supported by the observation that the small ditch which lies on the exterior of this feature, appears to cut into the innermost Iron Age rampart, and thus must post-date it. The earthworks may represent a reuse of the monument perhaps as a Roman signal station. None of these interpretations have been proved by excavation.

Location/access

The hillfort is located approximately 2.5km (1.5m) north-west of the village of Abbotsbury just off the B3157. The B3157 climbs steeply as it leaves Abbotsbury, and parking is available at several lay-byes close to the top of Abbotsbury Hill. Access to the hillfort is gained via footpaths from either the minor road running off the B3157 at 35580864 or from footpaths signed off the B3157 itself.
NGR 35550866
OS map OS Explorer OL 15

2 Badbury Rings Hillfort

Type Hillfort

Period Iron Age

Description

One of the most visited archaeological monuments in Dorset, Badbury Rings is a multivallate hillfort located within a rich archaeological landscape. The hillfort itself consists of a roughly circular enclosure comprising three circuits of bank and ditch which encloses 7.3ha of hilltop in the interfluve between the rivers Allen and Stour. Its positioning dominates the landscape for many square miles, a factor which must have been uppermost in the planning of this hillfort. Its potential therefore as a strategic focal point in the control of the immediate landscape is self-evident. There are three breaches in the ramparts which form entrances into the defences, located in the west, east and south-west. The origin and use of the south-western entrance has attracted some attention as it does not seem to be part of the initial design, but this is far from clear. The entrances themselves are fairly uncomplicated with the eastern comprising of in-turned ramparts, and the western of a more complex design involving outworks and a barbican between the outer and second circuit of ramparts. The outer circuit of rampart is considerably less imposing than the other two and is considered to be of a different phase, perhaps constructed as a response to the Roman invasion in AD 43.

The central occupation area is covered by a plantation that has its origins in the eighteenth century, which effectively masks any evidence of original features within the interior. Quite unusually for hillforts there is a spring located within the inner defences. The Romano-British phase of activity at this hillfort is dominated by the junction of two Roman roads 200m to the north of the outer rampart, and the presence of an extensive settlement located between Badbury and the village of Shapwick to the south-west. Recent geophysical survey is starting to identify an immense settlement area, which has often been thought to be associated with the settlement of Vindocladia mentioned in the Antonine Itinerary.

To the south-west of the hillfort are a small group of three round barrows lying at the side of the access road to the car park. All of them are probably of Early Bronze Age date and are exceptionally well preserved, although there is evidence to suggest that they have been dug into in antiquity.

Location/access
Badbury rings is located almost halfway between the towns of Wimborne Minster and Blandford Forum along the B3082. It is very well sign-posted from both towns and there is a large car park close to the monument. The monument is owned and maintained by the National Trust. The site is extremely popular with families and dog walkers so can be busy, especially during the summer and at weekends.
NGR 39641030
OS map OS Explorer 118

3 Banbury Hill Hillfort

Type Hillfort

Period Iron Age

Description
A small univallate hillfort located on a small rise of gravel within a belt of Kimmeridge clay. As with many of the lesser Dorset hillforts, Banbury has suffered through centuries of agricultural erosion. The single rampart survives as earth bank which never exceeds a height greater than 0.75m above that of the interior. Approached from outside of the monument, the bank does appear more massive (2m) above the top of the ditch. The ditch which originally would have encircled the bank, now appears largely infilled through silting and ploughing, and is best traced upon its southern circuit. The entrance to the hillfort consists of a simple breach in the rampart on the western side which has an outwork extending from its northern end creating a relatively narrow entry passage, over 75m long.

Location/access
The hillfort is situated on Banbury Hill 2km south of Sturminster Newton and 2km north-west of Okeford Fitzpaine. Footpaths traverse around the northern half of the earthworks, which can be accessed from the village of Broad Oak 378811124.
NGR 37891119
OS map OS Explorer 129

4 Bincombe Hill Barrow Group

Type Barrow Group

Period Bronze Age

Description

A barrow cemetery consisting of several well-preserved barrows. There is a triple-barrow which is enclosed by a single ditch at 3690208458. This group appears somewhat dispersed today but on careful inspection, one can see that the cemetery forms a rough semi-circle exposed to the east generally arranged on the 150–160m contour. The group is a small part of the greater group referred to as the Ridgeway Barrow Group which has 195 listed barrows, and forms one of the most extensive concentrations of round barrows in the British Isles. Some of the barrows have clearly been disturbed in antiquity, and many have also been subjected to modern ploughing and appear as low mounds within the fields. It is probable that some of the 'excavated' barrows are those investigated by Charles Warne in the middle of the nineteenth century but the exact locations of his excavations do not appear to have been recorded with any great precision.

Location/access

This group is located on private land on the summit of Bincombe Hill 400m east of the village of Bincombe. The barrows can be viewed quite effectively from footpaths (particularly the South West Coast Path) which runs to the south and the west.

NGR 36890846

OS map OS Explorer OL 15

5 Bindon Hill Hillfort

Type Hillfort

Period Iron Age

Description

Bindon Hill consists of a long earthen rampart some 2.5km in length, which along with the cliffs to the south and east encloses a massive 160ha of Bindon Hill. Sir Mortimer Wheeler excavated a small section of the rampart in 1950, but since this time there have been no further investigations. The site is part of extensive military ranges in the area and has been subject to periodic bombardment by army ordnance over several decades. There appears to be a single entrance located approximately 750m from the western end of the enclosure. Wheeler's excavations were targeted solely on the defences, which revealed a great deal regarding the constructional sequence, but little is known concerning the function of such a massive enclosure. His interpretations considered the fortifications to be a beach head protection for the natural harbour at Lulworth Cove which lies at its western foot, and to have been constructed *c.*400 BC.

Location/access

There is access via footpaths to the extreme western side of the enclosure from the villages of West Lulworth and Lulworth Cove. At certain times the army ranges are open and defined paths can be walked within the enclosure

NGR 38250803

OS map OS Explorer OL 15

6 Black Down Barrow Group

Type Barrow Group

Period Bronze Age

Description

Black Down is an excellent starting point to access a number of nearby burial monuments but also to see them within a wider landscape. The Black Down cemetery occupies the relatively open ground which is surrounded by the Black Down plantation. Approximately 10 round barrows can be seen within the immediate vicinity of the Hardy Monument which also occupies the site. The site appears somewhat chaotic, it being affected by gravel workings and a well-worn and rough and ready car park. Close to Black Down are a number of sites that are definitely worth the walk required to inspect them:

- Hell Stone Megalithic Cambered tomb (see separate entry), is located approximately 1km south-west of Black Down.
- Bronkham Hill lies along the Ridgeway that runs eastward from Black Down. Located on it is a linear barrow cemetery over 1.6km in length containing over 30 barrows, most of which are located on the line of the modern footpath (South West Coast Path).
- The group is a small part of the greater group referred to as the Ridgeway Barrow Group which has 195 listed barrows and forms one of the most extensive concentrations of round barrows in the British Isles.

Location/access

The car park at Black Down is located on a minor road which runs between Martinstown (Winterbourne St Martin) and Abbotsbury. Directions should be taken to the Hardy Monument where there is ample parking on private land.

NGR 36130876

OS map OS Explorer OL 15

7 Bradford Barrow

Type Round barrow

Period Bronze Age?

Description
This is certainly one of the largest round barrows in Dorset with a diameter of approximately 30m that survives to a height in excess of 6m. It is of a bowl-barrow form and could date to as early as the later Neolithic (however Grinsell considered that it was possibly Roman in origin evidenced by its 'conical' profile).

Location/access
This barrow is located in the Allen valley, 1.5km south of the village of Witchampton and 3km north-east of the hillfort at Badbury Rings. The barrow itself is located on private land but can be viewed from public right of way close to the monument. The nearest parking is at Badbury Rings or in the village at Witchampton.
NGR 39811046
OS map OS Explorer 118

8 Bulbury Camp Hillfort

Type Hillfort

Period Iron Age

Description
A much-denuded earthwork consisting of a single, and in places hardly discernible bank, enclosing an area of approximately 3.2ha. The site's aspect is fairly unusual as it lies on rising ground at an elevation of approximately 45m with higher ground to the north. The earthwork overlooks Lytchett Bay and Poole Harbour some 2 miles to the south-east. Today the single rampart has been much denuded and has clearly been affected by long periods of ploughing. It survives best in its south-western circuit where the elevation between ditch bottom and bank top is never more than 2m. Although never archaeologically excavated, finds recovered from an episode of draining the land in 1884 suggest that occupation dates to the first century AD and therefore may represent a response to the Roman invasion. A plan drawn during the late nineteenth century also suggests that the hillfort had opposed entrances to the east and west, conflicting with early OS maps which suggested entrances to the north and south. It therefore remains unresolved as to original articulation of the entrances serving this hillfort.

Location/access
This hillfort is likely to be disappointing to the visitor because of its exceedingly poor state of preservation. However, its aspect can be readily viewed from a public footpath to the north at Dolmans Hill (39290948). The hillfort is located 2km south-west of Lytchett Matravers at Higher Bulbury Farm.
NGR 39290942
OS map OS Explorer 118

9 Bussey Stool Park Hillfort

Type Hillfort

Period Iron Age

Description
An oval, univallate hillfort enclosing approximately 2ha on the southern end of a chalk spur. The single rampart has two entrances to the north-west and south-east. The site has no recorded archaeological excavation and subsequently little is known about it. Today virtually the whole of the fort is covered with thick undergrowth consisting mainly of trees. The bank is approximately 2m high and 10m wide at its base. The external ditch is 8m wide and approximately 1.5m deep. The site is also known as Caesar's Camp and lies within 200m (east of) a Roman road.

Location/access
The site lies due west of Farnham woods approximately 3km west of the village of Farnham. The fort is located on private land.
NGR 39301156
OS map OS Explorer 118

10 Buzbury Rings Hillfort

Type Hillfort

Period Iron Age

Description
Buzbury Rings is a form of Iron Age enclosure which is normally found further to the west in Cornwall or Devon. The monument is recognised as a hill-slope enclosure/fort which is located on an east-facing slope of Keynston Down overlooking the downland as it gradually falls down to the River Tarrant. This effectively means that the enclosure is vulnerable defensively from the north and north-west. As there is no obvious reason why the hillfort was not constructed

on the crest of the hill, one must assume that the choice of location was not driven by defence. The earthworks consist of an outer enclosure defined by a bank and ditch with a further inner enclosure similarly defined. The two earthwork enclosures are not concentric with each other. The outer bank and ditch, which appears kidney-shaped, encloses an area of almost 5ha whilst the smaller internal earthwork contains an area of 1ha. There does appear to be further earthworks of a more ephemeral nature within the enclosures, but their purpose is unclear. The entrance into the enclosure is likely to be in the south-west where the bank appears to in-turn.

The monument is entirely unique in the county and is further singled out by the outer bank having an internal ditch, reminiscent of earlier henge monuments. No excavation has taken place at the site. The monument is bisected by the modern road (B3082) and has also been partially 'landscaped' by a golf course, although the affected elements of both banks still survive in a modified form.

Location/access
Buzbury Rings is located 2km north-west of Tarrant Keyneston on the B3082 which links Wimborne Minster to Blandford Forum. The monument can be viewed from the roadside (which runs through it) but the rest of the property is on private land.
NGR 39191060
OS map OS Explorer 118

11 Came Down Barrow Group

Type Barrow Group

Period Bronze Age

Description
Came Down Barrow group consists of an extensive array of round barrows lying on high ground to the west of Down Wood. The group consists of few variant forms of round barrow including double-bowl, disc and bell types. Most of the group is contained within a golf course and while the surrounding landscape has been affected by some landscaping the barrows appear largely unaffected. The group is generally spread over a fairly large area but there is a notable focus for the group at 36880863. A number of these barrows were opened by Charles Warne in the second half of the nineteenth century.

Location/access
Although all of the barrows are on private land they can be viewed from the road which runs alongside Came and Down Woods which is approached by way of a minor road off the A354 Dorchester – Weymouth road signposted Broadmayne.
NGR 36850860
OS map OS Explorer OL 15

12   Castle Hill Hillfort

Type Hillfort

Period Iron Age?

Description

A little known site located in the upper reaches of the Frome valley. The enclosure, which captures approximately 1.75ha of the summit of a hilltop, appears to have done so by the artificial steepening of the hill-slope forming a defensible rampart which is breached by two entrances. The entrances are located to the north-east and north-west. Within the interior are the likely remains of a round barrow and some traces of agricultural terracing. The presence of agricultural terracing (presumably medieval) can also be seen on the lower slopes of the hill to the north of the enclosure.

Location/access

The site is located on the summit of Castle Hill overlooking the town of Cattistock to the south.
NGR 35941001
OS map OS Explorer 117

13   Chalbury Hillfort

Type Hillfort

Period Iron Age

Description

A hillfort, occupying a knoll of Lower Purbeck Limestone overlooking Weymouth Bay which lies to the south. This univallate hillfort encloses an area of approximately 3.3ha at an elevation of around 100-120m. The ramparts largely consist of a single bank with an exterior ditch that is pierced by a single entrance to the south-east. This entrance is a relatively simple affair consisting of a simple gap in the rampart with no discernible outworks or even in-turning of the bank. The gap in the defences further to the south-west is not thought to be original. The interior of the hillfort is littered with scoops and depressions that are almost certainly to be associated with storage pits and hut platforms/scoops. Partial excavation of this hillfort was undertaken in 1939 when trenches were cut into the rampart at two locations and where limited exploration of interior features was attempted. The excavations revealed that the hillfort appears to have been primarily occupied in the Early Iron Age with lesser evidence of activity in both the later Bronze Age and the Romano-British period. Artefacts recovered from the excavations could be considered to be typical of material recovered from contemporary sites elsewhere, consisting of pottery, personal ornaments and evidence for the grinding of grain (quernstone fragment) and spinning (spindle whorl). The site has unfortunately been partially damaged by modern quarrying on its western flanks and it may be possible that a number of the interior depressions and larger scoops may also be 'later' diggings for stone not associated with the original use of the monument.

Location/access

The hillfort is located 1km south east of the village of Bincombe and 1km north of Preston. The hillfort can be approached from a minor road that runs between Preston and Came Wood to the north. Whilst the monument is located on private land good views of its aspect can be made from the South West Coast Path to the north.

NGR 36950838

OS map OS Explorer OL 15

14 Chettle Long Barrow

Type Long barrow

Period Neolithic

Description

A well-preserved long barrow that lies on a south-east/north-west alignment. The mound survives as an earthen bank approximately 60m long, 10m wide and 2.5m high. There is no obvious trace of flanking quarry ditches although they almost certainly survive and have silted up over time. There is no record of archaeological investigation of this monument in recent times or by antiquarians, although it is recorded that part of the barrow was disturbed to make a grotto some time prior to 1767. During this work it is reported that a number of human bones were found, which are now presumably lost. The barrow has been incorporated into the current parish boundary separating Chettle from Tarrant Gunville. The monument is historically linked to the meeting place for the local hundred indicating the location's prominence as a place of significance spanning the millennia.

The lesser known long barrow located at 39501128 is a further excellent example. Alligned east-north-east/west-south-west this barrow is considerably longer (100m long, 10m wide and 2.25m high). It appears that the barrow was 'opened' in antiquity (*c*.1700) where a large number of bones and 'warlike' instruments were found which may suggest that the barrow also contained Saxon inhumations.

Location/access

The site of the barrow is quite accessible to view as it lies on the Jubilee Trail footpath between Chettle House and the village of Tarrant Gunville. The mound lies at an elevation of approximately 115m on an east-facing slope of Main Down, 1km east of Tarrant Gunville.

The barrow at 39501128 which is located in the grounds of Chettle House (400m south of the house) can be approached via a footpath which turns south off the Jubilee Way, west of Chettle village.

NGR 39371135

OS map OS Explorer 118

15 Chilcombe Hill Hillfort

Type Hillfort

Period Iron Age

Description
A bivallate hillfort enclosing 7.5ha of hilltop on Chilcombe hill. The defences consist of a ditch with both inner and outer bank. On the south-east side, the defences are likely to have partially slipped away leaving a ledge rather than an outer bank. The defences are breached in three places (east, north-west and south). Of these the southern appears to be a postern entrance whose origins and purpose is unclear. Both the eastern and north-western entrances have traces of 'passage ways' running into the interior which suggests use contemporary with the hillfort's occupation. There are traces of a round barrow near the north-west entrance.

The site has never been investigated intrusively and there are no obvious traces of occupation within the interior.

Location/access
The site is located midway between the villages of Askerswell and Chilcombe (approximately 1km from both). Although it is on private land it can be approached via a footpath/bridleway just to the north of Chilcombe.
NGR 35300920
OS map OS Explorer 117

16 Clandon Barrow

Type Round barrow

Period Bronze Age

Description
A large bowl barrow located in a very prominent position on the summit of Clandon Hill, which is the western limit of a chalk ridge that also attracted the builders of Maiden Castle 1km to the east. The barrow is approximately 27m in diameter and is over 5m high. It is included in this gazetteer primarily because of its significance and association with the Early Bronze Age Wessex I culture defined by Piggott in 1938 (see chapter 3). Edward Cunnington excavated the Barrow in 1882 and although the human remains of the primary interment were not found (probably never reached rather than implied absence), a cairn containing highly significant gold, bronze, amber and ceramic artefacts which was believed to be associated with a secondary interment was located. The finds are on display in the Dorchester Museum and are amongst the finest collection of grave goods recovered in southern England. The barrow also seems to have attracted later funerary use with Bronze Age cremations and two stone lined graves, probably of Romano-British date.

Location/access

The barrow is located 400m east of Winterbourne St Martin (Martinstown). The barrow is not easily accessible as it lies on private land and is not directly approachable by footpath. However, it is in a prominent position and can be seen very effectively from the bridleway that runs to its north.

NGR 36560890

OS map OS Explorer OL 15

17 Clubmen's Down Cross Dyke

Type Linear boundary (Ranch boundary?)

Period Later Bronze Age/Iron Age

Description

Although the county of Dorset has a large population of boundary dykes, probably the most easily viewed is the one located on Clubmen's Down in the north of the county. The dyke, which consists of a bank with inner and outer ditches, runs for approximately 250m crossing a ridge at the eastern end of Fontmell Down. These features are generally considered to be territorial divisions dividing areas of downland probably associated with animal management. They are thought to originate in the Later Bronze Age but many may have been constructed during the Iron Age.

Location/access

The Cross dyke is located 1km south-east of Compton Abbas and 2km south of Melbury Abbas. The site can be approached by footpath with car parking available at the top of Spread Eagle Hill (38851187).

NGR 38831184

OS map OS Explorer 118

18 Coney's Castle Hillfort

Type Hillfort

Period Iron Age

Description

The westernmost hillfort in Dorset, Coney's Castle occupies the southern end of a north-south ridge of Chert Beds. The natural slopes of the west face of the ridge mostly negate the need for ramparts but a ditch complete with an inner and outer bank bound the eastern and southern extents of the site. The monument has two distinct elements with a small and large enclosure abutting but separated by a ditch with inner and outer ramparts. Almost nothing is known about this monument historically, which has been badly affected by the construction of a road which bisects it (north–south) and a gravel pit at its northern end. The hillfort is likely to have had an entrance to its northern rampart but its form is now impossible to determine as the modern road has badly disturbed this area.

Location/access
The hillfort is easily accessed via the modern road that runs through it. The site is located in the Marshwood Vale approximately 3.5km north west of the village of Whitechurch Canonicorum. The site is owned and managed by the National Trust.
NGR 33720975
OS map OS Explorer 116

19 Culliford Tree Barrow Group

Type Barrow Group

Period Neolithic/Bronze Age

Description
This group of barrows stretching across three parishes (Whitcombe, Winterborne Came and Broadmayne) consists of at least 26 round barrows, a long barrow and a bank barrow. The group takes its name from a large bowl barrow (3699108547), which was excavated in 1858. The remains of this excavation can be seen in disturbance to the top and southern slopes of the barrow, where the lines of a trench can just be made out. This excavation unearthed four extended inhumations, which in all likelihood are secondary interments, the primary burial appears not to have been recovered.

The barrow is associated with the meeting place of the Hundred to which it gave its name. The barrow has a diameter in excess of 30m and is over 4m high. The trees, which cover it, were first planted in 1740. Most of the group is located in open farmland to the east of Came Wood and amidst these is an excellent example of a bank barrow (3702808533) that was originally identified by O.G.S. Crawford in 1938. The barrow lies on the summit of a chalk ridge at an elevation of approximately 150m. It is nearly 200m long and consists of a parallel-sided mound approximately 2m high with rounded termini (although the eastern end has been affected by the construction of the metalled road which just clips it). The quarry ditch for the mound is just visible on its southern flank but its companion to the north is barely discernible. The continuity in the location's importance can be clearly demonstrated with the later construction of round barrows at its western end and northern flank.

A number of barrows at the western end of the complex are contained within the privately-owned Came Wood nearby. Within the eastern part of this wood is a well-preserved example of a pond barrow some 15m in diameter which is bounded by a small bank. The group is a small part of the greater group referred to as the Ridgeway Barrow Group which has 195 listed barrows and forms one of the most extensive concentrations of round barrows in the British Isles.

Location/access
This very interesting group of barrows is located 2.5km west of Broadmayne on a
minor road linking Broadmayne to the A354 Weymouth – Dorchester road. There
are parking places alongside the road opposite Came Wood. Whilst all of the land
is private, many of the barrows can be viewed from the roadside very effectively
or from footpaths.
NGR 36990855
OS map OS Explorer OL 15

20 Deverel Barrow

Type Round barrow

Period Bronze Age

Description
A bowl barrow notable for giving its name to a cultural tradition of Middle –
Late Bronze Age burial, and its associated ceramic urns (Deverel-Rimbury). The
barrow was excavated in 1825 by W.A. Miles with an account published in the
following year. The barrow today shows little outward sign of its original pre-
nineteenth-century excavations. The surviving remains consist of a low mound
and a few stones surrounded by a wall. As one might expect for the nineteenth
century, the report is imprecise upon the objectives, methodology and results of
Miles' findings. Consequently, reconstruction of the original layout and
sequence of the barrow and its contents is considerably speculative, although the
dimensions were recorded as being 54ft in diameter and 12ft high (16.5 by
3.6m). The primary interment is thought to have been a cremation within a
collared urn, which predates the insertion of at least 20 cremations in Deverel-
Rimbury-type urns of bucket, barrel and globular forms. Most of the urns were
buried in pits and covered with stone slabs. The site of the barrow is part of a
small cemetery group on Deverel Down.

Location/access
The site of the barrow is located within a small copse surrounded by a wall, 3km
north-east of Milborne St Andrew. Although located on private land, the site is
closely by-passed by the Jubilee Trail footpath which goes close to the site as it
runs north from the A354 close to Longthorne Wood at 38220988.
NGR 38200990
OS map OS Explorer 117

21 Dorset Cursus

Type Cursus

Period Neolithic

Description
One of the 'jewels in the crown' of all the archaeological sites in Dorset. The Dorset Cursus is the longest known example of its type anywhere. The monument consists of a pair of parallel banks with external ditches, which form an enclosure nearly 10km in length and 100m wide. The monument traverses across Cranborne Chase beginning at Thickthorn Down (39691124) finally ending on Bokerley Down (40411192).

It is widely accepted that the monument was constructed in two principal stages, with the junction occurring on Bottlebush Down (40151157). Several funerary monuments are clearly associated with it, particularly long barrows which can be found both at, or close to, the terminals or within it. The monument whilst enormous in its scope had moderately constructed banks and ditches which has resulted in very little surviving as a visible upstanding monument. Much of the original earthwork has been levelled by centuries of ploughing, although probably the best-preserved section is to be found at its western terminal on Bottlebush Down. Most of the monument has been traced in recent years by recourse to crop or soil marks viewed from the air. Excavations in 1984 revealed ditches which were approximately 80cm in depth.

Location/access
The site is so large that it is crossed by several tracks, roads and paths; accessibility is not so much of a problem, even though all of it is on private land. The upstanding western terminal can be viewed from Thickthorn Down. An impression of the route of the Cursus can be appreciated from the Jubilee Trail at Gussage Down or from the mound of Ackling Dyke on Bottlebush Down where it crosses the B3081.
NGR 39701123 (Thickthorn Down terminal)
OS map OS Explorer 118

22 Dudsbury Hillfort

Type Hillfort

Period Iron Age

Description
Overlooking the River Stour and lying on the Tertiary Beds this hillfort would have held a commanding position overlooking the approaches to its east and west along the river valley. The hillfort's location takes advantage of a cliff, which lies above the river. Originally the ramparts chiefly consisted of a double rampart, however, the south-western flank of the fort lay above the precipitous slope which only required a single line of bank.

The interior of the hillfort has been subject to ploughing and has recently been partially developed as a golf course. Such developments have in part confused the determination of the original entrances to the hillfort, but of the current four entrances (east; north; south-west and west) those to the south-west and west are probably contemporary with the Iron Age occupation.

The site was partially excavated in 1921 by Heywood Sumner but appears to have been largely unproductive.

Location/access
The hillfort is located 4km west of Hurn (Bournemouth) airport alongside the B3073 at West Parley. The site is now a privately-owned golf course but a public footpath does cross it from east to west.
NGR 40770979
OS map OS Explorer OL 22

23   Dungeon Hill Hillfort

Type Hillfort

Period Iron Age

Description
Dungeon Hill earthworks enclose an area of approximately 3.5ha and encircle the summit of the same name. The earthworks consist of a single bank and ditch, oval in plan, with very slight traces of an additional outer bank on the eastern side. This additional bank is thought by some to be part of an all encompassing bank which has since mostly eroded away and is certainly common in a number of Dorset hillforts. The internal rampart survives to a relatively impressive height (over 2m), with an original entrance at the southern end. The interior shows no trace of internal features. The breaches in the eastern and western ramparts are considered to be modern. There are medieval strip-lynchets located on sloping ground on the eastern slopes below the hillfort.

Location/access
Dungeon Hill is located 2km north of Buckland Newton and can be approached by the B3146. The hillfort is under private ownership but a footpath runs along the foot of its eastern ramparts.
NGR 36891074
OS map OS Explorer 117

24   Eggardon henge and Barrow Group

Type Barrow Group

Period Neolithic/Bronze Age

Description

Located a few hundred metres east of Eggardon Hillfort is a relatively undistinguished group of round barrows which is otherwise notable for a monument which seems to sit somewhere between a henge monument and a very large disc barrow. The earthwork consists of a central mound of about 15m in diameter, which is surrounded by a ditch and outer bank that have a collective diameter of about 45m. The central mound has clearly been investigated in antiquity (there is evidence that the top of the mound has been disturbed), but there are no records of its findings. To further complicate matter,s the bank on its south-west side has a round barrow inserted into it, although the Royal Commission account considers the chronological relationship to be potentially the other way around. Slightly to the north of these features are three bowl barrows.

Location/access

The site is located at the junction of four minor roads 400m east of Eggardon Hillfort at 35470945 and 3km north-east of the village of Askerswell in West Dorset. The site is easily viewed from the roadside.

NGR 35460946

OS map OS Explorer OL 15

25 Eggardon Hillfort

Type Hillfort

Period Iron Age

Description

Probably one of the most overlooked of the larger hillforts in Dorset. The hillfort is located on a spur of chalk overlooking the vales to the west and in particular the Bride Valley to the south. The defences consist of three circuits of bank with ditches between them although at various points on the circuit there are variations to this. There is also an outwork to the south-west which seems to have been a later phase of construction, perhaps in response to a land-slip which damaged the ramparts above it, during the monuments occupation. The area enclosed by the hillfort (not including the south-western extension) exceeds 8ha and largely consists of level ground. During its occupancy the hillfort suffered a land slip on its southern side which resulted in a reworking of the defences at this point. Evidence for this landslide can clearly be seen from the interior whereby the internal bank along the whole of the southern middle section has slipped into the ditch below. The hillfort has two entrances to the south-east and the north-west. At both of these entrances there are considerable berms between the outer rampart and the next line of defence. Both entrances also show similar design in that the entrance to the interior through both of them required a diagonal approach, presumably to expose potential attackers to a greater length of defences. Such a design creates a formidable 'killing floor' that might also have doubled up as a temporary stock enclosure. The interior of the hillfort is littered with earthworks not all of which are contemporary with the Iron Age occupation. In addition to earlier round barrows, later field boundaries, and even a rather unique octagonal earthwork (that appears to have functioned as an arboretum and additionally as a navigational aid to coastal mariners), there are a large number of shallow depressions which appear to be storage pits of contemporary date to the hillfort.

The hillfort was evidently constructed over more than one phase, with clear evidence that the inner line of defences was strengthened with the reorganisation of the entrances and building of outworks (south and north-west).

Location/access
Eggardon is located 2.8km south-east of Powerstock and 7.2km east-north-east of Bridport. The southern half of the monument is owned by the National Trust and can be visited at any time. A particularly pleasant approach to the monument can be made via a minor road (considered to be a section of the Roman road running between Dorchester and Exeter), which leaves the A35 just east of Winterbourne Abbas, and runs along the high downs, almost parallel with the modern line of the A35.
NGR 35410948
OS map OS Explorer OL 15

26 Eweleaze Barn barrows

Type Barrow Group

Period Bronze Age

Description
A linear cemetery group in a landscape littered with the funerary remains of Bronze Age inhabitants of the region. This group is notable for the presence of what is almost certainly a quadruple-bell barrow. Multiple round barrows are relatively rare and are usually defined by the presence of an enclosing ditch (originally with a bank). This particular multiple-round barrow has, like so many others, been affected by centuries of agricultural damage, and consequently its uniqueness is not immediately apparent. The additional barrows in the group are a fairly good example of a linear cemetery that extends north-north-west from the multiple barrow. The group is a small part of the greater group referred to as the Ridgeway Barrow Group which has 195 listed barrows and forms one of the most extensive concentrations of round barrows in the British Isles.

Location/access
The Eweleaze Barn group is located on Four Barrow Hill which 1.5km south of Winterborne St Martin (Martinstown). The site which is located upon private land can be viewed from a bridleway which links Higher Ashton Farm (36580877) with the South West Coast Path.
NGR 36500871
OS map OS Explorer OL 15

27 Five Mary's Barrow Group

Type Barrow Group

Period Bronze Age

Description

This barrow group is an excellent example of a linear cemetery that contains three different types of round barrow. The cemetery consists of eight extant barrows that follow the line of the ridge running east-west. In the group are bowl, bell and pond barrows, all of which are damaged. Two of the barrows are likely to have been dug into by the Duchess of Berry before 1866 and with only one possible exception all of the others display similar signs of antiquarian diggings. Hutchins suggests that two barrows within this group had crouched inhumations associated with dear antlers as head adornment, but there is little else to substantiate the find.

Location/access

Five Mary's is located 1.5km west of Winfrith Newburgh and 1km north of Chaldon Herring. There is a footpath which runs alongside the barrows which can be reached from both of these villages.
NGR 37900842
OS map OS Explorer OL 15

28 Flower's Barrow

Type Hillfort

Period Iron Age

Description

Much of this impressive hillfort which is located on the coastal cliffs overlooking Worbarrow Bay has now fallen into the sea, and continuing cliff erosion means that annually more and more of this monument is being lost to the elements. The current remains consist of three sides of a bivallate hillfort with a surviving entrance to the south-east. The inner rampart encloses an area in excess of 2ha but it is impossible to be precise in regard to the area of the original enclosure. Speculatively it is likely to have been approximately twice its current size, but it is possible that the cliff edge always formed a natural defence to the south without any need for additional earthworks.

The ramparts are themselves very impressive with the innermost probably being the earliest. The northern stretch of the inner defences have within them traces of circular platforms which probably represent the site of contemporary round houses.

The only known excavation of this hillfort occurred in 1939 when a pit was excavated approximately 30m inside the entrance. Material recovered included sherds of Middle Iron Age pottery and a few slingstones.

Location/access
The hillfort at Flower's Barrow is located on land which forms part of the military ranges associated with Lulworth camp. The range walks are periodically opened up for public access and one such walk (which coincidentally forms part of the South West Coast Path) crosses the hillfort, entering by the original entrance and exiting to the west. The site can be accessed via the abandoned village of Tyneham where there is ample parking. The hillfort is 2km west of Tyneham.
NGR 38640805
OS map OS Explorer OL 15

29 Giant's Hill Settlement

Type Settlement

Period Iron Age

Description
The site consists of a number of associated earthworks, all of which are relatively well preserved. The site has been speculatively dated to having its origin in the Iron Age, on the basis of the form of its component parts and their analogy with better studied examples elsewhere. The site comprises a series of banks and enclosures that appear to be inter-linked and part of an agricultural settlement. There are traces of what appear to be hut circles and pits in the vicinity of the enclosures and there are traces of 'Celtic' field systems to the north-east. The focal point of the earthworks appears to be an oval enclosure (32m by 42m) which consists of a bank and ditch (much denuded) with traces of huts externally placed around its circumference.

Location/access
The group of earthworks are located 1km north-north-east of the village of Cerne Abbas. The site can be approached via a footpath that runs northwards from the foot of the Cerne Giant chalk hill-figure.
NGR 36691023
OS map OS Explorer 117

30 Grey Mare and Her Colts

Type Megalithic Tomb

Period Neolithic

Description
A megalithic chambered tomb, probably a simple variant of Severn-Cotswold type, which is now in a very ruinous state. The monument consists of a long mound approximately 40m in length and 20m wide. The mound is much disturbed but may have been originally as much as 3m high. The mound is aligned north-west/south-east and the megalthic chamber is located at the south-eastern end. The chamber

appears to consist of a shallow cresentic forecourt demarked by a façade of standing stones which runs on to form a peristalith around the circumference of the mound, although this has never been satisfactorily demonstrated by excavation. In the centre of the forecourt there exists the remains of an exposed single megalithic chamber. The megalithic chamber appears to be constructed from massive sarsens, a hard Tertiary conglomerate that in this area contains flint. Such sarsens are also to be found on other megalithic structures nearby (Hell Stone, Kingston Russell Stone Circle, Hampton Stone Circle and The Nine Stones – see separate entries). The chamber has partially collapsed with the capping stone having fallen into the chamber. The chamber appears to have been opened in the nineteenth century but little information survives as to the findings other than vague references to human bones and pottery.

Location/access
Located on the chalk plateau at an elevation of around 215m, 2km north–north-east of Abbotsbury and 2km west of Portesham, the site can be accessed via a footpath which is signposted from a lane off the Bishops Road between Abbotsbury and Portesham.
NGR 35840871
OS map OS Explorer OL 15

31   Gussage Hill Settlement

Type Settlement

Period Iron Age

Description
The earthworks on Gussage Down (also known as Gussage Cow Down) consist of a palimpsest of features dating to the prehistoric and Roman periods. Amongst the features which variously consist of a number of long barrows, the Dorset Cursus (see separate entry), 'Celtic' fields and linear dykes, is the site of an irregular shaped enclosure referred to as the Gussage Hill Settlement. The settlement consists primarily of a low bank with an external ditch enclosing an area of approximately 6.5ha. On the north-eastern side of the enclosure two further enclosures intrude into the main enclosure, which are circular in form and are approached via a funnelled entrance from the east. Both these enclosures enclose an area of between 0.5–0.75 acre. The smaller enclosures are generally considered to be stock or banjo enclosures with the larger enclosure thought to be chiefly for human settlement. Today only the eastern elements of the main enclosure and southernmost of the circular enclosures can be traced by earthworks, the remainder has been identified with the aid of aerial photography. Extending from the northern and south-eastern ends of the monument are extensive, surviving boundary dykes that are also thought to be related to stock control. To the east of the main enclosure and extending down the eastern slope of Gussage Hill are the extensive remains of field systems that are possibly contemporary with the settlement. Over the years surface pottery has been picked up in the vicinity of these

features which would suggest that the complex is Later Iron Age in origin but which was certainly still in occupation during the Roman occupation.

Location/access
The settlement is located on Gussage Down 2km east-south-east of Gussage St Andrew. The site can be approached via the Jubilee Trail footpath that runs through the earthworks, and is well worth the effort of the walk required to reach it. There is no car parking nearby. It should be noted that the settlement area also enables the viewing of two long barrows at 39951136/39931138 and the course of the Dorset Cursus (the latter long barrow is sited in the middle of the cursus).
NGR 39901140
OS map OS Explorer 118

32 Hambledon Hill Hillfort

Type Hillfort

Period Iron Age

Description
Arguably, this is one of the most visually impressive hillforts in the whole of southern England. The rampart defences enclose a spur of chalk that juts out into the Stour valley. The encircling ramparts consist chiefly of twin banks and ditches with a further counterscarp bank added beyond this. For the most part these defences have been cut into a hillside that already had reasonably steep sides. The builders would have been acutely aware that this technique would provide for immense ramparts for comparatively little effort. Inside the inner bank there is considerable evidence for the quarrying required for its construction in the form of shallow quarrying scoops, a technique quite widely adopted elsewhere. Changes to the alignment of the ramparts would suggest that the hillfort had a complex development and certainly was not constructed under a single design. The hillfort has possibly three principal construction phases evidenced by these changes which suggest that the hillfort expanded southwards on each occasion. The ramparts enclose a total area of more than 12ha, which was serviced by three entrances (north-east, south-west and south-east).

The interior of the hillfort evidences the remains of over 200 hut platforms scarped into the sloping sides of the hill. It remains conjectural of course, how many of these may have been occupied at any one time or indeed, what range of purposes they served. In addition to some early excavations by Edward Cunnington in 1894 further work was undertaken by Roger Mercer in the 1970s (see Hambledon Hill Neolithic Complex).

Location/access
Hambledon Hill is located between the villages of Childe Okeford and Shroton (Iwerne Courtney) and can be directly approached on foot from both villages via well-marked footpaths.

NGR 38451126
OS map OS Explorer 118

33 Hambledon Hill Neolithic Complex

Type Causewayed enclosure

Period Neolithic

Description
In addition to the remarkable Iron Age earthworks located on Hambledon Hill, there are other less well-defined features which herald an extensive period of occupation during the Neolithic period. The focal point of activity during the Neolithic appears to be the causewayed enclosure located to the east of the Iron Age defences. Further earthworks located on the adjacent Shroton and Stepleton spurs have also been attributed to the Neolithic and collectively they form a major complex dating from c.3200 BC. The main enclosure embraces an area of approximately 8ha and consists of a largely eroded bank with an external circuit of interrupted ditches in the traditional causewayed manner.

The site was subjected to a major excavation campaign, which commenced in 1974 and produced a range of interesting results, not least of which was the evidence for the ritual deposition of human skeletal remains in the causewayed ditches. The excavator believed that the activities within the ditches were synonymous with those being carried out on the enclosure interior that may suggest a place of excarnation. The earthworks on the Shroton Spur were included in the 1976 campaign of excavations and evidence emerged of a much more imposing earthwork (which Mercer refers to as a 'fortified barrier') but the ditch contained little evidence for the ritual practices carried out at the main enclosure. The activity on the Stepleton Spur has been dated by reference to the pottery styles unearthed (during the 1977-79 excavations) to be broadly contemporary, perhaps slightly later than the other earthworks. The activity indicates another causewayed enclosure but of a much smaller diameter than the main enclosure on the crown of Hambledon Hill. It is in the Stepleton enclosure that the skeleton of a young adult male was unearthed in 1978 who had a leaf-shaped arrowhead located in his thoracic cavity.

Location/access
Hambledon Hill is located 1km east of Childe Okeford and 1.5km west of Shroton (Iwerne Courtney). The remains of this complex are mainly limited to below ground survival but elements of the main causewayed enclosure can usually be seen from a vantage point on the ramparts of the Iron Age defences in the south-eastern segment, if ground and lighting conditions are right. Footpaths do traverse both the Shroton and Steepleton spurs.
NGR 38491122
OS map OS Explorer 118

34 Hampton Stone Circle

Type Stone Circle

Period Bronze Age

Description

The only example of a stone circle in Dorset to have been excavated in modern times, Hampton is one of a small number of examples in the county. The current positioning of the stones is a reconstruction based upon the results of the 1965 excavation, which showed that the stones were previously incorrectly placed. The original articulation of the stones provided for a circle of approximately 6m diameter which consisted of nine stones forming two arcs which were further conjoined by lengths of ditch. The plan recorded by Piggott in 1939 is now found to be incorrect, it having been derived from a reconstruction of the stones possibly undertaken in the seventeenth century or earlier.

The stones are of sarsen and are similar to those contained within the stone circles at Winterbourne Abbas (The Nine Stones) and Kingston Russell and the chambered tombs Grey Mare and Her Colts and the Hell Stone (see separate entries).

Location/access

The reconstructed remains of Hampton Stone Circle are to be found 1km north-west of Portesham and can be approached via the South West Coast Path as it leaves a minor road north of Portesham at 36010869. The site is located on private land.
NGR 35960865
OS map OS Explorer OL 15

35 Hell Stone

Type Megalithic Tomb

Period Neolithic

Description

The monument that survives today is largely the product of restoration under-taken in 1866 and consequently it is now impossible to reconstruct faithfully the original articulation of its megalithic components. The results of the restoration are almost certainly incorrect. The stones are today contained within a badly destroyed mound which has recently been disturbed by the construction of a dew pond. The mound that survives is a relatively low earthwork (30m long by 14m wide by 1.5m high) that may have once completely covered the stones, in much the same manner as that postulated for the nearby chambered tomb of Grey Mare and Her Colts. There are no records relating to the recovery of funerary remains. It is likely that the monument was similar in design to that suggested for Grey Mare but without more detailed examination by excavation the determination of its likely original form is highly speculative.

Location/access
The monument is located on private land on Portesham Hill 1.5km south-west of the Hardy Monument and 1km north of Portesham. The South West Coast Path passes near to it between Hampton Barn and Blackdown Barn.
NGR 36060867
OS map OS Explorer OL 15

36 Hengistbury Head

Type Hillfort

Period Bronze Age/Iron Age

Description
The site at Hengistbury Head is probably best known as the location of a promontory hillfort defined by two large banks each complete with outer ditches which effectively cut off the end of a peninsula which juts out into the English Channel and creates a natural harbour. It is this factor which clearly attracted the builders of the hillfort. However, earlier inhabitants, as long ago as the Upper Palaeolithic period preceded the Iron Age occupants of the promontory. During the Bronze Age, the site was utilised for funerary purposes with nine recorded examples of round barrows being found within the territory bounded by the later Iron Age defences. One of the barrows contained a rich Wessex type II cremation, which may suggest that the site was part of a trading network linking the continent to Wessex.

The Iron Age defences have a single entrance through the centre and the more massive inner rampart is approximately 3m above the surrounding ground level. Excavations carried out between 1979-84 by Professor Barry Cunliffe in the interior of the defences demonstrated extensive occupation dating from *c.*500BC to the Roman period.

Location/access
Hengistbury Head is located 1.5km south of Christchurch and is well signposted from both Christchurch and Bournemouth. The site is owned by Christchurch Borough Council and access is possible at any time. There are extensive car parks at the site.
NGR 41640910
OS map OS Explorer OL 22

37 Hod Hill Hillfort

Type Hillfort

Period Iron Age

Description
One of the better known hillforts of Dorset, located in the Stour Valley in the
north of the county. The hillfort was partially excavated by Sir Ian Richmond
between 1951-8. The site consists of a multivallate set of ramparts in a rectangular
plan, which encloses approximately 22ha of hilltop/side. The ramparts are made
up of a triple defensive line of bank and ditch to the north and parts of the south
with a double line to the east. The western flanks of the hillfort have a lesser need
of such arrangements as the natural slopes of the hill are at their steepest where
they tumble down into the meandering River Stour which lies at the base of the
hill at this side. However, there are elements of a single rampart to the west but it
may be that these defences were never finished. The excavations by Richmond
demonstrated that the hillfort was constructed in three phases with the massive
inner rampart being the earliest, which remains an impressive earthwork even after
two millennia of erosion. The bank is over 4.5m high with an outer ditch over 6m
deep and 12m wide. The final phase of prehistoric construction would appear to
be in response to the impending threat of Roman invasion when the defences
were hurriedly strengthened. All this appears to have been fruitless as Richmond's
excavation suggests the hillfort was taken with minimal fuss. The north-west
corner of the hillfort had, rather unusually, a Roman fort constructed in it, which
appears to have happened very early in Vespasian's annexation of the region. It is
likely that Hod Hill is one of the twenty hillforts (oppida) referred to by
Suetonious, in his account of Vespasian's campaign in the tribal territory of
the Durotrigans.

Location/access
The monument of Hod Hill is owned by the National Trust and can be accessed
at any reasonable time. Located 5.5km north-west of Blandford Forum the site can
be reached via a turning off the A350 (signposted Childe Okeford) with limited
parking available a kilometre along this road. A (steep) signposted path leads up to
the monument.
NGR 38571106
OS map OS Explorer 118

38 Kingston Russell Stone Circle

Type Stone Circle

Period Bronze Age

Description

One of the few stone circles in the county and certainly the largest surviving example. The site consists of 18 recumbent sarsens (see entry for Grey Mare and Her Colts). The plan of the stones is ovoid, measuring 24m by 28m. Whilst the stones are all recumbent today at least one was recorded by Hutchins as being erect before the middle of the nineteenth century. The site has not been excavated nor has it been extensively studied. On the basis of examples elsewhere in England it is tentatively dated to the Early Bronze Age.

Location/access

The monument is located upon a broad ridge of open downland, and can be reached via a footpath from near to Gorwell Farm (see entry for Grey Mare and Her Colts). It is certainly best viewed when the grass is short, which otherwise masks the stones (if the field is under arable it is similarly best to visit the site after the harvest). Whilst the monument is on private land, access can be gained at any reasonable time.

NGR 35770878

OS map OS Explorer OL 15

39 Knowlton Barrow Groups

Type Barrow Group

Period Neolithic/Bronze Age

Description

Surrounding the henge complex at Knowlton is an extensive array of barrow cemeteries clustered in three distinct groups. Almost all of the barrows have long since been levelled by agricultural activity but their presence has been largely determined through the analysis of aerial photographs taken over many years. Certainly a few of the larger barrows survive as low earthworks but over 95 per cent of them survive predominantly as 'ring ditches' (the encircling quarry ditch from which the original mound material was dug). The cemeteries are referred to as the Southern, Central and Northern groups and collectively contain as many as 180 barrows/ring ditches and possibly many more. Although the great majority of the barrows cannot be seen in the field the site is worth visiting to view the associated monuments in this highly important ritual landscape of the Later Neolithic and Early Bronze Age.

Location/access

The site is located along the B3078 Cranborne to Wimborne road. The site is approached via a minor road (Lumbar Lane) off the B3078 at 40251101. Whilst most of the monuments are on private land a good view of the visible archaeology can be found from the banks of the Church henge, where there is also limited roadside parking.

NGR 40251100

OS map OS Explorer 118

40 Knowlton Circles and The Great Barrow

Type Henge

Period Neolithic

Description

The group of earthworks at Knowlton is located on the periphery of Cranborne Chase and represents an intense period of monument building towards the end of the Neolithic *c.*2600 BC–2200 BC. Our understanding of the major components of this complex is still rather limited with excavations restricted to a small exploratory trench on one of the monuments (Southern Circle) in 1994 by Bournemouth University. The major monuments in the group consist of four enclosures and a large round barrow: the Central or Church Circle – 40241103; The Southern circle – 40251100; The North circle – 40231104, a circular enclosure (The Old Churchyard) 40221103 and The Great Barrow 40251102.

The central and Southern Circles are almost certainly classic henge monuments defined primarily by their tell-tale inner ditch. Little is known of their precise function but they are almost certainly ceremonial. The Northern circle also has an inner ditch with a now levelled outer bank. This may mark it out as another ceremonial henge, however, its ditch and bank appear not to complete a circuit giving the monument a D-shaped plan which marks it out as unique, if indeed it is a henge type structure.

The 'Old churchyard' is the smallest of all the Circles and notably the ditch is external to the bank. It is unclear as to its date or function, but it appears not to be associated with the Norman church located in the Central Circle as the name was probably appended to the earthworks in the eighteenth or nineteenth century, after the church had been abandoned. The Great Barrow which is usually associated with the Knowlton Circles Group of Barrows is mentioned here because of the association of large round mounds often linked with some of Wessex's other major henge monuments, i.e. Avebury - Silbury Hill.

The relative uniqueness of this group lies in the clustering of henge type monuments, which is extremely rare. With the exception of the Central Circle many of the other monuments are now difficult to see. However, traces of the henge bank of the Southern Circle can still be seen in the fields to the east of the B3078 close to new Barn Farm. The 'Old churchyard' can be seen as a slight mound in the field to the north-east of the Central circle. The North Circle is marked by a small cluster of trees (mainly yews) to the north–north–west of the Central circle. The Great barrow is largely undamaged but the mound is covered in trees and dense undergrowth to the east of the Central Circle.

Location/access

The site is located along the B3078 Cranborne to Wimborne road. It is approached via a minor road (Lumbar Lane) off the B3078 at 40251101. Whilst most of the monuments are on private land a good view of the visible archaeology can be made from the banks of the Church henge, where there is also limited roadside parking.
NGR 40251100
OS map OS Explorer 118

41 Lambert's Castle

Type Hillfort

Period Iron Age

Description

The earthworks at Lambert's Castle comprise a single bank and ditch which enclose the northern end of a greensand spur that overlooks the Marshwood Vale in the eastern extreme of the county. Very little is known about this site, although the uprooting of trees in a storm of 1990 allowed for the only recorded archaeological inspection of the ramparts themselves. Observations at this time suggest that the hillfort's defences were initially constructed as box ramparts, which are normally associated with the earlier Iron Age. There also appeared to be evidence of re-facing of this rampart with a stone-built wall that consisted of faced chert boulders. The ramparts enclose an area of approximately 1.5ha.

Location/access

The site of Lambert's Castle is located 1km south-west of Marshwood and can be reached via the B3165. The site is owned and managed by the National Trust and access is generally available. The Wessex Way footpath runs through the middle of the site and there is parking nearby.
NGR 33710990
OS map OS Explorer 129

42 Lewesdon Hillfort

Type Hillfort?

Period Iron Age?

Description

Slight traces of earthworks located on Lewesdon Hill are the potential remains of a fortified hill which benefits from naturally steep, scarped slopes. The platform at the summit of the hill is approximately 1ha in extent. There are traces of a berm or possibly a silted-up ditch located on the less precipitous northern slopes of the hill and there are similar traces at the southern and western ends of the site. Much of the hill has been subjected gravel extraction and the fact that the hill is covered in dense woodland makes further interpretation extremely speculative.

Location/access

The site is located in dense woodland 1km south of the village of Broadwindsor in the extreme west of the county. It is owned and managed by the National Trust and access is possible at any time.
NGR 34361012
OS map OS Explorer 116

43 Long Bredy Cursus

Type Cursus

Period Neolithic

Description
One of only three or four currently identified cursus monuments located in the
county. The cursus at Long Bredy can only be seen through the benefit of aerial
photography when the ground conditions are correct. The cursus is located close
to the bank barrow on Martin's Down with which it is probably contemporary.
There are no traces of the monument visible at ground level. A second cursus just
to the north, recently observed from the air, suggests that this part of the Neolithic
landscape was of some significance.

Location/access
The cursus is located 100m north-east of the bank barrow on Martin's Down (see
separate entry).
NGR 35790912
OS map OS Explorer OL 15

44 Maiden Castle Hillfort

Type Hillfort

Period Neolithic/Iron Age

Description
Almost certainly the most widely known archaeological monument in Dorset,
Maiden Castle is a major feat of Iron Age construction. However, its location as a
place of human activity begins in a much earlier period when society was
beginning to undertake large monumental constructions. During the excavations
undertaken by Sir Mortimer Wheeler in 1934-8, underneath the first phase of the
Iron Age defensive circuit, he found elements of two concentric lines of causewayed ditches. The banks usually associated with such structures were not found
by Wheeler's excavation team, having been destroyed probably by the later Iron
Age workings of the first hillfort. Pottery found during the excavations is of a type
referred to as Windmill Hill ware and is associated with the Early Neolithic period
dating to before 3000 BC. Later excavations undertaken by Neil Sharples in
1985-6 produced radiocarbon determinations which suggest that the initial phase
of construction may have been as early as 3800 BC.

Following the abandonment of the causewayed enclosure, a long mound was
constructed several decades later whose purpose remains unclear. This long mound
was constructed over the top of the earlier enclosure and consisted of a linear bank
over 540m long and 18m wide, flanked by quarry ditches. The mound is very
difficult to trace today as it has been levelled over the centuries. Although no burials

have been located from within the mound, the skeletons of two children were found by Wheeler at its eastern end that were dated to the Neolithic period.

After an extensive period whereby the site was unoccupied, the site was then chosen as the place to construct a defensive enclosure in the Iron Age. The Iron Age activity at Maiden Castle is very complex if only because with few exceptions it is one of the most intensively studied monuments of its type in north-western Europe. However construction and occupation of the hillfort can be simplified into three main periods:

Period 1 – Construction of the initial hillfort comprising the enclosure on the eastern hill with a single rampart (*c*.600 BC).

Period 2 – Construction of an extended hillfort now enclosing both the eastern and western hills including the construction of two additional ramparts to the south and a one to the north. At this time the entrances, which are essentially those that survive today, were largely developed (*c*.400–350 BC).

Period 3 – Gradual breakdown of organisation within the hillfort, reduction of attention paid to the defences. Increased use of the hillfort for agricultural purposes. Some evidence for refurbishment of ramparts towards the end of this period (*c*. 300 BC– AD 50).

The defences in total enclose an area of 17.2ha.

Location/access

Maiden Castle is easily approached by road being signposted off the A354 (Weymouth Road) 1km south of Dorchester town centre. The access road runs through a modern estate and ends in a gravelled car park at the foot of the northern slopes of the hill on which the hillfort is located. Access to the monument is available at any time.

NGR 36690884

OS map OS Explorer OL 15

45 Martin's Down Bank Barrow

Type Bank barrow

Period Neolithic

Description

Bank barrows appear to be a highly localised variant of the long barrow tradition. There are three, possibly four examples in Dorset with that on Martin's Down being an excellent example of the type. With the exception of that found within the ramparts of Maiden Castle none of these monuments has been excavated archaeologically. Martin's Down bank barrow, like its contemporaries, consists of an exceptionally long parallel-sided bank with flanking quarry ditches. The Martin's Down example is 197m long, 13m wide and approximately 1.75m high. The barrow shows signs of having been damaged in antiquity – with a gap cut through it three quarters along its length towards its north-eastern end.

Location/access
The monument can be approached via a footpath that leaves the A35 at the junction with a minor road that is signposted to Long Bredy (35700914).
NGR 35710911
OS map OS Explorer OL 15

46   Maumbury Rings

Type Henge

Period Neolithic

Description
Until the excavation of this monument between 1908-13 by Harold St George-Gray this embanked enclosure was understood to be a surviving example of a Roman amphitheatre, which of course it was, but there was considerable speculation concerning its possible earlier origins. The excavations, however, clearly demonstrated that its origin was much older, having been originally constructed in the Later Neolithic as a henge monument. The henge has been significantly remodelled by both the Roman reworking of the monument and much later on when it was utilised by Cromwell's Parliamentary forces for the defence of Dorchester.

The surviving earthworks that are now enclosed within a small park defined by a police station, a railway line and a road are still, however, quite impressive. The Neolithic monument consisted of a bank that was originally 3m in height. Inside the bank there is a suggestion of a ditch but this had been severely truncated by the construction of the floor of the Roman amphitheatre. During the excavations a series of 18 shafts cut into the base of the ditch were discovered; it is likely that these shafts continued in a circle with a diameter of 52m, on the inside of the henge bank. What is quite spectacular about these shafts is that they were excavated to an average depth of 10m below the contemporary ground surface.

Location/access
The monument is located on the A354 (Weymouth Road) close to Dorchester South Railway Station. There are large car parks on the opposite side of the road and the earthworks can be visited at any time.
NGR 36900899
OS map OS Explorer OL 15

47   Mistleberry Hillfort

Type Hillfort

Period Iron Age

Description

Located on the Dorset-Wiltshire boundary this earthwork appears to be an unfinished example of a small univallate hillfort. It occupies the southern slope of a spur overlooking Handley Common on Cranborne Chase. The earthworks are now all contained within Mistleberry Wood. They consist of a bank, which nowhere survives much above a height of 1.25m, with an external ditch. The plan of the enclosure appears to be oval but as at least a third of the western circuit was never completed, it is only possible to estimate the enclosed area, which is a little under 1ha.

Location/access

The earthworks are located 2km north of the village of Sixpenny Handley. The site can be glimpsed through the trees via a footpath which follows the county boundary and leaves a minor road at Pribdean Wood where there is limited parking available at 40041195.

NGR 39961195

OS map OS Explorer 118

48 Mount Pleasant Henge and Conquer Barrow

Type Henge

Period Neolithic

Description

Mount Pleasant was partially excavated in 1970-1 by Geoffrey Wainwright. The banks of this monument have been seriously eroded by agricultural activity but enough survives to determine an enclosure which bounded 5ha and which contained an inner ditch. This marks out the monument as a henge monument dating to the later part of the Neolithic period. The original enclosure had four entrances and contained within the enclosure was a timber-built structure, circular in plan, consisting of five concentric circles of post-holes. The structure is not unlike others discovered at Woodhenge and Durrington Walls in Wiltshire and all of these examples are difficult to interpret. The excavator considered the structure to have been roofed and to have been used for communal purposes. The timber structure was later replaced by a setting of stones and pits and the enclosure itself was superseded by a huge timber palisade that followed the line of the henge on the inside of ditch. This second phase of major activity is thought to correspond with Beaker use of the site. Conquer barrow is a large round mound constructed over the henge bank in the western circuit of the enclosure. Like the henge, the barrow has suffered through the effects of agricultural damage.

Location/access

The site of both these monuments is located on the extreme eastern edge of the Dorchester conurbation at Max Gate. There is little of the earthworks to see that survive above ground. The site is on private ground.

NGR 37100899

OS map OS Explorer OL 15

49 Nettlecombe Tout Hillfort

Type Hillfort

Period Iron Age

Description

A very poorly understood earthwork which is located on a broad, relatively level spur on the edge of the Blackmore Vale. It is unclear whether the hillfort is unfinished or whether it has been partially destroyed. The earthworks consist of a 320m line of bank with an external ditch which turns at its north-western end and rapidly peters out. At the south-western end of the rampart there appears to be the remains of an entranceway with a suggestion of a protective outwork. The earthworks were constructed where there is little natural slope, but where there are gaps, defences may have been unnecessary due to the natural steepness of parts of the hill.

Location/access

The site is located 3km south of the village of Mappowder and 2.5km north-west of Plush. The earthworks can be viewed from the nearby Wessex Ridgeway footpath that runs 200m to its south.
NGR 37371032
OS map OS Explorer 117

50 Nine Barrow Down (Ailwood Barrow Group)

Type Barrow Group

Period Neolithic/Bronze Age

Description

An impressive linear barrow group consisting of 18 barrows in all (1 long barrow, 17 bowl barrows). As seen in other barrow groups around the county the association and continuity in funereal landscapes over time is demonstrated here with the locale being adopted by Neolithic and Bronze Age occupants of the area. All of the barrows are strung out along the chalk ridge although the long barrow and some of the round barrows are found slightly off the crest of the ridge lying on the southern slope. The long barrow has parallel sides and there are slight traces of its original flanking ditches to be seen around the mound's perimeter. Several of the barrows show signs of disturbance with at least one having been dug by W.A. Miles in the early nineteenth century.

Location/access

This barrow group is located on the chalk ridge which extends between East Hill (39610824) and Godlingston Hill (40180812). A footpath extends along the ridge and can be accessed at various points. The nearest access point to the barrows however is that from a footpath that leaves the viewing point on the B3351 at

40070818, and ascends the Ridgeway northwards over Kingswood Down and Nine Barrow Down.

NGR 39950816

OS map OS Explorer OL 15

51 Nine Stones Stone Circle

Type Stone Circle

Period Bronze Age

Description

This unusually sited and small stone circle consists of nine sarsen stones of a local sarsen conglomorate arranged in a circle with a diameter of approximately 8m. All the stones are set into the ground and appear to be upright. The stones vary in height but most are between 0.50m-0.75m. Two of the stones are considerably taller than the others, measuring 2m and 2.2m. The current articulation of the stones may not be entirely original, although Hutchins account of the stones in 1876 essentially mirrors the modern description quoted above. Warne's account of the stones in 1872 suggests the presence of a tenth stone but a drawing by Stukely dated 1723 only shows nine stones. The site has not been excavated but is probably attributable to the Early Bronze Age period *c*.2000-1700 BC.

Location/access

The Nine Stones is located beside the busy A 35, 750m west of the village of Winterbourne Abbas in west Dorset. It lies within a wooded area beside the South Winterbourne stream. It can be visited at any time.

NGR 36100904

OS map OS Explorer OL 15

52   North Poorton Hillfort

Type Hillfort

Period Iron Age

Description

A small univallate hillfort that encloses approximately 0.5ha of the end of a chalk ridge. The defences consist of artificially created scarps which accentuate the general steep hill-side slopes at the north, south and west sides. There is a transverse ditch cut across the narrow neck of ridge to the east. The enclosure is a rounded triangle in plan.

Location/access

The hillfort, which is on private land is ringed by footpaths with the Jubilee Trail running across the ridge to the monument's east. The site lies 1km south-east of the village of Mapperton and 1km north-west of North Poorton.

NGR 35110988
OS map OS Explorer 117

53 Oakley Down Barrow Group

Type Barrow Group

Period Neolithic/Bronze Age

Description
One of the better preserved of the Dorset barrow cemeteries, Oakley Down Barrow group is located in the extreme north-east of the county on Cranborne Chase. The barrow group consists of at least 31 barrows comprising of a range of round barrow forms including bowl, bell, saucer and disc. The siting of the cemetery group is close to a Neolithic Long Barrow (Wor Barrow) which might have influenced its location. The number of the barrows were investigated by Sir Richard Colt-Hoare and William Cunnington in the early part of the nineteenth century, and many of the barrows carry the excavation scars of these intrusions at their centres. The recording of the excavations was sufficiently well done that Colt-Hoare created a numbered plan which was cross-indexed with details of the findings made during the excavation. The finds made in this group are amongst the 'richest' anywhere in Wessex and constitute a funerary complex which would have been in use for a period of about 300–400 years in the Early Bronze Age. Many of the artefacts found in this group are now to be found in Devizes Museum in Wiltshire.

Location/access
This barrow group is located 2km south-east of the village of Sixpenny Handley, immediately north of the junction of the A354 and the B3081. The majority of the cemetery can be found within a triangle of pasture formed by the A354, B3081 and the Roman road (Ackling Dyke). The barrows are best viewed collectively from an elevated position, which is possible from a point on Ackling Dyke (40161163), where there is also limited off road parking. The barrows can be approached on foot from this point via the path that runs north along Ackling Dyke.
NGR 40181173
OS map OS Explorer 118

54 Penbury Knoll Hillfort

Type Hillfort

Period Iron Age

Description
The earthworks at Penbury Knoll probably represent a small unfinished univallate hillfort located at the north-eastern extremities of the county. The interior of the hillfort is bounded by a bank to the north and west (which rises approximately 2m

above the interior ground surface) with scarping occurring throughout its southern extent. Much of the area has been affected by quarrying, presumably for the capping of gravel that lies on top of the chalk ridge at this point. Some of the quarry pits that are to be found to the rear of the northern rampart are possibly contemporary with the rampart's construction. There is no evidence for the construction of an external ditch at any point in the monument's defensive circuit. There is little clear indication where the entrance to the fort would have been, if indeed it ever had one, as in all likelihood the construction was never completed. The hillfort occupies a dominant position at the head of the River Crane, over-looking large parts of Cranborne Chase to the west.

Location/access
The earthworks are located 1km south-east of the village of Pentridge from where the site can be accessed via footpaths.
NGR 40401171
OS map OS Explorer 118

55 Pilsdon Pen Hillfort

Type Hillfort

Period Iron Age

Description
Located on the highest point of Dorset this hillfort occupies the end of a spur with steep natural slopes on every aspect but that of the north-west. The hillfort has a 'flattened' oval plan and encloses an area of approximately 3ha. The defences are relatively uniform throughout, consisting of twin sets of bank and ditch with a final outer conterscarp bank. At the north-west end there is a platform between the first and second ramparts. As is common with a number of hillforts the inner rampart can hardly be traced from the interior. Of the four observable entrances through the earthworks today, three are probably original (those at the south-east; south-west and the north) and all are relatively simple affairs with no additional outworks. It should be noted however, that the case for a south-eastern entrance may be exaggerated by occurrence of land slip.

On the inside of the enclosure are a number of features, which were substantially investigated by Peter Gelling between 1964-71. A number of post and gulley, or slot type round houses were identified, but also rather contentiously, a rectilinear feature defined by gulleys and interpreted by Gelling as a large Iron Age timber rectilinear structure, now generally considered to be much more recent in date.

Location/access
Pilsdon Pen hillfort is located 3km south-west of Broadwindsor and can be approached via footpath from the B3164 at 34141009. The site is owned and managed by the National Trust with access at all times.
NGR 34131013
OS map OS Explorer 116

56 Pimperne Long Barrow

Type Long barrow

Period Neolithic

Description
One of the best examples of a long barrow in Dorset and certainly one of the largest and better preserved. The mound which is orientated south-east/north-west survives as a parallel-sided earthen mound, 110m long, 28m wide and 2.75m high. It lies on the parish boundary between Tarrant Hinton and Pimperne, a not unusual occurrence where ancient monuments frequently were incorporated into territorial land divisions. Traces of the associated quarry ditches can still be faintly traced flanking the mound but they do not appear to enclose its ends. Common with other parallel-sided variants in the long barrow tradition there is no discernible 'high end' which would usually indicate the functional part of the mound in the more common wedge or trapezoidal forms. There are no records of it having been excavated but on typological grounds it is thought to date to the earlier Neolithic period *c*.3000 BC.

Location/access
The barrow can be accessed via a footpath which leads off the A354 Blandford-Salisbury Road, opposite the access road to Blandford Army camp at 39181102.
NGR 39171105
OS map OS Explorer 118

57 Pins Knoll Settlement

Type Settlement

Period Iron Age

Description
Pins Knoll is located on a chalk spur which overlooks the Bride Valley and has been identified as a settlement site consisting of a number of huts which probably formed an agricultural farmstead dating to the Iron Age. In addition to the huts, excavation has revealed a number of storage pits, one of which contained traces of carbonised grain, a corn-dryer and a range of artefacts including loom weights and sling stones.

Location/access
The site is located 1km west of the village of Litton Cheney on the lower southern slopes of Hodders Hill. There are no visible earthworks at the site which is on private land.
NGR 35410905
OS map OS Explorer OL 15

58 Poor Lot Barrow Group

Type Barrow Group

Period Neolithic/Bronze Age

Description

Alongside Oakley Down barrow Group (see separate entry) Poor Lot Barrow Group near Winterbourne Abbas is the most impressive collection of surviving barrows in Dorset. As with Oakley Down there is also a suggestion of continuity in the use of the landscape in prehistory, as this predominantly Early Bronze Age cemetery has a geographical association with long barrows, in this case two examples.

The Bronze Age components of the cemetery consist of at least 44 barrows comprising 7 bell types, 1 double-bowl, 6 disc, 4 pond, 2 bell-disc, 2 triple-bowls and 22 bowls.

The cemetery is located near the head of the South Winterbourne Valley along its southern flanks on Black Down. The cemetery group is notable for the inclusion of some of the so-called 'fancy barrows' which are variants in the normal form and can be often associated with southern Dorset. Four of the disc barrows can be included within these variants which have a small ditch close to the central mound and also have conspicuously smaller overall diameters than the usual Wessex type. Of all the barrows in this group the only ones to have been excavated in recent times appear to be two of the pond barrows which were investigated by Richard Atkinson in 1952 and again in 1953. Both excavations appear to have revealed little and have never been fully published but do suggest that in both cases the barrows represent features associated with ritual and the burial rite, although they did not appear to contain burials themselves. Little dating evidence is available for this group but it presumably must lie in the period 2000 BC – 1500 BC for the round barrows.

Location/access

The site is located alongside the busy A35, 3km west of the village of Winterbourne Abbas (1km south-east of Kingston Russell). The site can be approached and crossed via a footpath which runs south-east of the A35 at 35900908. The barrows are located however on private land.
NGR 35890907
OS map OS Explorer OL 15

59 Poundbury Hillfort

Type Hillfort

Period Iron Age

Description

The hillfort of Poundbury has for a long time been dominated by its larger and arguably contemporary companion, Maiden Castle. Located on the upper chalk at an elevation of around 100m, with the River Frome meandering at its northern feet, Poundbury is by any standards an impressive hillfort. Enclosing an area in excess of 5ha, the twin sets of bank (excepting the northern flank) and ditches form a trapezoidal plan. The inner bank is relatively well-preserved although the outer defences do appear to be much denuded and badly damaged. The only original entrance appears to be that located in the centre of the eastern line of defences adjacent to modern Dorchester, and comprised of a simple gap in the defensive curtain that now lies over the 1855 railway tunnel excavated under the hillfort.

The hillfort has undergone two phases of significant archaeological investigation with excavations in 1938 and again in 1971. The excavations of 1938 took place on the western line of defences and enabled the excavator to determine that the ramparts represented two phases of construction. The inner bank was constructed first and consisted of a timber-faced palisade where the earth was likely to have been partially derived from internal quarries. This bank was later enlarged by dump construction. The external bank and ditch was a later development being constructed of a simple dump construction. Dating of the initial rampart construction is not altogether clear but is likely to be around the sixth century BC, with the major remodelling of the inner bank and building of the outer bank probably taking place in the first century AD. The 1971 excavations took place outside the hillfort to the north east of the eastern entrance at the site of an extensive Roman cemetery.

Location/access
The site is located on the north-western perimeter of modern Dorchester and is approached via a minor road at the junction of the town's Military Museum (signposted to Bradford Peverell).

NGR 36830912

OS map OS Explorer OL 15

60 Povington Heath Barrows

Type Barrow Group

Period Bronze Age

Description
At least 24 barrows are located within the confines of Povington Heath which are all contained within the army ranges used for artillery training in the Purbeck Hills. Most of them have been used for target practice in the past and have suffered accordingly.

Location/access
The barrows are spread around Povington Heath, which is located to the north of the Purbeck Hills, 2km north of the abandoned village of Tyneham and 2km east of East Lulworth. The barrows are all located within Army ranges and access can be restricted.

NGR 38760840

OS map OS Explorer OL 15

61 Rawlsbury Camp Hillfort

Type Hillfort

Period Iron Age

Description
A very prominently located hillfort, Rawlsbury is oval in plan whose defences enclose an area of over 2ha. The defences consist of two banks each with an external ditch. The inner and outer defences are separated at the northern and southern extremities by a wide berm. It is likely that the two ramparts represent two distinct phases of construction although it remains unclear which ramparts represent the earlier phase. The entrance to the hillfort is located on its eastern side where easy access to the hillfort would have been undertaken along the spur. The entrance consists of a simple gap in the inner ring of rampart with an outwork created by the outer rampart of the northern circuit. However, the full complexity of the entrance is marred by disturbance to the earthworks at this point and it is unclear as to the articulation of the southern ramparts. The ramparts elsewhere survive reasonably intact with the inner rampart rising to a height of 1.75m above the inner ground level and the outer bank survives to a similar extent above the intervening berm on the northern side. The ditches, however, are extremely variable in their depth throughout their circuit, which is mostly attributable to silting and to some extent damage from later workings.

Location/access
Rawlesbury is located 3km south-west of the village of Ibberton on a spur of Bulbarrow Hill. The hillfort is easily accessed via footpaths. The Wessex Ridgeway footpath runs through the hillfort traversing along its southern ramparts. Parking is possible on Bulbarrow Hill.
NGR 37671057
OS map OS Explorer 117

62 Rempstone Stone Circle

Type Stone Circle

Period Bronze Age

Description
Both the monument and the site which it inhabits has been much disturbed, which makes the description and evaluation of this site very difficult. The site survives as eight (only five of which are erect) irregularly shaped gritstone boulders positioned in an arc on a west-facing slope close to the foot of Nine Barrow down. The monument now lies within a wood that seems to have been disturbed by late eighteenth–century clay workings, which have destroyed the southern third of the monument. The original diameter of the stone circle would have been in the region of 26m making it the second largest stone circle in the county. There is a

suggestion that the site may have had an associated avenue or processional way of stones leading to/from it, when in 1957 J. Calkin noted the presence of a short section of parallel stones (3m apart) nearly a kilometre to the west of the circle. The stones used in the construction of the circle are almost certainly from the local Bagshot Beds. The site probably dates to the Early Bronze Age *c.*2000 BC.

Location/access
The site is located within woods beside the B3351, 4km east of Corfe castle and 5km west of Studland. The monument is on private land.
NGR 39940821
OS map OS Explorer OL 15

63 Ridge Hill Barrow Group

Type Barrow Group

Period Bronze Age

Description
The Ridge Hill group of barrows consists of at least 38 barrows stretched along the South Dorset Ridgeway between a disc-bell barrow close to Gould's Bottom (36630866) in the east and a bell barrow (36380868) in the west. The Ridge Hill group is part of an extensive linear cemetery which has the Bronkham Hill Group to the west. Many of the barrows in this group appear not to have been disturbed although at least six of them were opened by William Cunnington between 1884–1888. The now very much denuded barrow at 3657408662 contained one of the richest Bronze Age burial deposits in
Wessex with an inhumation that also contained extensive grave goods including a flint mace head and a three riveted bronze dagger. Secondary deposits included a cremation with three grooved and riveted daggers, gold mountings for a dagger pommel and a small flanged copper axe. All of the barrows in the group are round types and probably date to *c.*2000–1500 BC. The group also lies in close proximity to the Eweleaze Barn Group (see separate entry). The group is a small part of the greater group referred to as the Ridgeway Barrow Group which has 195 listed barrows and forms one of the most extensive concentrations of round barrows in the British Isles.

Location/access
The centre of this group lies 2km south of Winterbourne St Martin (Martinstown), and all the barrows can be accessed via the South West Coast Path that runs alongside them.
NGR 36640866
OS map OS Explorer OL 15

64 Ringmoor Settlement and Field System

Type Settlement

Period Iron Age

Description

The earthworks at Ringmoor lie on Turnworth Down above the village of Turnworth in North Dorset. The earthwork features present on the site consist of a number of enclosures associated with roads and fields that are likely to be Iron Age in origin. The current focus of the earthworks appears to be an oval enclosure measuring approximately 48m by 36m defined by a bank and ditch with an entrance on its eastern arc. The enclosing bank survives as a relatively diminutive earthwork, being no more than 0.75m in height with a footprint of approximately 3m. The ditch, which lies on the outside of the bank, has largely silted up but can be traced throughout its entire circuit. On the northern arc of the enclosure there are slight traces of an outer bank but it is unclear as to whether or not this feature was entirely concentric with the other earthworks.

The entrance is embellished with an outwork which extends from its south side in an arc northwards. There are traces of disturbance on the interior of the enclosure but it is unclear as to whether or not this is contemporary with the original use of the enclosure or its initial abandonment. Approximately 400m west (and up-slope) of this enclosure lie the remains of what is likely to have been a second enclosure. An arc of bank and ditch survives to a length of approximately 80m but the remainder of the area was destroyed in the construction of Ringmoor Cottage, which is now itself ruined. A third enclosure located 200m south of the oval enclosure has been identified via the use of aerial photography. This enclosure is slighter larger than its neighbour to the north, having a diameter of approximately 65m. Associated with all these enclosures and linking them all is an embanked track or road system that is approximately 3-5m wide. Surrounding both the enclosures and the trackways is an extensive field system that appears to entirely contemporary with them. Although the site has never been subjected to intrusive investigation the form of the earthworks are entirely consistent with enclosed farmstead units of the Iron Age/Romano British periods.

Location/access

The site is located 1km north-east of the village of Turnworth and is approached via a minor road which links the villages of Winterbourne Whitechurch with that of Okeford Fitzpaine. The earthworks are owned by the National Trust and can be visited at anytime. They can be approached via The Wessex Ridgeway path from the direction of the car park at Okeford Hill (38131094).
NGR 38091085
OS map OS Explorer 117

65 Seven Barrow Plantation barrow Group

Type Barrow Group

Period Neolithic/Bronze Age

Description
This small cluster of barrows consists of twelve barrows contained within a small plantation (known as Seven Barrow Plantation). Within a collection of round barrows is a long barrow approximately 70m long and 15m wide. The barrows are in various states of preservation and at least one or two of them have been excavated in antiquity.

Location/access
The barrows are located on the south-west slope of Penn Hill, 1km south-west of the village of Bradford Peverell. A footpath runs through the plantation.
NGR 36470924
OS map OS Explorer OL 15

66 Shearplace Hill

Type Settlement

Period Later Bronze Age

Description
One of very few settlement sites in the county which are securely dated to the Later Bronze Age. Excavated in 1961 by Philip Rahtz, the remains on Shearplace Hill consists of a number of enclosures which are integrated with trackways which in turn are associated with relict field boundaries. The main enclosure consists of a rectangular area bounded by a bank with an exterior ditch. The entrance into this enclosure was facilitated by a gap in the boundary in the south-west corner which probably served as the original entrance. Within this enclosure lay the remains of two post-built round houses. The activity undertaken within the enclosure and the evidence of the surrounding features are entirely consistent with a small farmstead. Shearplace Hill was one of the first sites to benefit from the application of radiocarbon dating in the county with a subsequent determination being drawn from amalgamated samples with a date range of 1360–1000 BC.

Location/access
The site is located 1km south-south-east of Sydling St Nicholas. Although the site has been subjected to the rigours of a excavation there are still topographical remains on the site, however, the remains are best viewed in relation to the wider landscape. The site can be approached via footpaths from Sydling St Nicholas which in part trace the route of one of the tracks associated with the settlement.
NGR 36400985
OS map OS Explorer 117

67 Shipton Hill Hillfort

Type Hillfort?

Period Iron Age

Description
Can only be seen as a hillfort within the broadest definition of the term. Certainly the top of this Greensand topped hill has been partially and artificially strength-ened as a defensive settlement with the introduction of steepened slopes to the north and south. Lower down the northern and southern slopes there are the remains of a bank and ditch but as with the upper slopes, such earthworks have not been extended around the ends. The site was examined in the 1950s when early Iron Age pottery was discovered and also a hoard of over 1,000 sling stones which lends support to its interpretation as a hillfort.

Location/access
Shipton Hill is located 1km north-west of the village of Shipton Gorge. The site can be accessed via footpath from Loders Lane at 35030923.
NGR 35080921
OS map OS Explorer OL 15

68 Spetisbury Rings

Type Hillfort

Period Iron Age

Description
Otherwise known as Crawford Castle, Spetisbury Rings is a hillfort of univallate construction sited no doubt by its builders to dominate the valley of the River Stour which it overlooks to the north-east and south-west. The remains of the hillforts defences are fairly well preserved although the construction of a railway cutting in 1857 destroyed part of the single rampart and ditch on its eastern circuit. The rampart appears to be unfinished in areas particularly to the west where the rampart joins the only entranceway and also on the southern extent where the rampart is truncated by the railway cutting. The most visually impressive section of the rampart is in its southern angle where it reaches a height of 8m above the ditch bottom (5m above the interior).

The entrance to the hillfort is located at its north-western corner and is a rela-tively simple gap with slightly everted ends to the banks. Just outside this entrance are the clear remains of a short stretch of bank which appear to be the remains of an outwork, probably a hornwork which extends from the northern bank. It is not entirely clear as to whether this hornwork was ever completed or if it has suffered from erosion since its initial construction. The interior of the hillfort has been ploughed and there are no traces of features surviving.

The excavation of the railway revealed a mass grave of approximately 120 individuals recovered in both 1857 and 1858, but the precise circumstances went largely unrecorded. At least two of the skeletons exhibited injuries that indicated that they had come to a violent end. Artefacts recovered at the time included iron spear heads, which have led to interpretations that the deposit is a war cemetery associated with the initial Roman conquest of the area. However, this remains unproved although the unfinished nature of the defences would certainly suggest a hurriedly built hillfort, possibly a response to a large scale threat which is likely to be contemporary with Vespasian's march through the area.

Location/access
The site is located adjacent to the A350 Blandford – Poole road in the village of Spetisbury, 250m from the junction of the A350 and the B3075. The earthworks are situated on private land but can be visited by footpath. The footpath can be joined at its junction with the B3075 at 39171018.
NGR 39151020
OS map OS Explorer 118

69 Sturminster Newton Hillfort

Type Hillfort

Period Iron Age

Description
Within a much disturbed area on top of a steep-sided triangular spur of Corallian Limestone lie the fragmentary remains of what was almost certainly an Iron Age hillfort. The sites early origins are masked by structural elements of a tenth to fourteenth-century manor house complex that survived intact until the Dissolution. The likely prehistoric remains appear to be mainly in the south-west where a bank and ditch effectively cut off the remainder of the promontory which extends to the north-east. The bank survives to a height of approximately 3-4.5m with its outer ditch surviving to a depth of 6.5m. The position of the hillfort, is like that of Spetisbury to the south, located directly above the River Stour (see separate entry).

Location/access
The hillfort is located 1km south-south-west of the town of Sturminster Newton, on the southern side of the River Stour adjacent to the impressive medieval bridge. The ramparts at the western end of the hillfort can be seen via footpath which leaves the A357 at 37841135. The remains are located on private land.
NGR 37841134
OS map OS Explorer 129

70 Tenant's Hill Settlement and Field System

Type Settlement

Period Iron Age

Description
Located on small spur of Tenant's Hill to the north of Kingston Russell Stone Circle (see separate entry) lie the remains of a modest irregularly shaped earthwork which has the characteristics of an Iron Age defended farmstead. The earthworks consist of a low bank (approximately 1m high) which has an accompanying external ditch that is mostly silted up, but whose upper edges are clearly visible. The single entrance to the enclosure is to be found in its southern arc and consists of a simple gap. To the south of this gap are the remains of an outwork that protects the entrance and creates a banked approach from the east. Approximately 20m to the south of this outwork there is an earthen bank which appears to mimic the line of the outwork at its eastern end, which runs for approximately 200m and ends with a banked hollow. The interior of the hollow appears much disturbed and may have been artificially deepened in recent times. The purpose of this feature is unclear but its origin does appear to be tied to the main enclosure. Approximately 50m to the west of these earthworks are traces of rectangular field-banks that may also be contemporary with the settlement remains.

Location/access
The settlement remains are located 1.5km south-west of the village of Little Bredy and are best approached from the direction of the Kingston Russell Stone Circle, 500m to the south. For further details see entry for Kingston Russell Stone Circle.
NGR 35770882
OS map OS Explorer OL 15

71 Thickthorn Long barrows and Dorset Cursus

Type Long barrow and cursus

Period Neolithic

Description
Two long barrows are located on Thickthorn Down close to the south-western terminal of the Dorset Cursus. The southernmost of the two barrows was excavated in 1933 by Stuart Piggott and revealed three secondary interments but no primary deposit. The secondary interments were all female, and appear to be dated to the Early Bronze Age. The barrow itself is of course much earlier in date with Neolithic Impressed ware pottery being found in the secondary fills of the barrows quarry ditches. The mound (as with its companion) appears to have been deliberately aligned south-east north-west to align with the cursus terminal. Both mounds are over 30m long and are approximately 20m wide and 2.75m high. The mound

excavated by Piggott is one of a number of barrows located on Cranborne Chase that have characteristic U-shaped ditches which appear to occur nowhere else.

Location/access

The barrows (and the western terminal of the Dorset Cursus) are located 1km south-east of Thickthorn Cross cross-roads on the A354 Salisbury-Blandford road at 39651130. The monuments can be accessed from fottpaths via stiles from the road, although vehicles need to be left at the cross-roads, where there is limited parking.

NGR 39711123

OS map OS Explorer 118

72 Two Gates Long Barrow

Type Chambered Tomb?

Period Neolithic

Description

The possible site of a chambered tomb, referred to by Charles Warne in the nineteenth century. There is little confirming the site's authenticity today and therefore it must be treated with caution.

Location/access

The site is located on Compton Down 1km south-west of the village of West Compton. There is no public access to the site although a footpath crosses the field in which the monument was recorded to be located by Warne in the middle of the nineteenth century.

NGR 35540937

OS map OS Explorer OL 15

73 Valley of Stones

Type Prehistoric quarry

Period Neolithic/Bronze Age

Description

The majority of megalithic remains found within west Dorset are made from a type of sarsen which is a conglomerate whose availability is fairly restricted to the area known as the Valley of Stones within the Bride Valley. It is fairly certain that this small but significant group of monuments were supplied with material from this source, nearly all of which are located within 7km of the valley. The stones occur thinly spread along the sides and bottom of this dry valley.

Location/access

The Valley of Stones is located 2km north-north-west of Portesham. The land is privately owned, but the valley can be observed from a minor road (called the Bishop's Road) which runs along the southern ridge above the valley.

NGR 35970877

OS map OS Explorer OL 15

74 Weatherby Castle Hillfort

Type Hillfort

Period Iron Age

Description

A much-overlooked example of an Iron Age hillfort that occupies the southern end of a chalk spur on downland above the village of Milborne St Andrew. This multi-vallate hillfort encloses the highest point of the spur, including 6.4ha of downland. The inner rampart consists of a bank and ditch that makes excellent use of the natural slope to create an impressive barrier which appears much larger than it actually is. A similar approach was taken with the second outer line of ramparts. There would appear to have been only one entrance to the fort, which is located on its eastern side and was protected by an external length of rampart. The entrance through the inner rampart is gained via an opening in the rampart line, which has been out-turned at both ends creating a passageway. The broad gap in the inner defences to the north of the western entrance is not thought to be original.

The site loses much of its dominant impact because of the dense plantation that has grown upon it. This not only effectively masks the whole of the interior but is almost certainly seriously damaging the surviving archaeology. The site has not been excavated but Charles Warne records in his nineteenth-century volume *Ancient Dorset* that he picked sherds of Roman pottery from the site.

Location/access

The hillfort is located 1.5km south of the village of Milbourne St Andrew and 2.25km north-east of Tolpuddle. The site is located on private ground but is accessible via a footpath from a minor road which runs between Milborne St Andrew and Briantspuddle. The footpath leaves the minor road at 38090963.

NGR 38070963

OS map OS Explorer 117

75 West Hill Barrow Group

Type Barrow Group

Period Bronze Age

Description

A group of 10 round barrows, nine of which constitute a linear cemetery aligned south-west north-east on a prominent spur of the Ridgeway. All of the barrows lie on the crest of the spur, a position of prominence which clearly was the intention of the builders. Most of the group is now very badly damaged by agricultural activity and at least one of them was opened by Charles Warne in the middle of the nineteenth century. With the exception of one pond barrow all of the other barrows are thought to be bowl types.

Location/access
This group is located 2km east of the village of Bincombe and can be approached via the South West Coast Path which ascends West Hill via a minor road at 36970845.
NGR 37000847
OS map OS Explorer OL 15

76 Woodbury Hillfort

Type Hillfort

Period Iron Age

Description
Enclosing an area of just over 5ha, Woodbury consists of a single bank and ditch with an outer counterscarp bank. The inner rampart is over 6m high and 12m wide with a ditch 1.75m deep and 9.5m wide. The counterscarp bank, the first line of defence, is 9m wide and it accentuates the steep slopes of the natural hill. The weakest stretch of the defences lies to the north where a saddle connecting the chalk spur of Woodbury Hill where the main ridge is located. Here the outer defences of the counterscarp bank have been constructed 65m further to the north, however this line of defence is very poorly preserved having been badly affected by subsequent ploughing. The original main entrance to the hillfort is probably to be found along the south-west arm of the defences but this is complicated by a more recent access road/track which enters the monument at this point. There are several other breaches in the ramparts but all of them appear to be largely unconnected with the original construction of the hillfort. The hillfort holds a commanding position overlooking the lower reaches of the River Piddle (Trent) before it joins the River Frome. The interior has obviously been affected by post-Iron Age activity and no obvious contemporary features are identifiable. The interior was the location for a chapel for which the footings survived and were observed by Hutchins in the late eighteenth century. The date of the chapel is thought to be of fifteenth-century date.

Location/access
Woodbury Hill is located 1km due east of Bere Regis and can be approached via a minor road from the A35 sign-posted to Woodbury Hill. The hillfort is on private land but a public footpath bisects the monument.
NGR 38560948
OS map OS Explorer 117

77 Woolsbarrow Hillfort

Type Hillfort

Period Iron Age

Description

Located on a gravel knoll this small, univallate hillfort encloses an area of 1ha and has been severely damaged and eroded by gravel workings (no longer active) which have almost completely destroyed the interior. The ramparts consist of a single bank and ditch, constructed some 7m below the summit of the knoll. The ditch is located on the inside of the bank, a feature which is not particularly unusual in hillfort construction where the angle of slope allows for this without compromising the effectiveness of the defensive circuit. Part of the interior was excavated during the late nineteenth century when a local antiquarian examined what was thought to be a burial mound but with negative results.

The entrance to the hillfort is located in the south-east corner of the ramparts but its original form has been damaged by a modern track.

Location/access

Located within Wareham forest this hillfort is now surrounded by plantation but can be reached from footpaths to the south. The site lies approximately 5km north-west of Wareham and is approachable only by foot.

NGR 38930925

OS map OS Explorer 117

78 Wor Barrow

Type Long barrow

Period Neolithic

Description

This Neolithic long barrow was totally excavated by General Pitt-Rivers during 1893-4 and is included within this gazetteer because of the significance it holds for the discipline of archaeology. As is common with the process of excavation the barrow is almost totally destroyed and the earthworks which are located where it once stood are an arena created by the General for the holding of exhibitions and games. The excavation of this site, in association with a number of excavations elsewhere on Cranborne Chase, proved to be a watershed in the development of excavation techniques, with the General being rightly regarded as the 'father of British Archaeology'.

Location/access

The site is located 1.5km east of Sixpenny Handley and very close to the Oakley Down Barrow Group (see separate entry). Wor Barrow can be viewed from the viewpoint located on Ackling Dyke (40181159). The site is on private land.

NGR 40121173

OS map OS Explorer 118

FURTHER READING

Although this volume has been prepared and written to include only essential references within the main narrative, this should not detract from the great body of work that has been consulted in its execution. I have therefore included within the following bibliography all of the texts used which the reader may wish to consult for detail. In addition, for those who wish to undertake some more general reading on prehistory, the main bibliography is preceded by a short list of recommended titles under some basic themes. The list is far from exhaustive and by its nature, highly selective.

General Prehistory

Bradley, R., 1984. *The social foundations of prehistoric Britain*. London. Longman.

Darvill, T., 1987. *Prehistoric Britain*. London. Batsford.

Green, M., 2000. *A Landscape Revealed: 10,000 Years on a Chalkland Farm*. Stroud. Tempus.

Marsden, B.M., 1984. *Pioneers of Prehistory: Leaders and Landmarks in English Archaeology (1500-1900)*. Ormskirk, G.W. & A. Hesketh.

Megaw, J. and Simpson. D., 1988 (fourth ed.) *Introduction to British Prehistory*. Leicester. Leicester University Press.

Parker Pearson, M., 1993. Bronze Age Britain. London. Batsford.

Russell, M., 2002. *Prehistoric Sussex*. Stroud. Tempus.

Taylor, C., 1983. *Village and Farmstead: A History of Rural Settlement in England*. London. George Philip & Son.

The Neolithic

Ashbee, P., 1970. *The Earthen Long Barrow in Britain*. London. J.M. Dent & Sons Ltd.

Daniel, G.E., 1950. *The Prehistoric Chamber Tombs of England & Wales*. Cambridge. Cambridge University Press.

Kinnes, I., 1992. *Non-Megalithic Barrows and Allied Structures in the British Neolithic*. British Museum Occasional Papers 52. London. British Museum.

Oswald, A., Dyer, C. and Barber, M., 2001. *The Creation of Monuments: Neolithic Causewayed Enclosures in the British Isles*. Swindon. English Heritage.

Thomas, J., 1999. *Understanding the Neolithic*. London. Routledge

Wainwright, G., 1989. *The Henge Monuments: Ceremony and Society in Prehistoric Britain*. London. Thames and Hudson.

The Bronze Age

Burgess, C., 1980. *The Age of Stonehenge*. London. Dent & Sons.

Burl, A., 1976. *The Stone Circles of the British Isles*. London. Yale University Press.

Case, H., 1977. The Beaker culture in Britain and Ireland, in Mercer, R. (ed.). *Beakers in Britain and Europe*. Oxford. BAR Supplementary series 26, 71-101.

Parker Pearson, M., 1993. Bronze Age Britain. London. Batsford.

Piggott, S., 1938. The Early Bronze Age in Wessex. *Proceedings of the Prehistoric Society* 3, 52-106.

The Iron Age

Cunliffe, B., 1991. *Iron Age Communities of Britain*. (third ed.) London. Routledge

Harding, D.W., 1974 *The Iron Age in Lowland Britain*. London. Routledge & Kegan Paul.

Reynolds, P.J., 1979. *Iron Age Farm: The Butser Experiment*. London. Collonade.

BIBLIOGRAPHY

Aitken, G.M. and G.N., 1990. Excavations at Whitcombe, 1965-1967. *Proceedings of the Dorset Natural History and Archaeology Society* 112, 57-94.

Ashbee, P., 1970. *The Earthen Long Barrow in Britain*. London. J.M. Dent & Sons Ltd.

Atkinson ,R.J.C., Piggott, C.M. & Sandars, N.K., 1951. *Excavations at Dorchester, Oxon*. Oxford

Barclay, A. and Bayliss, A., 1999. 'Cursus monuments and the radiocarbon problem' in: A. Barclay and J. Harding, (eds) *Pathways and ceremonies: The cursus monuments of Britain and Ireland*. Neolithic Sudies Group Seminar Papers 4. Oxford. Oxbow, pp 11-29.

Barrett, J. Bradley, R. and Green, M., 1991. *Landscape Monuments and Society: The Prehistory of Cranborne Chase*. Cambridge. Cambridge University Press.

Bowen, H.C., 1990. *The Archaeology of Bokerley Dyke*. London. HMSO.

Bradley, R., 1976. *Maumbury Rings, Dorchester: The Excavations of 1908-1913*. Oxford. Society of Antiquaries of London.

Bradley, R., 1984. *The Social Foundations of Prehistoric Britain*. London. Longman.

Bradley, R., 1993. *Altering the Earth: The Origins of Monuments in Britain and Continental Europe*. Edinburgh. Society of Antiquaries of Scotland Monograph Series Number 8.

Bradley, R., and Entwisle, R. 1985. Thickthorn Down long Barrow – A New Assessment. *Proceedings of the Dorset Natural History and Archaeological Society* 107, 174-176.

Brailsford, J.W., 1986.' The Early Iron Age Sequence at Hod Hill' in I. Richmond, *Hod Hill. Vol 2. Excavations carried out between 1951 and 1958 for the Trustees of the British Museum*. London. The Trustees of the British Museum, 147.

Burgess, C., 1980. *The Age of Stonehenge*. London. Dent & Sons.

Burl, A., 1976. *The Stone Circles of the British Isles*. London. Yale University Press.

Calkin, B., 1959. 'Some Archaeological Discoveries in the Isle of Purbeck pt II – A possible avenue to the Rempstone Circle' *Proceedings of the Dorset Natural History and Archaeology Society*, 81, 114-6.

Calkin, B., 1966. Some records of Barrow excavations re-examined. *Proceedings of the Dorset Natural History and Archaeology Society*. 88, 128-148.

Case, H., 1977. The Beaker culture in Britain and Ireland, in Mercer, R. (ed). *Beakers in Britain and Europe*. Oxford. BAR Supplementary series 26, 71-101.

Catherall, P.D., 1974. The Excavation of a Circular Enclosure and a Cairn at Litton Cheney, Dorset. *Proceedings of the Dorset Natural History and Archaeological Society* 96, 52.

Cunliffe, B., 1968. Excavations at Eldon's Seat, Encombe, Dorset. *Proceedings of the Prehistoric Society*, 34, 191-237.

Cunliffe, B., 1984. *Danebury: an Iron Age Hillfort in Hampshire. Vol. 1, The Excavations, 1969-1978*. London. CBA Res. Rep. 48.

Cunliffe, B., 1987. *Hengistbury Head, Dorset. Vol 1 The Prehistoric and Roman Settlement 3500 BC-AD 500*. Oxford. Oxford University Committee for Archaeology Monograph No 13.

Cunliffe, B., 1991. *Iron Age Communities of Britain*. (third ed.) London. Routledge.

Daniel, G.E., 1950. *The Prehistoric Chamber Tombs of England & Wales*. Cambridge. Cambridge University Press.

Darvill, T., 1987. *Prehistoric Britain*. London. Batsford.

Davies, S.M. Stacey, L.C. and Woodward, P.J., 1985. 'Excavations at Allington Avenue, Fordington, Dorchester, 1984/5: Interim Report'. *Proceedings of the Dorset Natural History and Archaeological Society*, 107, 101-110.

Drew,C.D. and Piggott, S., 1936. 'The Excavation of long Barrow 163a on Thickthorn Down, Dorset'. *Proceedings of the Prehistoric Society*, 2, 77-96.

Ellison, A. and Rahtz, P., 1987. ' at Hog Cliff Hill, Dorset'. *Proceedings of the Prehistoric Society*. 53. 223-269.

Farrah, R.A.H., 1955. 'An Early Iron Age fort on Shipton Hill, Shipton Gorge'. *Proceedings of the Dorset Natural History and Archaeology Society*, 77, 135-136.

Farwell, D.E., and Molleson, T.I., 1993. *Poundbury Vol. 2. The Cemeteries*. Dorchester. Dorset Natural History and Archaeological Society Monograph series No 11.

Gelling, P., 1977. 'Excavations on Pilsdon Pen, Dorset, 1964-71' *Proceedings of the Prehistoric Society*, 43, 263-286.

Green, C.J.S., 1987. *Excavations at Poundbury. Vol. 1: The Settlements*. Dorchester. Dorset Natural History Archaeological Society Monograph, 7

Green, C., Lynch, F. and White, H., 1982. 'The Excavation of Two Round Barrows on Launceston Down, Dorset (Long Crichel 5 and 7)'. *Proceedings of the Dorset Natural History and Archaeology Society*. 104, 39-57.

Green, M., 2000. *A Landscape Revealed: 10,000 Years on a Chalkland Farm*. Stroud. Tempus.

Gresham, C.A., 1939. 'Spettisbury Rings, Dorset'. *Archaeological Journal* XCVI, 114-131.

Grinsell, L.V., 1959. *Dorset Barrows*. Dorchester. Dorset Natural History & Archaeological Society.

Grinsell, L.V., 1982. *Dorset Barrows* Supplement. Dorchester. Dorset Natural History & Archaeological Society.

Harding, D.W. and Blake, I.M., 1963. An Early Iron Age Settlement in Dorset. *Antiquity* 37. 63-4

Harding, D.W., 1974 *The Iron Age in Lowland Britain*. London. Routledge & Kegan Paul.

Hawkes, C.F.C., 1931. Hillforts. *Antiquity*, 5, 60-97.

Hawkes, C.F.C., 1947. 'Britons, Romans and Saxons round Salisbury & in Cranborne Chase: Reviewing the excavations of general Pitt-Rivers 1881-1897'. *Archaeological Journal* CIV, 27-81.

Hawkes, C.F.C., 1959, The ABC of the British Iron Age. *Antiquity*. 33. 170-82

Hutchins, J., 1861. (Third ed) *History and Antiquities of the County of Dorset*. Westminster. J.B. Nicholson & Son.

Kinnes, I., 1992. *Non-Megalithic Barrows and Allied Structures in the British Neolithic*. British Museum Occasional Papers 52. London. British Museum.

Marsden, B.M., 1984. *Pioneers of Prehistory: Leaders and Landmarks in English archaeology (1500-1900)*. Ormskirk, G.W. & A. Hesketh.

Oliver, V.L., 1922. 'The Helstone'. *Proceedings of the Dorset Natural History and Archaeology Society*. 42, 36-41.

Oswald, A., Dyer, C. and Barber, M., 2001. *The Creation of Monuments: Neolithic Causewayed Enclosures in the British Isles*. Swindon. English Heritage.

Parke, A., 1953. 'The Excavation of a Bell-Barrow, Oakley Down, Wimborne St Giles'. *Proceedings of the Dorset Natural History and Archaeology Society*. 75. 36-44.

Petersen, F.F., 1981. *The Excavation of a Bronze Age Cemetery on Knighton Heath, Dorset*. Oxford. BAR British Series 98.

Piggott, S., 1937. 'The Excavation of a Long Barrow in Holdenhurst Parish, near Christchurch, Hants'. *Proceedings of the Prehistoric Society*, 3, 1-14.

Piggott, S., 1938. 'The Early Bronze Age in Wessex'. *Proceedings of the Prehistoric Society*, 3, 52-106.

Piggott, S., 1945. 'The Chambered Cairn of 'The Grey Mare and Colts''. *Proceedings of the Dorset Natural History and Archaeology Society*, 67, 30-33.

Piggott, S., and C.M., 1939. Stone and Earth Circles in Dorset. *Antiquity* 13, 138-158.

Piggott, S., and C.M., 1944. *Excavation of Barrows on Crichel and Launceston Downs, Dorset*. Archaeologia 90, 47-80.

Pitt Rivers, A.L.F., 1898. *Excavations in Cranborne Chase* IV. Privately Printed.

Proudfoot, E.V.W., 1963. Excavation of a Bell Barrow in Edmonsham, Dorset. *Proceedings of the Prehistoric Society*, 29, 395-425.

Putnam, B., 1998. *The Prehistoric Age (Discover Dorset)* Stanbridge. Dovecote Press.

Rahtz, P., 1962. Excavations at Shearplace Hill, Sydling St. Nicholas, Dorset, England. *Proceedings of the Prehistoric Society*. 28, 289-328.

Richardson, K.M., 1940. 'Excavations at Poundbury, Dorchester, Dorset, 1939'. *Antiquaries Journal*, 20, 429-448.

Richmond, I., 1986. *Hod Hill Vol. 2. Excavations carried out between 1951 and 1958 for the Trustees of the British Museum*. London. The Trustees of the British Museum.

Reynolds, P.J., 1979. *Iron Age Farm: The Butser Experiment*. London. Collonade.

Russell, M., 2002. *Prehistoric Sussex*. Stroud. Tempus.

Sharples, N.M., 1991. *Maiden Castle: Excavations and field survey 1985-6*. English Heritage Archaeological Report No.19. London. Historic Buildings and Ancient Monuments Commission.

Smith, I.A. and Evans, J.G., 1968. 'Excavation of Two Long barrows in North Wiltshire'. *Antiquity*, XLII, 138-142.

Smith, R.J.C., Healy, F. Allen, M.J. Morris, E.L. Barnes, I. and Woodward, P.J., 1997. *Excavations along the route of the Dorchester bypass, Dorset 1986-8*. Wessex Archaeology Report 11

Strabo., *The Geography*. IV.5.2.

Taylor, C., 1970. *Dorset*. London. Hodder and Stoughton

Taylor, C., 1983, *Village and Farmstead: A History of Rural Settlement in England*. London. George Philip & Son.

Thomas, J., 1999. *Understanding the Neolithic*. London. Routledge.

Wainwright, G., 1966. 'The Excavation of Hampton Stone Circle, Portesham, Dorset'. *Proceedings of the Dorset Natural History and Archaeology Society* 88, 122-127.

Wainwright, G., 1968. 'The Excavation of a Durotrigian Farmstead near Tollard Royal in Cranbourne Chase, Southern England'. *Proceedings of the Prehistoric Society* 3, 102-137.

Wainwright, G., 1979. *Mount Pleasant, Dorset: Excavations 1970-1971*. London. Society of Antiquaries (Research Report 37).

Wainwright, G., 1979b. *Gussage All Saints: An Iron Age Settlement in Dorset*. London. Department of Environment Archaeological Reports No.10

Wainwright, G., 1989. *The Henge Monuments: Ceremony and Society in Prehistoric Britain*. London. Thames and Hudson.

Wainwright, G. and Switsur, V., 1976. 'Gussage All Saints – a chronology'. *Antiquity*, 50, 32-39.

Warne, C., 1866. Celtic Tumuli of Dorset. London. John Russell Smith

Warne, C., 1872. *Ancient Dorset*, Bournemouth

Wheeler, R.E.M., 1943. *Maiden Castle, Dorset*. Research Report of the Committee of the Society of Antiquaries London, 12.

Wheeler, R.E.M., 1953. 'An early Iron Age 'Beach-Head' at Lulworth, Dorset'. *The Antiquaries Journal*, 33, 1-13.

Whimster, R., 1977. 'Iron Age burial in southern Britain'. *Proceedings of the Prehistoric Society*, 43, 317-327.

Whimster, R., 1981. *Burial Practices in Iron Age Britain. A Discussion and Gazetteer of the Evidence c.700 BC–AD 43*. Oxford. BAR British Series 90.

White, D.A., 1970. The Excavation of an Iron Age Round Barrow near Handley, Dorset, 1969. *Antiquaries Journal*, 50, 26-36.

White, D.A., 1982. *The Bronze Age Cremation Cemeteries at Simons Ground, Dorset*. Dorchester. Dorset Natural History and Archaeology Society Monograph 3.

Whitley, M., 1943. Excavations at Chalbury Camp, Dorset, 1939. *Antiquaries Journal* 23. 97-121.

Woodward, A., 2000. *British Barrows: A Matter of Life and Death*. Stroud. Tempus.

INDEX

Page numbers in **bold** refer to text illustrations.